2 Longman Academic Reading Series

READING SKILLS FOR COLLEGE

Kim Sanabria

Dedication

To Victor, Kelly, and Carlos.

Longman Academic Reading Series 2: Reading Skills for College

Copyright © 2014 by Pearson Education, Inc.
All rights reserved.

Pearson Education, 10 Bank Street, White Plains, NY 10606

Staff Credits: The people who made up the **Longman Academic Reading Series 2** team, representing editorial, production, design, and manufacturing, are Pietro Alongi, Margaret Antonini, Rosa Chapinal, Aerin Csigay, Ann France, Gerry Geniusas, Françoise Leffler, Amy McCormick, Liza Pleva, Massimo Rubini, and Robert Ruvo.

Cover image: The Loupe Project/Shutterstock
Text Composition: TSI Graphics

Library of Congress Cataloging-in-Publication Data
Böttcher, Elizabeth.
Longman Academic Reading Series / Elizabeth Bottcher.
volumes cm
Includes index.
ISBN 978-0-13-278664-5 (Level 1)—ISBN 978-0-13-278582-2 (Level 2)—
ISBN 978-0-13-276059-1 (Level 3)—ISBN 978-0-13-276061-4 (Level 4)—
ISBN 978-0-13-276067-6 (Level 5)
1. English language—Textbooks for foreign speakers. 2. Reading comprehension—Problems, exercises, etc. 3. College readers. I. Title.
PE1128.B637 2013
428.6'4—dc23

2013007701

ISBN 10: 0-13-278582-X
ISBN 13: 978-0-13-278582-2

Printed in the United States of America
1 2 3 4 5 6 7 8 9 10—V082—18 17 16 15 14 13

CONTENTS

Welcome to the *Longman Academic Reading Series*, a five-level series that prepares English-language learners for academic work. The aim of the series is to make students more effective and confident readers by providing **high-interest readings on academic subjects** and teaching them **skills and strategies** for

- effective reading
- vocabulary building
- note-taking
- critical thinking

Last but not least, the series encourages students to **discuss and write** about the ideas they have discovered in the readings, making them better speakers and writers of English as well.

High-Interest Readings On Academic Subjects

Research shows that if students are not motivated to read, if reading is not in some sense enjoyable, the reading process becomes mechanical drudgery and the potential for improvement is minimal. That is why high-interest readings are the main feature in the *Longman Academic Reading Series*.

Varied High-Interest Texts

Each chapter of each book in the series focuses on an engaging theme from a wide range of academic subjects such as psychology, cultural studies, multicultural literature, and health science. The reading selections in each chapter (two readings in Level 1 and three in Levels 2–5) are chosen to provide different and intriguing perspectives on the theme. These readings come from a variety of sources or genres—books, textbooks, academic journals, newspapers, magazines, online articles—and are written by a variety of authors from widely different fields. The Level 2 book, for instance, offers two poems about cultural identity by Li-Young Lee and Aurora Levins Morales, an interview with the inspirational "Tony the Traveller," a textbook excerpt on Bloom's Taxonomy, and an online article on types of intelligence, including a quiz—all challenging reading selections that spark students' interest and motivate them to read and discuss what they read.

Academic Work

The work done in response to these selections provides students with a reading and discussion experience that mirrors the in-depth treatment of texts in academic coursework. Although the readings may be adapted for the lower levels and excerpted for the upper levels, the authentic reading experience has been preserved. The series sustains students' interest and gives a sample of the types of content and reasoning that are the hallmark of academic work.

Skills and Strategies

To help students read and understand its challenging readings, the *Longman Academic Reading Series* provides a battery of skills and strategies for effective reading, vocabulary building, note-taking, and critical thinking.

Effective Reading

The series provides students with strategies that will help them learn to skim, scan, predict, preview, map, and formulate questions before they begin to read. After they read, students are routinely asked to identify main ideas as well as supporting details, progressing through the chapter from the "literal" to the "inferential." Students using this series learn to uncover what is beneath the surface of a reading passage and are led to interpret the many layers of meaning in a text. Each text is an invitation to dig deeper.

Vocabulary Building

In all chapters students are given the opportunity to see and use vocabulary in many ways: guessing words in context (an essential skill, without which fluent reading is impossible), identifying synonyms, recognizing idioms, practicing word forms as well as using new words in their own spoken and written sentences. At the same time, students learn the best strategies for using the dictionary effectively, and have ample practice in identifying roots and parts of words, recognizing collocations, understanding connotations, and communicating in the discourse specific to certain disciplines. The intentional "recycling" of vocabulary in both speaking and writing activities provides students with an opportunity to use the vocabulary they have acquired.

Note-Taking

As students learn ways to increase their reading comprehension and retention, they are encouraged to practice and master a variety of note-taking skills, such as highlighting, annotating, paraphrasing, summarizing, and outlining. The skills that form the focus of each chapter have been systematically aligned with the skills practiced in other chapters, so that scaffolding improves overall reading competence within each level.

Critical Thinking

At all levels of proficiency, students become more skilled in the process of analysis as they learn to read between the lines, make inferences, draw conclusions, make connections, evaluate, and synthesize information from various sources. The aim of this reflective journey is the development of students' critical thinking ability, which is achieved in different ways in each chapter.

Speaking and Writing

The speaking activities that frame and contribute to the development of each chapter tap students' strengths, allow them to synthesize information from several sources, and give them a sense of community in the reading experience. In addition, because good readers make good writers, students are given the opportunity to express themselves in a writing activity in each chapter.

The aim of the *Longman Academic Reading Series* is to provide "teachable" books that allow instructors to recognize the flow of ideas in each lesson and to choose from many types of exercises to get the students interested and to maintain their active participation throughout. By showing students how to appreciate the ideas that make the readings memorable, the series encourages students to become more effective, confident, and independent readers.

The Online Teacher's Manual

The Teacher's Manual is available at www.pearsonelt.com/tmkeys. It includes general teaching notes, chapter teaching notes, answer keys, and reproducible chapter quizzes.

CHAPTER OVERVIEW

All chapters in the *Longman Academic Reading Series, Level 2* have the same basic structure.

Objectives

BEFORE YOU READ

A. Consider These Questions/Facts/etc.

B. Your Opinion *[varies; sometimes only Consider activity]*

READING ONE: [+ *reading title*]

A. Warm-Up

B. Reading Strategy

[Reading One]

COMPREHENSION

A. Main Ideas

B. Close Reading

VOCABULARY *[not necessarily in this order; other activities possible]*

A. Guessing from Context

B. Synonyms

C. Using the Dictionary

NOTE-TAKING *[in two reading sections]*

CRITICAL THINKING

READING TWO: [+ *reading title*]

A. Warm-Up

B. Reading Strategy

[Reading Two]

COMPREHENSION

A. Main Ideas

B. Close Reading

VOCABULARY *[not necessarily in this order; other activities possible]*

A. Guessing from Context

B. Synonyms

C. Using the Dictionary

CRITICAL THINKING

LINKING READINGS ONE AND TWO

READING THREE: [+ *reading title*]

A. Warm-Up

B. Reading Strategy

[Reading Three]

COMPREHENSION

A. Main Ideas

B. Close Reading

VOCABULARY *[not necessarily in this order; other activities possible]*

A. Guessing from Context

B. Synonyms

C. Using the Dictionary

D. Word Forms

NOTE-TAKING *[in two reading sections]*

CRITICAL THINKING

AFTER YOU READ

BRINGING IT ALL TOGETHER

WRITING ACTIVITY

DISCUSSION AND WRITING TOPICS

Vocabulary

Self-Assessment

Each chapter starts with a definition of the chapter's academic subject matter, Objectives, and a Before You Read section.

A short **definition of the academic subject** mentioned in the chapter title describes the general area of knowledge explored in the chapter.

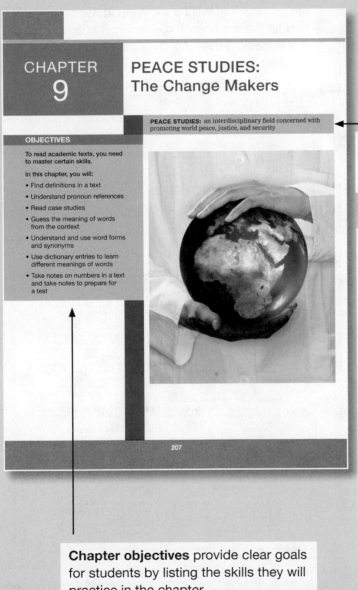

CHAPTER
9

PEACE STUDIES:
The Change Makers

PEACE STUDIES: an interdisciplinary field concerned with promoting world peace, justice, and security

OBJECTIVES

To read academic texts, you need to master certain skills.

In this chapter, you will:

• Find definitions in a text
• Understand pronoun references
• Read case studies
• Guess the meaning of words from the context
• Understand and use word forms and synonyms
• Use dictionary entries to learn different meanings of words
• Take notes on numbers in a text and take notes to prepare for a test

207

The **Before You Read** activities introduce the subject matter of the chapter, using a mix of information and questions to stimulate students' interest.

BEFORE YOU READ

Ⓐ Consider These Facts

How much do you know about world poverty? Read the facts below and fill in the blanks with your guess. Then check your answers at the bottom of the page.

1. There is no sanitation in _____ percent of the world.

2. Women in developing countries have to walk _____ miles to get water each day.

3. Globally, women earn _____ percent less than men.

4. The richest 20 percent of the world's population earns _____ percent of the world's income.

5. Worldwide, _____ children die from poverty every day.

Ⓑ Your Opinion

Answer the questions. Check (✓) the appropriate box. Then discuss your answers with a partner. If you answered yes, give more details.

	Yes	No
Have you ever . . .		
1. felt strongly about a serious world problem?	☐	☐
2. been involved in a group project?	☐	☐
3. taken on a leadership role?	☐	☐
4. had an idea about how to improve the lives of others?	☐	☐

Answers
1. 33, 2. 4, 3. 50, 4. 75, 5. 30,000

208 CHAPTER 9

Chapter objectives provide clear goals for students by listing the skills they will practice in the chapter.

Each of the three reading sections in a chapter starts with a Warm-Up activity and a Reading Strategy presentation and practice, followed by the reading itself.

The **Warm-Up** activity presents discussion questions that activate students' prior knowledge and help them develop a personal connection with the topic of the reading.

Reading One sets the theme and presents the basic ideas that will be explored in the chapter. Like all the readings in the series, it is an example of a specific genre of writing (here, a textbook excerpt).

READING ONE: Social Entrepreneurship

Ⓐ Warm-Up

An *entrepreneur* is a person who operates a business, especially a new one. A *social entrepreneur* approaches a social problem with a business model. Read the list of qualities of a good social entrepreneur. Rank them in order of importance (1 being the most important) in solving serious social problems. Then share your ideas with a partner.

_____ knowing powerful people

_____ having close friends

_____ being idealistic

_____ being young and energetic

_____ having innovative ideas

_____ having a lot of money

_____ being creative

_____ your own idea: _____

Ⓑ Reading Strategy

Finding Definitions

If you are unfamiliar with an important word or concept in a text, especially if it is in the title or appears more than once, **scan the text carefully to find whether it is defined.** You will often find an explanation of important words immediately before or after them.

Look at the title of the reading and then scan the text to find answers to the questions.

1. Who are social entrepreneurs, and what do they do?
2. What characteristics do social entrepreneurs have?

Now read the text. If you come across unfamiliar words, scan the text to find the definitions.

Peace Studies: *The Change Makers* **209**

The **Reading Strategy** box gives a general description of a reading strategy, such as finding definitions, and the reasons for using it. The **activities** below the box show students how to apply that strategy to the reading.

SOCIAL ENTREPRENEURSHIP

WE HAVE IDEAS: Now we have to make them happen!

1   At the age of 80, sculptor Henry Moore said: "The secret of life is to have a task, something you do your entire life, something you bring everything to, every minute of the day for your whole life. And the most important thing is: It must be something you cannot possibly do." With these words, he captured the idealism and determination of one of the fastest growing programs of study: social entrepreneurship. Although this term was not commonly used until the 1970s, today there are programs in the field in some of the highest-ranking universities in the world.

2   Social entrepreneurs identify **daunting** world challenges. For example, they may see the need to protect the environment, provide universal health care, or promote **literacy**. They look for creative new ideas to implement large-scale, long-term change in the world. Many social entrepreneurs have a background in business, but they also have persistence, vision, **courage**, and commitment. Their projects typically involve large numbers of people working in their own communities.

3   Social entrepreneurs are people who are trying to improve the lives of others, especially those living in underserved[1] communities. The Skoll Foundation, an organization committed to peace and **sustainability**, defines them as "society's change agents: creators of innovations that disrupt the status quo[2] and transform our world for the better."

4   Social entrepreneurs are said to share various characteristics:
Ambitious: They tackle major social issues. These might include increasing the college enrollment rate of low-income students or fighting poverty in developing countries.
Mission-Driven: Although their projects may be profitable, they measure their success in terms of the social progress they are able to make.
Strategic: They improve systems, create solutions, and invent new approaches. They are intensely focused and **relentless** in their **pursuit** of a social vision.
Resourceful: Because they have limited access to capital[3], social entrepreneurs are **exceptionally skilled** at gathering and **mobilizing** human, financial, and political **resources**.
Results-Oriented: Ultimately, social entrepreneurs produce measurable returns. These results transform existing realities, open up new pathways for the marginalized and disadvantaged, and unlock society's potential to effect social change.

5   Of course, the idea of innovation and social transformation is not new, but the models used by social entrepreneurs are fresh and exciting.

[1] *underserved:* inadequately provided with essential services

[2] *the status quo:* the way things are

[3] *capital:* wealth or financial assets

210   CHAPTER 9

A Poverty-Free World

1 According to official statistics, almost half the world —over three billion people—live on less than $2.50 a day. They do not have access to the basic needs of food, water, **shelter**, clothing, health care, and education, and they have little hope of ever escaping from their situation. Millions more live on much less than that.

2 Muhammad Yunus was troubled by the cycle of poverty[1] in his native land, Bangladesh, one of the poorest countries on earth. He started visiting villages across the country, where he would go to people's houses and talk to them, trying to understand their life. He was **struck** by the fact that a small amount of money could make so much difference in their lives. For example, he met a 21-year-old basket maker, Sufiya Begum, trying to raise her three children on next to nothing. He realized that if she could get a **loan** of just a few dollars, she could operate more efficiently and her business could be **transformed**, but no bank would lend her any money, saying she would never pay it back.

Muhammad Yunus (left) received the Nobel Peace Prize for his work with the poor.

3 Yunus felt that, poor or not, people should be able to borrow money. He believed in human potential and thought that, given a chance, even the illiterate and the uneducated could build on the skills they had and pull themselves out of poverty. Yunus founded the Grameen Bank ("gram" means "village" in Bangla), to give small loans to the world's poorest, especially women. In addition to microfinancing[2], the bank also distributed educational information about health, farming, and innovative technological ideas so that people could take their **destiny** into their own hands. Respect, dignity, and opportunity were among the goals they **envisioned** for the world's poorest citizens. Yunus and Grameen were awarded the Nobel Peace Prize in 2006. **Incidentally**, 97 percent of **borrowers** do pay back their loans.

4 Grameen has had an impact on many people. More than 100 countries worldwide have been inspired by its success and have created similar programs. Yunus is hopeful for the future. He said: "We have created a slavery-free world, a smallpox-free world, an apartheid[3]-free world. Creating a poverty-free world would be greater than all these **accomplishments** while at the same time reinforcing them. This would be a world that we could all be proud to live in."

[1] *cycle of poverty:* a set of events by which poverty, once it starts, is most likely to continue
[2] *microfinancing:* making small amounts of money available temporarily
[3] *apartheid:* an official policy of racial segregation, formerly practiced most notably in South Africa

Peace Studies: *The Change Makers* **217**

Reading Two addresses the same theme as Reading One, but from a completely different perspective. In most cases, it is also an example of a different genre of writing (here, an online article).

Reading Three addresses the same theme as Readings One and Two, but again from a different perspective from the first two. And in most cases, it is also an example of a different genre (here, a case study).

B Reading Strategy

Reading Case Studies

Case studies are often used to illustrate course concepts. Case studies are **generalized applications of theories that students encounter**. When you read a case study, ask yourself: What information does it provide? What concepts does the case study illustrate?

Now read the case study and determine what information it provides and how it illustrates the concept of social entrepreneurship.

All readings have **numbered paragraphs** (with the exception of literary readings that have numbered lines) for easy reference. The **target vocabulary** that students need to know in order to read academic texts is set in boldface blue for easy recognition. Target vocabulary is recycled through the chapter and the level.

The Barefoot College

1 Rajasthan is a region in northern India where people face huge challenges, such as a lack of formal education, widespread poverty, hunger, and health problems that affect people on a daily basis.

2 Sanjit Bunker Roy felt devastated by these problems. He wanted to find a way to address **famine** and water **shortage** for those from backgrounds less **affluent** than his own. Roy did not accept the idea that illiteracy was an **insurmountable** barrier to progress. He did not think a **lack** of education should necessarily prevent people from developing their skills. Instead, he **emphasized** the idea that the very poor should have access to modern ideas that could help them address problems that were immediate and relevant to them. In addition, he saw potential in what local villagers *did* know. For example, in Rajasthan there are examples of rainwater-collecting mechanisms that are hundreds of years old. Roy showed that in an educational environment that **targets** concrete problems, people are capable of rapidly learning about new technology and combining it with their existing skills.

3 In 1972, he moved to Rajasthan to establish the Barefoot College, which teaches its students—many of them semi-literate older women—how to use solar power to generate electricity and how to harvest[1] rainwater. The college has dirt floors and no chairs or other basic facilities. The students do not receive formal certificates. However, as a result of Roy's visionary efforts, they do have **demonstrable** results. The "graduates" of the college have installed solar energy panels in 750 remote villages and made drinking water and **sanitation** available to over 2½ million children.

4 Roy's critics thought he would not be able to succeed. He was inspired by the words of Gandhi[2], who said: "First they ignore you, then they laugh at you, then they fight you, and then you win." The Barefoot College model has now spread to over 28 countries in the least developed parts of the world.

[1] *harvest:* collect
[2] Mahatma Gandhi (1869–1948) inspired Roy. He supported civil rights and freedom, and worked tirelessly to improve the situation of the poor.

Most readings have **glosses** and **footnotes** to help students understand difficult words and names.

Each reading in the chapter is followed by Comprehension and Vocabulary activities.

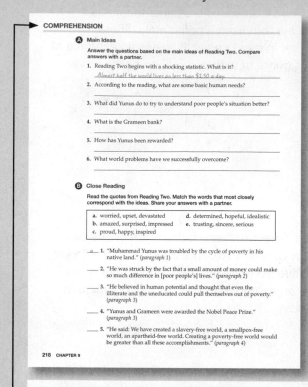

The **Vocabulary** activities focus on the target vocabulary in the reading, presenting and practicing skills such as guessing meaning from context or from synonyms, using a dictionary, and understanding word usage.

The **Comprehension** activities help students identify and understand the main ideas of the reading and their supporting details.

The **Synonyms** activity also helps students understand the meaning of the target vocabulary in the reading, but here for each target word students are given synonyms to match or choose from.

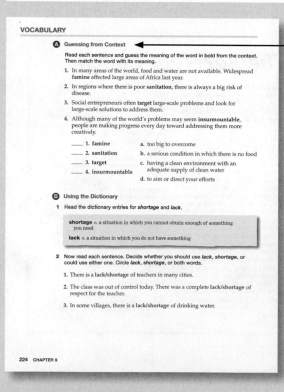

The **Guessing from Context** activity helps students guess the meaning of the target vocabulary by encouraging them to go back to the reading to find clues in the context, and base their guesses on these clues.

B Using the Dictionary

1 Read the dictionary entries for *gift*, *prime*, *stem*, and *will*.

> **gift** *n.* **1** a present that you give to someone **2** a natural ability to do something
>
> **prime** *adj.* **1** very important, very good **2** describes a number that can only be divided by itself and one
>
> **stem** *v.* **1** to develop or originate from something else **2** to stop something from spreading or growing
>
> **will** *n.* **1** the determination to do what you have decided to do **2** a legal document that shows what to do with your money and possessions when you die

2 Now read each sentence. Mark which entry, *1* or *2*, explains the way the word in bold is used.

1. ____ **a.** Many savants have serious disabilities, but they also have remarkable **gifts**.

   ____ **b.** Perhaps their greatest **gift** to the world is making people think differently about unusual people.

2. ____ **a.** Daniel Tammet has such advanced math abilities that he can tell if a number is **prime** within seconds.

   ____ **b.** The reason Tammet is such a **prime** subject for researchers is that he can explain his condition.

3. ____ **a.** Tammet's abilities seem to **stem** from a combination of factors.

   ____ **b.** Researchers are trying to **stem** the apparent increase in autism worldwide.

4. ____ **a.** When she dies, my mother wants to leave some of her savings for autism research in her **will**.

   ____ **b.** Many autistic children have a very strong **will** and are determined to have their way.

Psychology: Theories of Intelligence **125**

Using the Dictionary shows students how to understand a dictionary entry for some of the target words. Students choose the appropriate meaning of the word as it is used in the reading and in other contexts.

B Word Forms

1 Fill in the chart with the correct word forms. Some categories can have more than one form. Use a dictionary if necessary. An *X* indicates there is no form in that category.

	NOUN	VERB	ADJECTIVE
1.	awareness	X	*aware*
2.	abolition/abolitionist		X
3.			articulate/
4.	compassion	X	
5.		X	sincere/
6.	trust		

2 Complete the biographies with the correct form of the words.

Sojourner Truth was a famous participant in the

___*abolitionist*___ movement, a movement to end
  1. (abolition/abolish/abolitionist)

slavery in the United States. As a person who was born into

slavery herself, she was uniquely _____
                                    2. (aware/awareness)

of the need to fight for equality for all. She spoke with great

_____ and _____ about the rights of
  3. (sincerity/sincere)   4. (compassion/compassionate)

African Americans and women.

  Abraham Lincoln was America's 16th president. He is best known for

leading his country through the Civil War and for ending slavery. He

was also an _____ person, well
            5. (articulation/articulate)

known for his sayings. One of his famous statements has

to do with believing in other people. He said: "The people

when rightly and fully _____ will
                        6. (trust/trusted/trusting)

return the _____."
            7. (trust/trusted/trusting)

186 CHAPTER 8

Word Forms helps students expand their vocabulary by encouraging them to guess or find out the different forms some of the target words can have. Then students are challenged to use the forms correctly.

Two of the three reading sections in a chapter have a Note-Taking activity. All three reading sections end with a Critical Thinking activity. The Linking Readings One and Two activity comes at the end of the Reading Two section.

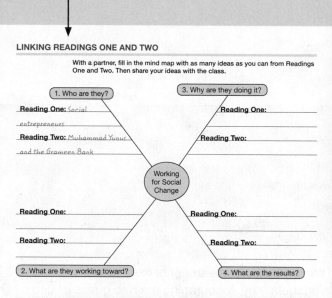

NOTE-TAKING: Taking Notes on Numbers in a Text

When you take notes on an informational reading, make sure you correctly identify what any **numbers** in the reading refer to.
EXAMPLE:
3 billion (*paragraph 1*) = the number of people in the world who live on a very small amount of money.

Read the numbers in bold. Go back to Reading Two. Circle the numbers. In your own words, write down what the numbers refer to. Share your responses with a partner.

1. **half** (*paragraph 1*): *fraction of the world that lives on a very small amount of money*
2. **$2.50** (*paragraph 1*): _____
3. **21** (*paragraph 2*): _____
4. **2006** (*paragraph 3*): _____
5. **97** (*paragraph 3*): _____
6. **100** (*paragraph 4*): _____

CRITICAL THINKING

Discuss the questions in a small group. Be prepared to share your opinions with the class.

1. Why do you think Yunus was interested in visiting people's houses and speaking to them face to face? What was the value of this personal interaction?
2. How do you think microfinancing can help people succeed? Do you believe this is a good strategy? Explain.
3. Yunus refers to the elimination of slavery, smallpox, and apartheid. What other problems, in your view, do we need to end and why?
4. How does the nursery rhyme before the reading represent Yunus's strategy?

The **Note-Taking** activity teaches students to use skills such as circling, underlining, writing margin notes, categorizing, outlining, and summarizing information to increase their reading comprehension.

The **Linking Readings One and Two** activity leads students to compare and contrast the ideas expressed in the first two readings. It helps students make connections and find correlations between the two texts.

LINKING READINGS ONE AND TWO

With a partner, fill in the mind map with as many ideas as you can from Readings One and Two. Then share your ideas with the class.

1. Who are they?
Reading One: *Social entrepreneurs*
Reading Two: *Muhammad Yunus and the Grameen Bank*

3. Why are they doing it?
Reading One: _____
Reading Two: _____

Working for Social Change

Reading One: _____
Reading Two: _____

Reading One: _____
Reading Two: _____

2. What are they working toward?
4. What are the results?

READING THREE: The Barefoot College

Ⓐ **Warm-Up**

Look at the photo and describe what you see to a partner. Explain the feelings that you experience.

The **Critical Thinking** activity encourages students to analyze and evaluate the information in the reading. This activity develops students' critical thinking skills and their ability to express their opinions coherently.

Each chapter ends with an After You Read section, a Vocabulary chart, and a Self-Assessment checklist.

The **After You Read** activities go back to the theme of the chapter, encouraging students to discuss and write about related topics using the target vocabulary of the chapter.

AFTER YOU READ

BRINGING IT ALL TOGETHER

Review the characteristics of social entrepreneurs that Reading One lists. Then work with a partner. Explain whether you believe Yunus and Roy have these characteristics. Give specific examples.

READING ONE: SOCIAL ENTREPRENEURS	READING TWO: MUHAMMAD YUNUS	READING THREE: SANJIT BUNKER ROY
• ambitious		Sanjit Bunker Roy was very ambitious because he wanted to tackle a huge problem — famine.
• mission-driven		
• strategic	Muhammad Yunus was very strategic. His strategy was to make small amounts of money available to very poor people.	
• resourceful		
• results-oriented		

Peace Studies: *The Change Makers* **227**

The **Vocabulary chart**, which lists all the target vocabulary words of the chapter under the appropriate parts of speech, provides students with a convenient reference.

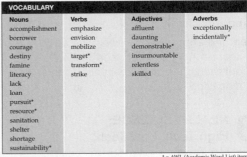

VOCABULARY

Nouns	Verbs	Adjectives	Adverbs
accomplishment	emphasize	affluent	exceptionally
borrower	envision	daunting	incidentally*
courage	mobilize	demonstrable*	
destiny	target*	insurmountable	
famine	transform*	relentless	
literacy	strike	skilled	
lack			
loan			
pursuit*			
resource*			
sanitation			
shelter			
shortage			
sustainability*			

* = AWL (Academic Word List) item

SELF-ASSESSMENT

In this chapter you learned to:

- ○ Find definitions in a text
- ○ Understand pronoun references
- ○ Read case studies
- ○ Guess the meaning of words from the context
- ○ Understand and use word forms and synonyms
- ○ Use dictionary entries to learn different meanings of words
- ○ Take notes on numbers in a text and take notes to prepare for a test

What can you do well? ✍

What do you need to practice more? ✍

Peace Studies: *The Change Makers* **229**

The **Self-Assessment** checklist encourages students to evaluate their own progress. Have they mastered the skills listed in the chapter objectives?

SCOPE AND SEQUENCE

CHAPTER	READING	VOCABULARY
1 CULTURAL STUDIES: The Lessons of Travel **Theme:** What we can learn from travel **Reading One:** *Tony the Traveller* (an online article) **Reading Two:** *The Benefits of Studying Abroad* (a newspaper article) **Reading Three:** *The Way of St. James: A Modern-Day Pilgrimage* (a magazine article)	• Skim a text to get an overview • Rank the benefits of studying abroad in order of importance • Preview a text using visuals • Find correlations between two texts • Decide if a main idea is true or false • Identify the main ideas of a text • Predict main ideas by writing questions • Understand the details that support the main ideas	• Understand and use synonyms, suffixes, definitions, and different word forms • Guess the meaning of words from the context • Use the Vocabulary list at the end of the chapter to review the words learned in the chapter • Use this vocabulary in the After You Read speaking and writing activities
2 MULTICULTURAL LITERATURE: Writing about Cultural Identity **Theme:** How to express and talk about cultural identity **Reading One:** *Mangoes and Magnolias* (a book excerpt) **Reading Two:** *Poems about Personal Identity* (a book excerpt) **Reading Three:** *Book Review of Mixed: An Anthology of Short Fiction about the Multiracial Experience* (a magazine article)	• Visualize images to understand a story • Identify poetic devices • Scan a text for specific information • Find correlations between two texts • Decide if a main idea is true or false • Complete the main ideas of a text • Understand the details that support the main ideas	• Guess the meaning of words from the context • Use dictionary entries to learn different meanings of words • Understand and use expressions and synonyms • Study the usage of certain phrases and idioms • Use the Vocabulary list at the end of the chapter to review the words, phrases, and idioms learned in the chapter • Use this vocabulary in the After You Read speaking and writing activities
3 HEALTH SCIENCE: High Tech, Low Tech, No Tech **Theme:** How technology in health care helps people **Reading One:** *Robots Improve Health Care, Helping Doctors, Nurses, and Patients* (a magazine article) **Reading Two:** *A Simple Diagnosis* (a textbook excerpt) **Reading Three:** *Water Is Shown to Help People Lose Weight* (a newspaper article)	• Predict the content of a text from its title • Predict the content of a text from its first paragraph • Find correlations between two texts • Decide if a main idea is true or false • Identify the main ideas of a text • Put the main ideas of a text in order • Understand the details that support the main ideas	• Guess the meaning of words from the context • Understand and use synonyms and word forms • Use the Vocabulary list at the end of the chapter to review the words learned in the chapter • Use this vocabulary in the After You Read speaking and writing activities

NOTE-TAKING	CRITICAL THINKING	SPEAKING/WRITING
• Use a graphic organizer • Organize notes in columns	• Express opinions and support your opinions with examples from a text or from your own experience and culture • Use a chart to compare types of travel • Analyze and evaluate information • Infer information not explicit in a text • Draw conclusions • Find correlations between two texts • Make connections between ideas • Synthesize information and ideas	• Discuss your opinions on travel, your reactions to journal entries, and why someone might make a pilgrimage • Write questions before reading a passage to help you get the main ideas of a text • Write a two-paragraph journal entry about a travel experience • Discuss a number of topics about travel with a small group of classmates • Choose one of the topics and write a paragraph about it
• Identify the basic parts of a story • Highlight the basic elements of a book review	• Answer questions based on information in a text or on your own experience and culture • Use a chart to compare the topics of two texts • Determine and explain your opinions on statements about a text • Analyze and evaluate information • Infer information not explicit in a text • Draw conclusions • Find correlations between two texts • Make connections between ideas • Synthesize information and ideas	• Discuss your reaction to visual images in a story • Write responses to two emails • Discuss your opinions on multiculturalism and cultural identity • Write two paragraphs about a personal experience • Discuss a number of topics about multiculturalism with a small group of classmates • Choose one of the topics and write a paragraph or two about it
• Use an outline • Use a flowchart	• Use a chart to determine the disadvantages of using robots in health care • Determine and explain your opinions on statements about a text • Express opinions and support your opinions with examples from a text or from your own experience and culture • Use a chart to compare the topics of two texts • Analyze and evaluate information • Infer information not explicit in a text • Draw conclusions • Find correlations between two texts • Make connections between ideas • Synthesize information and ideas	• Discuss your reactions to the idea of using robots for health care and to a scientific study • Discuss advantages and disadvantages of robotic innovations, and how certain groups might benefit from them • Discuss your opinion on diagnosing illnesses • Discuss how different groups might benefit from health-care innovations • Organize a panel discussion on the topic of improving health care • Write a paragraph reacting to advice from an old wives' tale • Discuss a number of topics about technology, health care, and healthy lifestyles • Choose one of the topics and write a paragraph or two about it

CHAPTER	READING	VOCABULARY
4 EDUCATION: The Task of the Teacher **Theme:** Different approaches to education **Reading One:** *Bloom's Taxonomy* (a textbook excerpt) **Reading Two:** *The Mayonnaise Jar and Two Cups of Coffee* (an online article) **Reading Three:** *A Teacher's Lasting Impression* (a magazine article)	• Preview a text using visuals • Predict the content of a text from its title and first paragraph • Recognize the narrative structure of a text • Find correlations between two texts • Identify the main ideas of a text • Evaluate the main ideas of a text • Put the main ideas of a text in order • Understand the details that support the main ideas	• Guess the meaning of words from the context • Use dictionary entries to learn different meanings of words • Understand and use word forms, synonyms, suffixes, and literal and figurative meanings • Use the Vocabulary list at the end of the chapter to review the words learned in the chapter • Use this vocabulary in the After You Read speaking and writing activities
5 PSYCHOLOGY: Theories of Intelligence **Theme:** What intelligence is and how we learn **Reading One:** *Types of Intelligence* (an online article) **Reading Two:** *Transforming Students' Motivation to Learn* (a textbook excerpt) **Reading Three:** *The Extraordinary Abilities of Daniel Tammet* (a magazine article)	• Understand and identify a text's purpose • Use the KWL method to get the most out of a text • Retell a text to monitor understanding • Find correlations between two texts • Decide if a main idea is true or false • Complete the main ideas of a text • Put the main ideas of a text in order • Understand the details that support the main ideas	• Guess the meaning of words from the context • Understand and use word forms • Use dictionary entries to learn different meanings of words • Study the usage of certain phrases and idioms • Use the Vocabulary list at the end of the chapter to review the words, phrases, and idioms learned in the chapter • Use this vocabulary in the After You Read speaking and writing activities

NOTE-TAKING	CRITICAL THINKING	SPEAKING/WRITING
• Use underlining to identify factual information • Use color coding to distinguish different types of information	• Evaluate lower-order and higher-order skills, according to Bloom's Taxonomy • Express opinions and support your opinions with examples from a text or from your own experience and culture • Use a chart to evaluate information in a text • Determine and explain your opinions on statements about a text • Complete a diary to determine the educational purpose behind a teacher's lessons • Interpret quotes and how they relate to a text • Analyze and evaluate information • Infer information not explicit in a text • Draw conclusions • Find correlations between two texts • Make connections between ideas • Synthesize information and ideas	• Discuss your opinions on learning, a good education, what makes a good teacher, and your reaction to learning skills • Role-play Benjamin Bloom, the professor (from the reading), and Mrs. Monell (from the reading) • Write two paragraphs about a favorite teacher • Discuss a number of topics about education with a small group of classmates • Choose one of the topics and write a paragraph or two about it
• Fill in a chart • Make triple entry notes	• Complete a chart to correlate types of intelligences with the questions in an intelligence quiz • Express your opinions and support them with examples from a story • Hypothesize about someone else's point of view • Analyze and evaluate information • Infer information not explicit in a text • Draw conclusions • Find correlations between two texts • Make connections between ideas • Synthesize information and ideas	• Discuss your opinions on intelligence debates, what you think a cartoon means, and types of intelligence • Take an intelligence quiz and then discuss your reactions • Write two paragraphs about intelligence • In a small group, discuss topics related to intelligence • Choose one of the topics and write a paragraph or two about it

CHAPTER	READING	VOCABULARY
6 BUSINESS: **The Changing Workplace** **Theme:** Different career choices in today's workplace **Reading One:** *The One Week Job: 52 Jobs in 52 Weeks* (an online article) **Reading Two:** *Flip Flops and Facebook Breaks: Millennials Enter the Workplace* (a newspaper article) **Reading Three:** *Eight Keys to Employability* (a magazine article)	• Preview a text by reading section headings • Use the 3-2-1 strategy to review a text • Deal with difficult words or expressions • Find correlations between two texts • Complete the main ideas of a text • Identify the main ideas of a text • Decide if a main idea is true or false • Understand the details that support the main ideas	• Guess the meaning of words from the context • Understand and use word forms, synonyms, word usage, and prefixes • Study the usage of an idiom • Use the Vocabulary list at the end of the chapter to review the words and idiom learned in the chapter • Use this vocabulary in the After You Read speaking and writing activities
7 MATH: Developing a Love of the "Language of Science" **Theme:** What can be done to increase interest in math **Reading One:** *A Mathematician's Lament* (a book excerpt) **Reading Two:** *What's Wrong with Math Education?* (an online article) **Reading Three:** *Angels on a Pin* (a magazine article)	• Understand an author's point of view • Understand an author's purpose • Scan a text for time markers to understand the sequence of events • Scan a text to identify an author's purpose • Find correlations between two texts • Identify the main ideas of a text • Decide if a main idea is true or false • Understand the details that support the main ideas	• Understand and use definitions, word forms, and word usage • Guess the meaning of words from the context • Use the Vocabulary list at the end of the chapter to review the words learned in the chapter • Use this vocabulary in the After You Read speaking and writing activities
8 PUBLIC SPEAKING: **Messages and Messengers** **Theme:** The importance of public speaking and public speeches **Reading One:** *The Power of Public Speech* (a magazine article) **Reading Two:** *The Best Way to Structure a Speech* (an online article) **Reading Three:** *Famous American Speeches* (a textbook excerpt)	• Skim by reading topic sentences • Understand rhetorical modes • Examine footnotes • Find correlations between two texts • Identify the main ideas of a text • Use paraphrasing to explain the main ideas • Decide if a main idea is true or false • Complete the main ideas of a text • Understand the details that support the main ideas	• Guess the meaning of words from the context • Understand and use word forms and word usage • Use dictionary entries to learn different meanings of words • Use the Vocabulary list at the end of the chapter to review the words learned in the chapter • Use this vocabulary in the After You Read speaking and writing activities

NOTE-TAKING	CRITICAL THINKING	SPEAKING/WRITING
• Label paragraphs • Write margin notes	• Complete an outline of a reading • Express your opinions and support them with examples from a story • Complete a chart to correlate career choices with personality types • Interpret quotes and how they relate to a text • Analyze and evaluate information • Infer information not explicit in a text • Draw conclusions • Find correlations between two texts • Make connections between ideas • Synthesize information and ideas	• Discuss your career interests, the changing workplace, and characteristics of good employees • Write a paragraph about careers and work • Discuss topics related to careers and work • Choose one of the topics and write a paragraph or two about it
• Identify topic sentences • Paraphrase	• Express your opinions and support them with examples from a text or from your own experience and culture • Analyze and evaluate information • Come up with an appropriate title for a reading • Infer information not explicit in a text • Draw conclusions • Find correlations between two texts • Make connections between ideas • Synthesize information and ideas	• Discuss your feelings about math and math education • Discuss how math is related to a number of other areas • Discuss your reactions to comments about math education and to an anecdote about a math exam • "Freewrite" a paragraph or two answering a question about math education • Discuss in a small group topics related to math • Choose one of the topics and write a paragraph or two about it
• Research a person or topic • Use a chart to group ideas	• Identify rhetorical modes in speeches • Express your opinions and support them with examples from a text or from your own experience and culture • Use a chart to compare the topics of two texts • Analyze and evaluate information • Infer information not explicit in a text • Draw conclusions • Find correlations between two texts • Make connections between ideas • Synthesize information and ideas	• Discuss the qualities of public speakers and issues addressed in speeches • Discuss your experience as a public speaker • Write a one-page speech on an issue you feel strongly about • Discuss in a small group topics related to public speaking • Choose one of the topics and write a paragraph or two about it

CHAPTER	READING	VOCABULARY
9 PEACE STUDIES: The Change Makers **Theme:** People and organizations who are promoting peace and social justice **Reading One:** *Social Entrepreneurship* (a textbook excerpt) **Reading Two:** *A Poverty-Free World* (an online article) **Reading Three:** *The Barefoot College* (a case study)	• Find definitions in a text • Understand pronoun references • Read case studies • Find correlations between two texts • Complete the main ideas of a text • Identify the main ideas of a text • Understand the details that support the main ideas	• Guess the meaning of words from the context • Understand and use word forms and synonyms • Use dictionary entries to learn different meanings of words • Use the Vocabulary list at the end of the chapter to review the words learned in the chapter • Use this vocabulary in the After You Read speaking and writing activities
10 URBAN STUDIES: Living Together **Theme:** How cities develop and how people react in urban environments **Reading One:** *City Fact Sheet* (an online article) **Reading Two:** *The Future of Cities* (a magazine article) **Reading Three:** *Won't You Be My Neighbor?* (a newspaper article)	• Read a fact sheet • Read aloud to determine the main idea of a text • Recognize the difference between narration and opinion • Find correlations between two texts • Identify the main ideas of a text • Put the main ideas of a text in order • Understand the details that support the main ideas	• Guess the meaning of words from the context • Use dictionary entries to learn different meanings of words • Understand and use positive and negative meanings of words • Use the Vocabulary list at the end of the chapter to review the words learned in the chapter • Use this vocabulary in the After You Read speaking and writing activities

NOTE-TAKING	CRITICAL THINKING	SPEAKING/WRITING
• Take notes on numbers in a text • Take notes to prepare for a test	• Express your opinions and support them with examples from a text or from your own experience and culture • Identify what numbers refer to in a text • Analyze and evaluate information • Infer information not explicit in a text • Draw conclusions • Hypothesize about someone else's point of view • Find correlations between two texts • Make connections between ideas • Synthesize information and ideas	• Discuss your opinions on social entrepreneurship and on the meaning of a nursery rhyme • Write a paragraph about an organization promoting positive change • Discuss topics related to social entrepreneurship in a small group • Choose one of the topics and write a paragraph or two about it
• Use abbreviations and symbols to take notes • Take notes on a timeline	• Express your opinions and support them with examples from a text or from your own experience and culture • Use a chart to compare the main ideas of two texts • Express your opinions on information presented in a text • Interpret quotes and how they relate to a text • Analyze and evaluate information • Infer information not explicit in a text • Draw conclusions • Find correlations between two texts • Make connections between ideas • Synthesize information and ideas	• Discuss the differences between and your opinions on life in the city and life in a town • Discuss your relationships with your neighbors • Write a short essay on life in the city or a neighbor • Discuss in a small group topics about cities and urban life • Choose one of the topics and write a paragraph or two about it

ACKNOWLEDGMENTS

I would like to express my profound gratitude to the many people who have helped to shape the Longman Academic Reading Series.

Massimo Rubini, our Acquisitions Editor, has been an inspiring, competent, and gracious force. Françoise Leffler, who coordinated much of the editorial work, has also been an extremely supportive guide. I worked closely with development editor Gerry Geniusas. A keen eye for detail, the ability to inspect and question, and the tact to deal with missteps are difficult qualities to find in a single person, but she possesses them all! I am so grateful for the help of these talented individuals.

Then I would also like to thank editor Amy McCormick; Rosa Chapinal, who took care of the maze of permissions enquiries; Jill Krupnick, who worked tirelessly on permissions contracts; Jane Lieberth, for her perceptive oversight of the manuscript during its various iterations; and Jaime E. Lieber, Senior Production Editor, for her patience as I prepared the manuscript.

To dear students and colleagues at Eugenio María de Hostos Community College, to my series co-authors, and to other friends who have assisted me with suggestions, my most sincere appreciation.

Kim Sanabria

Reviewers

The publisher would like to thank the following reviewers for their many helpful comments.

Jeff Bette, Naugatuck Valley Community College, Waterbury, Connecticut; **Kevin Knight**, Japan; **Melissa Parisi**, Westchester Community College, Valhalla, New York; **Jason Tannenbaum**, Pace University, Bronx, New York; **Christine Tierney**, Houston Community College, Stafford, Texas; **Kerry Vrabel**, GateWay Community College, Phoenix, Arizona.

CHAPTER 1

CULTURAL STUDIES:
The Lessons of Travel

CULTURAL STUDIES: an interdisciplinary field concerned with the study of contemporary culture worldwide. It may include the study of literature, history, media, language, and art. Many cultural studies programs include study-abroad courses so that students can learn about countries other than their own.

OBJECTIVES

To read academic texts, you need to master certain skills.

In this chapter, you will:

- Skim a text to get an overview
- Preview a text using visuals
- Predict main ideas by writing questions
- Understand and use synonyms, suffixes, definitions, and word forms
- Guess the meaning of words from the context
- Use a graphic organizer
- Organize notes in columns

Consider This Information

1   Read the information about travel. The items in bold type are incorrect. Work in a small group and guess what the correct information might be. Then check your answers at the bottom of the page.

Travel has been a popular activity for centuries. Nowadays, tourism is a major industry worldwide. The word "traveler" (or "traveller," as it is spelled in the United Kingdom) comes from **Latin**, and the word "tourist" was first used in the **14th century**.

The world's top travel destination is France, and the second most popular destination is **China**. A foreign tourist is defined as a person who stays in another country longer than **72 hours** and less than **one year**.

2   Discuss the questions with a partner.

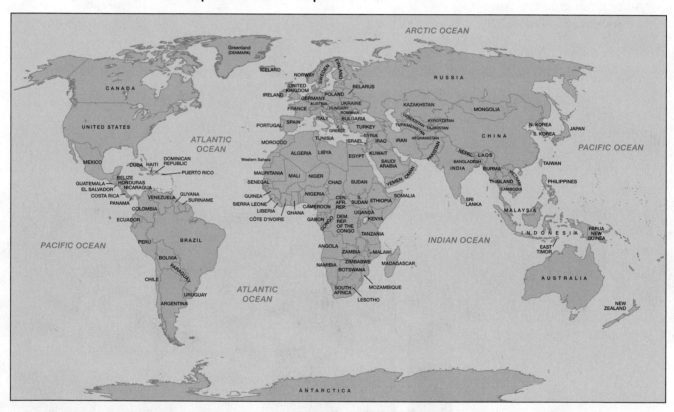

1. Look at the map and show a partner where you have traveled. Give as many details as possible. For example, what did you do? Who traveled with you? How long were you there?

2. Did you enjoy your trips? What did you learn?

3. Where would you like to travel in the future, and why?

A **Warm-Up**

> Tony Giles, whose nickname is "Tony the Traveller," has written a book about his world travels called *Seeing the World My Way*. What is your favorite way of "seeing the world"? Which of the following activities would your perfect trip include?

Check (✓) all that apply. Add an idea of your own. Then share your ideas with the class.

☐ eating new foods

☐ sightseeing and visiting monuments

☐ meeting local people

☐ learning about a place's history

☐ listening to local music

☐ taking photographs

☐ keeping a journal

☐ your own idea: _____

B **Reading Strategy**

Skimming

Skimming is a method of getting **a general overview of a text**. When readers skim a complete passage or part of any text, they read three to four times as fast as usual.

Skim the first paragraph of the reading. Then answer the questions.

1. Who is Tony? _____

2. Where has he been, and what has he done? _____

_____

Now read the website to check your answers.

Tony the Traveller

1 Tony Giles, from England, loves to travel, and people who meet him are **amazed** by his **determination**. Tony has been to every continent on earth and swum in all the major oceans. He travels alone, although he points out that travelers are rarely alone for long. He has gone bungee jumping, taken mud baths, cruised Antarctica, fed penguins, explored ancient ruins, and slept at campsites.

2 Tony claims to travel for more or less the same reasons other young people do. He talks about the sense of adventure, the urge[1] to escape from **conventional** life and the trappings of responsibility, and the **challenge** of doing something new. He documents his experiences on his website and has written a book, called *Seeing the World My Way*.

Bungee jumping is one of the amazing activities Tony has done.

3 What makes Tony truly **remarkable**, however, is that unlike most travelers, he is completely blind and 80 percent deaf. He says: "People often ask why a blind person would want to travel the world when they can't see anything when they get there. It is a good question from a sighted person's[2] **perspective**, but traveling is more than just seeing the beautiful scenery or landscape with your eyes. It concerns using all the body's senses. It is being able to engage with people, feeling different textures, being **exposed** to an alternative, exciting culture, emerging into another country, and returning home knowing more than I did before I left. Meeting the people, enjoying the food, the sounds, the smells, the atmosphere—I can take it all in."

4 Tony adds: "Traveling allows me to experience the world in a multitude of ways. It **enables** me to obtain a great global education that books only hint at. Tasting **unknown** foods, hearing new music, and feeling the contours and gradients[3] of mountains, valleys, and rivers cannot really be achieved at home or in the study environment—you have to travel to experience life.

5 I can travel because of four things—**confidence**, wanting to travel, good mobility skills, and planning. That's all anyone needs. I have proved that nothing—not even disabilities[4]—can stop you living a full life. If you want it, and have a heart for it, you can achieve anything. I desired it so badly that I traveled around the world solo twice. And if I can do it, so can you."

---

[1] *urge:* wish, desire

[2] *sighted person:* a person who is able to see

[3] *gradients:* slopes or inclines

[4] *disabilities:* physical or mental conditions that limit movements or activities

COMPREHENSION

A Main Ideas

Read each statement. Decide if it is *True* or *False* according to the reading.
Check (✓) the appropriate box. Discuss your answers with a partner.

	TRUE	FALSE
1. Tony is a young man who cannot travel.	☐	☐
2. Tony is different from other young travelers in that he is totally blind and 80 percent deaf.	☐	☐
3. What Tony likes most about traveling is the beautiful scenery.	☐	☐
4. Tony thinks that he can learn more from traveling than from books.	☐	☐

B Close Reading

Read the questions. Cross out the one answer that is not correct. Share your
answers with a partner.

1. What do we know about Tony?

   a. ~~his age~~

   b. his origin

   c. his activities

2. What has Tony done in his travels?

   a. He has swum in all the major oceans of the world.

   b. He has been to all of the world's seven continents.

   c. He has traveled to all the countries in the world.

3. What does Tony say about most young people?

   a. They like adventure.

   b. They enjoy new challenges.

   c. They are not responsible.

(continued on next page)

4. What has Tony done to record his travels?

    a. He has written a book.

    b. He has made a movie.

    c. He has set up a website.

5. When sighted people ask why Tony wants to travel, what is his response?

    a. He feels angry.

    b. He explains his reasons patiently.

    c. He thinks it is a good question.

6. What does traveling allow Tony to do?

    a. have new experiences

    b. get a global education

    c. appreciate staying at home

VOCABULARY

 Synonyms

Complete the journal entry about travel with the words from the box. Use the synonym (a word or phrase similar in meaning) in parentheses to help you select the correct word.

challenge	conventional	exposed	remarkable
confidence	enables	perspective	unknown

    I first experienced the urge to travel when I was young. I suppose I

thought that traveling would be a _____*challenge*_____, and I definitely
                      1. (test of my abilities)

wanted to see the world from another _____. I wanted to
                              2. (point of view)

get away from my old, _____ routine.
                    3. (traditional)

    When I first started to travel, I had great _____ in
                                4. (trust)

myself. Even though I had many strange and interesting experiences with

_____ people and places, I quickly caught the "travel
      5. (new)

bug." I have learned many new languages, which _____
                                   6. (makes it possible for)

me to communicate with others.

Being _____ to new cultures, languages, and foods
7. (introduced)

was not always easy, but I have to say that traveling has been the most

_____ experience of my life and has changed me in many
8. (incredible)

ways. The writer Mary Anne Radmacher said: "I am not the same, having

seen the moon shine on the other side of the world." That's exactly how I feel.

B **Word Forms**

1 Fill in the chart with the correct word forms. Some categories can have more
than one form. Use a dictionary if necessary. An **X** indicates there is no form in
that category.

	NOUN	VERB	ADJECTIVE
1.	amazement	amaze	amazed/amazing
2.			challenging
3.		X	confident
4.			determined
5.	exposure		
6.			known/unknown

2 Complete the pairs of sentences with the correct form of the words. Choose
from the forms in the chart. Share your answers with a partner.

1. **a.** Most people are filled with ____amazement____ when they learn about

Tony Giles.

b. Tony is an _____ person.

2. **a.** Although Tony is disabled, he still enjoys _____ activities.

b. When Tony travels, he faces both physical and emotional _____.

3. **a.** Tony believes strongly in his own ability. He is _____ that if

you really want to do something, you can.

b. His _____ has inspired many other people.

4. **a.** Tony has a strong sense of purpose. He is a person with great

_____.

b. Tony is _____ to visit as many countries as he can.

(continued on next page)

5. **a.** On his website, Tony points out that travel _____ people to situations they might not face at home.

    b. Tony feels that _____ to new experiences is one of the best parts about traveling.

6. **a.** Tony _____ that other travelers find his story inspiring.

    b. One person wrote on his blog: "Tony, you have opened my mind! Now I'm not so afraid of _____ experiences."

NOTE-TAKING: Using a Graphic Organizer

One of the easiest ways to take notes is to **use a graphic organizer**, which is a visual representation of ideas. You may set up an organizer in many ways. A basic format is to divide the ideas into categories around a central topic. This is sometimes called a "mind map." This helps you organize the information you read in a way that makes sense to you, and then later to remember the information quickly and efficiently.

Go back to the reading and read it again. Take notes on the graphic organizer. Share your notes with a partner.

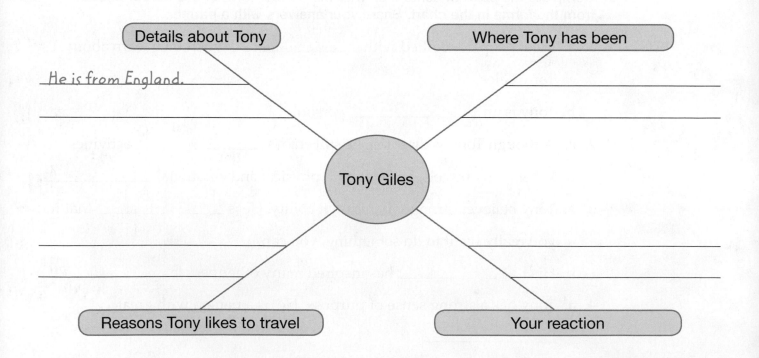

CRITICAL THINKING

Discuss the questions in a small group. Be prepared to share your answers with the class.

1. Do you believe that young people enjoy traveling more than older people? Do you think that young people enjoy different types of travel? Explain.

2. Tony talks about "conventional life and the trappings of responsibility." What do you think he means? Do you agree or not? Explain.

3. Many people think of traveling as seeing new sights, or places. The word "sightseeing" emphasizes this idea. However, Tony reminds us that we use all our senses to experience our world. How have you used all of your senses when you have traveled? Give examples.

4. Tony believes that learning from books is not as educational as traveling. He says: "You have to travel to experience life." What do you think he means by this statement? Do you agree or not? Explain.

5. Tony says that if people want something very badly, they can achieve it, and many visitors to his website have indicated that they find this idea very inspiring. Why do you think Tony's story has had such an effect on them? What effect does his story have on you?

READING TWO: The Benefits of Studying Abroad

 A Warm-Up

> Some students get the chance to study abroad, that is, spend a short period studying in another country. Many people believe that this is an experience that all students should have.

1 Read some of the benefits of studying abroad. Put them in order of importance, with 1 being the most important and 10 being the least important. Add an idea of your own.

_____ It is a good way to learn a foreign language.

_____ It exposes students to different cultures and lifestyles.

_____ It helps students develop skills that classrooms cannot provide.

_____ It allows students to learn about themselves.

_____ It helps students make friends around the world.

_____ It improves employment opportunities.

_____ It helps students become more informed about the world.

_____ It allows students to share their own culture with others.

_____ It opens people's minds.

_____ Your own idea: _____

2 With a partner, decide which are the three most important benefits of studying abroad. Then share your answers with the class.

B Reading Strategy

Previewing Using Visuals

Many readings in college textbooks are accompanied by **visual images**, like photos, illustrations, and charts, to illustrate the text. Sometimes the images also have captions. Previewing visual material, particularly reading the captions, **can help you understand the text better**.

Look at the two photos and captions in the reading. Then discuss the questions with a partner.

1. What do the photos show?

2. What do the captions tell you about the benefits of studying abroad?

Now read the entire text to check your answers.

The Benefits of Studying Abroad

By Professor Jason Flora

1   The philosopher St. Augustine (354–430) declared: "The world is a book, and those who do not travel read only a page." Many educators agree. Colleges in the United States are promoting study-abroad programs, noting the language and cultural skills that participants gain. Students, too, value the experience of traveling and studying abroad. They say it can be a **rewarding**, even **life-changing** experience. In fact, participating in study-abroad programs, even for short periods, can have a significant **impact** on university students, leaving an **indelible** mark on their lives. Why does travel make such an impact?

2   To begin with, study-abroad participants have firsthand[1] learning opportunities not offered through

Seeing original artwork in a museum is an inspiring experience for study-abroad participants. It is often more powerful than book learning.

_____
[1] *firsthand:* based on personal experience

"book learning" in traditional classroom settings. An art student who contemplated a Velásquez painting in a museum after studying Spanish painting remarked: "I feel like I have lived through a textbook. I didn't have to *read* everything; I was able to *live* everything."

3   In addition, travel seems to **sharpen** the human senses—sight, hearing, touch, taste, and smell. Philosopher David Hume (1711–1776) also suggested that experiencing beauty "enlarges the sphere both of our happiness and misery" and makes us **sensitive** to "pains as well as pleasures." And of course, travel also makes students more sensitive to current events, opening their minds

When study-abroad participants write about their experiences, they reflect more deeply on what they are learning.

and helping them to understand the world's challenges. Even when students traveling abroad encounter difficulties, they are learning important lessons.

4   A **fundamental** component of learning is **self-reflection**, the process of thinking carefully about your values and beliefs. That is why I ask my students to keep a journal about their experiences. Writing about what they see and do makes it easier for them to understand the **overwhelming** emotions they may feel. A student in my class observed: "When I walked in that room and saw Michelangelo's *David* standing at the other end, 14 feet tall, my eyes filled with tears. Happy tears. I never thought it could be so amazing, so glamorous. I don't really know how to describe it; I'm **speechless**. . . . The craftsmanship was amazing and the detail made me cry. The whole thing was extraordinary."

5   As a college professor, I recognize that studying abroad enhances[2] higher education. It allows students to make connections, to challenge themselves, and to better understand themselves and others. No wonder more and more educators are trying to make the study-abroad experience available to as many students as they can.

---

[2] *enhances:* improves

COMPREHENSION

A **Main Ideas**

Check (✓) the statements that best express the main ideas in the reading. Discuss your answers with a partner.

☐ **1.** Many colleges in the United States now have study-abroad programs.

☐ **2.** Students who participate in study-abroad programs do better on tests.

☐ **3.** Studying abroad is generally a positive experience for students.

☐ **4.** More professors are supporting study-abroad programs.

B Close Reading

Read each statement. Decide if it is *True* or *False*, or if there is *No Information* found in the reading. Check (✓) the appropriate box. Discuss your answers with a partner.

	TRUE	FALSE	NO INFORMATION
1. Students like to travel so that they can tell people about their own culture.	☐	☐	☑
2. In order for study-abroad programs to be effective, they should be as long as possible.	☐	☐	☐
3. Traditional classrooms do not provide as many firsthand experiences as studying abroad.	☐	☐	☐
4. When students travel, they often become more sensitive to the world around them.	☐	☐	☐
5. The problems students sometimes face when studying abroad makes the experience less valuable.	☐	☐	☐
6. In Professor Flora's opinion, writing about what you experience when studying abroad helps you learn more.	☐	☐	☐
7. According to Professor Flora, it is easier to explain your emotions in spoken words than in writing.	☐	☐	☐

VOCABULARY

A Definitions

Match each word with its definition. Use a dictionary if necessary.

_d_ 1. indelible	a. bringing many benefits
____ 2. life-changing	b. alters or transforms your life
____ 3. rewarding	c. appreciating beauty or emotions
____ 4. sensitive	d. permanent, doesn't go away
____ 5. overwhelming	e. amazing or incredible

B Guessing from Context

> Looking up every unfamiliar word in the dictionary is not an effective way to read. It is much better to **guess the meaning of unfamiliar words from the rest of the sentence or paragraph (the context)** and keep reading. You can use the dictionary after you get the main idea of the reading.

Read the instant messages between two professors who have just returned from a study-abroad program. Try to guess the meaning of each word in bold from other words in context. Underline the words that help you guess. Then write your guess on the line. Compare answers with a partner.

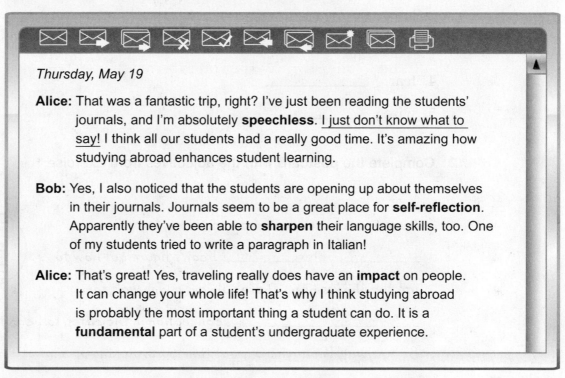

Thursday, May 19

Alice: That was a fantastic trip, right? I've just been reading the students' journals, and I'm absolutely **speechless**. I just don't know what to say! I think all our students had a really good time. It's amazing how studying abroad enhances student learning.

Bob: Yes, I also noticed that the students are opening up about themselves in their journals. Journals seem to be a great place for **self-reflection**. Apparently they've been able to **sharpen** their language skills, too. One of my students tried to write a paragraph in Italian!

Alice: That's great! Yes, traveling really does have an **impact** on people. It can change your whole life! That's why I think studying abroad is probably the most important thing a student can do. It is a **fundamental** part of a student's undergraduate experience.

1. speechless   *unable to say anything*

2. self-reflection _____

3. sharpen _____

4. impact _____

5. fundamental _____

C **Suffix: -less**

> A suffix comes at the end of a word. **The suffix -less** means "without."
> When you add -less to a **noun**, the word becomes an **adjective**.
>
> **EXAMPLE:**
> *speech* (noun) + **-less** = **speechless** (adjective meaning "without speech")
> • I was **speechless**. I did not know what to say.

1 Change the nouns into adjectives by adding the suffix -less.

1. effort _effortless_

2. harm _____

3. hope _____

4. fear _____

5. wire _____

2 Complete the postcard with the adjectives from Exercise 1.

Hi everyone! I've been meaning to call, but it's

_____ hopeless _____! I can't figure out how to
     1.

use the phones here. There's always a long wait for

_____ connection in the cafes, so I can't Skype.
     2.

But anyway, I'm having a great time. I am picking up a lot of Italian,

and it feels _____ because I'm not studying it in a
     3.

book—I just repeat what people say. That has to be the best way to learn

another language! We're having a lot of fun, too. My roommate went

parachute jumping, which seemed scary to me, but he was absolutely

_____, so maybe I'll give it a try, too. Our room is
     4.

pretty nice, but the other day we saw a big spider in the room! It looked scary,

but they told us it was _____. Anyway, can't wait to
     5.

tell you more . . .

CRITICAL THINKING

1 Divide the class into five groups. Each group should read one of the entries from students' journals.

	JOURNAL ENTRY
Student 1	I was on my way to the airport when I realized I had lost my passport. At first I was so scared! But when I went back to the hotel, the receptionist immediately understood what I was trying to say. She ran to my room and found my passport under the bed! I burst into tears. Then she called a taxi and explained my problem to the driver. He made sure I made it to the airport in time. I was so grateful to these people. How can I ever repay their kindness?
Student 2	I was traveling in the Caribbean, and I went to a local festival. A little girl wanted to see my camera, so I showed it to her and let her take a few pictures. My friend said: "Don't do that! She might run away with your camera." But I knew that wouldn't happen. This little girl was so sweet, so innocent. I let her play with the camera for a long time, and then she gave it back and ran off with the other children. I never learned this little girl's name, and I really don't know anything about her, but I will never forget her smile.
Student 3	*I was on my way back to the hostel when it started to rain. There was a restaurant in the square, and I went in, but it was full of people watching a sports game on TV. I wasn't sure what sport it was—I'd never seen it before. I felt a bit uncomfortable because I was an obvious stranger, but I didn't want to go out in the rain, so I ordered some tea. Two hours later, I was still there. Some older men were trying to explain the game to me, and even though I didn't really understand what they were saying, I had a great time.*
Student 4	When I was in Asia, I took a photo of a fruit seller, who was selling oranges in a market. I went back two years later, trying to find the man again, but I couldn't. I had brought a copy of the photo with me, because I thought it was so beautiful. I showed the picture to some other fruit sellers, and then one of them took out his cell phone and made a call. He passed me the phone, and I assumed the orange seller was on the line. I couldn't understand a word, but it was a beautiful moment. Everyone seemed to think it was quite funny.
Student 5	*I was hiking in the mountains, and suddenly a rain cloud came over and it started to pour. A woman emerged from a small house with a chair, which she put down under a tree. She motioned for me to sit down. She disappeared for a while, and then came out with a hot bowl of soup. This woman was so poor, but she wanted to share what she had with me, and she refused to take the money I offered to her.*

2 Make new groups of five people, one person from each group. Using your own words, tell the group about the entry you read.

3 As a class, discuss your reactions to the journal entries.

LINKING READINGS ONE AND TWO

Discuss the questions in a small group. Be prepared to share your answers with the class.

1. How do both authors explain how travel affects the senses?

2. According to the authors, what lessons can you learn from travel?

READING THREE: The Way of St. James: A Modern-Day Pilgrimage

 Warm-Up

For thousands of years, people of all religions have made pilgrimages, journeys to places with religious or spiritual significance. Today, around 100 million people make this kind of journey every year.

A pilgrimage to Taj Mahal

Discuss the questions in a small group.

1. Have you heard of these pilgrimage sites? What do you know about them?
   - Lourdes, France
   - Lhasa, Tibet
   - Varanasi, India
   - Mecca, Saudi Arabia
   - Stonehenge, United Kingdom

2. Are there any pilgrimage sites in your country? Do you know anyone who has made a pilgrimage? Why might someone make a pilgrimage?

B **Reading Strategy**

Predicting Main Ideas

Writing questions before you read a passage can help you **predict (guess) the main ideas** of a text. You may ask questions of any kind; using question words— **who**, **what**, **where**, **when**, **why**, and **how**—is one way to generate interesting questions. Of course, it is possible that not all your questions will be answered, but many of them will be.

With a partner, write questions about the reading using question words. Share your questions with the class.

Who _____?

What _____?

Where _____?

When _____?

Why _____?

How _____?

Now read the article to see if your questions are answered.

The Way of St. James: A Modern-Day Pilgrimage

By Meike Heukels

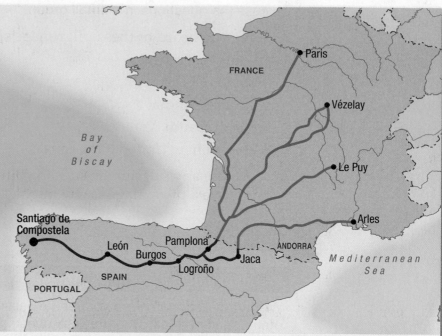

The Way of St. James (El Camino de Santiago), an important Christian medieval pilgrimage, is still popular today. The trail follows an ancient Roman trade route across northern Spain to Santiago de Compostela, where St. James is buried.

1   Every year, tens of thousands of pilgrims make the journey from various places in Europe to Santiago. They come from all over the world, from Japan, Brazil, Sweden, Namibia. They travel mostly on foot, but also by bicycle and even on horseback. Some of them walk for religious reasons, but many others want to see the countryside, have adventures, meet other people, or get away from **frantic** modern life.

2   I walked the trail for over three months with other pilgrims to gain **insight** into people's **motivation** for making this journey. Why would they walk hundreds of miles across a country with nothing more than a backpack, carrying only their most necessary belongings? What made them put up with **exhaustion**, physical **discomfort**, loneliness, and **uncertainty** about their basic needs? I found that they were looking for hope and **renewal**. Indeed, for many pilgrims, their journey turned into one of the most extraordinary[1] experiences of their lives.

3   Imagine yourself walking on a path where millions of footsteps have gone before you. Imagine returning to the basics: food, movement, sleep, and friendship. When there is rain, it rains for everybody. When there is sunshine, it warms everybody. When somebody needs help, there is always a helping hand. If you return to a life of **simplicity**, the only wish that you have left is to share what you have with other people.

4   Many of the pilgrims arrive in Spain planning to walk alone, to take time for themselves. But once they are on the road, most of them grow and **blossom**, like flowers. They experience the beauty of sharing stories, laughter, and food with others. When people leave stress and daily occupations behind, they find a new person inside themselves. And life looks very different when you are not in a rush.[2] When you are walking for eight hours a day, you have time to give the world your full attention. Butterflies become beautiful creatures, people become unique stories, and walking becomes a **meditation**.

---

[1] *extraordinary:* unusual, remarkable

[2] *in a rush:* in a hurry

COMPREHENSION

A **Main Ideas**

Read each main idea from the reading. Find the paragraph that contains each of the main ideas in the reading. Write the paragraph number. Discuss your answers with a partner.

1. PARAGRAPH __2__ In order to study the people who walked the trail, the author walked it herself.

2. PARAGRAPH _____ She wanted to discover why people make this journey.

3. PARAGRAPH _____ The *Way of St. James* is a popular pilgrimage route.

4. PARAGRAPH _____ Many pilgrims change their plans when they begin walking.

5. PARAGRAPH _____ When you make your life less complicated, you want to share what you have with others.

6. PARAGRAPH _____ There are many physical discomforts on the trail.

B **Close Reading**

Discuss the questions with a partner. If necessary, read the text again.

1. How many pilgrims walk the trail every year?

2. What three ways do the pilgrims travel?

3. How long did the author walk the trail?

4. How many miles do people walk?

5. What are four things that the pilgrims must put up with?

6. What does the author say happens to the pilgrims once they are on the road?

VOCABULARY

A Synonyms

Read the sentences. Match each word in bold with its synonym. Compare answers with a partner.

1. My life is so **frantic**. I always have to meet deadlines, and I seem to run around all day.

2. I wish I could return to a life of **simplicity**. I think my life was easier and less complicated when I was younger.

3. My son has been interested in Eastern philosophy for some time. In fact, he practices **meditation** every day.

4. He has decided to go on a long trip alone in India. At first, I didn't understand his **motivation** for doing that, but now I understand that he needs to get away from everything.

5. He may find it difficult, since his Hindi is pretty basic, but I think after a few weeks, his language skills are going to really **blossom**.

_c_ 1. **frantic**	**a.** develop
___ 2. **simplicity**	**b.** reasons
___ 3. **meditation**	**c.** busy
___ 4. **motivation**	**d.** deep thoughts
___ 5. **blossom**	**e.** ease, less difficulty

B Word Forms

1 Fill in the chart with the correct word forms. Some categories can have more than one form. Use a dictionary if necessary. An **X** indicates there is no form in that category.

	NOUN	VERB	ADJECTIVE
1.	insight	X	insightful
2.	motivation		
3.	simplicity	X	
4.	meditation		
5.	renewal		renewed /
6.	comfort / discomfort		comfortable /
7.	exhaustion		
8.	certainty /	X	certain /

2 Complete the summary with the correct form of the words. Choose from the forms in parentheses.

In her _____*insightful*_____ passage on a popular pilgrimage,
1. (insight / insightful)
Heukels examines the _____ of the thousands of
2. (motivation/motivate/motivated)
people who return to the _____ life, carrying nothing
3. (simplicity/simple)
but a backpack full of their belongings, and walk across Spain. On the way,
she discovers that when people _____ about their
4. (meditation/meditate/meditated)
experiences, they feel that they are _____. At times
5. (renewal/renew/renewed)
the pilgrims are not _____, and they are frequently
6. (comfort/comfortable)
_____ and _____ about exactly
7. (exhaustion/exhaust/exhausted)   8. (uncertainty/uncertain)
where they are going. However, most people find that sharing their walk with

others is a life-changing experience.

NOTE-TAKING: Organizing Notes in Columns

> **Organizing notes in columns** allows you to categorize the information you learn from a reading. It also allows you to summarize a reading effectively.

1 Use the following categories to organize your notes in columns. Share your notes with a partner.

SOME COUNTRIES PILGRIMS COME FROM	SOME REASONS PILGRIMS MAKE THE JOURNEY	SOME CHALLENGES PILGRIMS FACE	SOME BENEFITS OF MAKING THE PILGRIMAGE
• Japan	• religious reasons	• exhaustion	• experience the beauty of sharing with others
•	•	•	•
•	•	•	•
•	•	•	•

(continued on next page)

2 With a partner, make an oral summary of the text. Use your notes and these phrases as a guide.

- The text explains that . . .
- The author wanted to know . . .
- She discovered that . . .

CRITICAL THINKING

Decide whether these are examples of benefits or challenges one might face on a pilgrimage. Check (✓) the appropriate box. Discuss your ideas with a partner.

☐ traveling on foot

☐ spending time with people you've never met before

☐ sharing your food, water, and other belongings

☐ sleeping outside

☐ walking eight hours a day

AFTER YOU READ

BRINGING IT ALL TOGETHER

Fill in the chart with as many ideas as you can. Then discuss your ideas in a small group. Use some of the vocabulary you studied in the chapter (for a complete list, go to page 24).

TYPE OF TRAVEL	THINGS YOU MIGHT LIKE	THINGS YOU MIGHT FIND DIFFICULT	THINGS YOU MIGHT LEARN
Traveling alone			
Traveling as part of a study-abroad program			
Making a religious or spiritual pilgrimage			

WRITING ACTIVITY

Write a journal entry about a travel experience. Follow these instructions. Use at least three of the words you studied in the chapter.

1. Choose a trip you have taken, either in your own country or in another country. Select one experience, either good or bad, that had an effect on you.

2. Write a journal entry about this experience. You should aim to write two paragraphs. In your entry:

   a. Give details about the experience you are describing. For example, what did you do? Who were you with? Where were you? What happened? Try to remember as much as you can.

   b. Explain what the experience taught you or made you think about. Did it change you in any way, or make you understand yourself or others better? Explain.

   c. If you can, find a photo of the experience you are describing. Use it to help you remember details.

DISCUSSION AND WRITING TOPICS

Discuss these topics in a small group. Choose one and write a paragraph about it. Use the vocabulary from the chapter.

1. All of the readings suggest that modern life tends to make us too busy to appreciate the world around us, and that traveling is a way to correct this problem. Do you agree with this opinion? Why or why not?

2. Do you think there is a difference between a "tourist" and a "traveler"? If so, what is it?

3. As more and more people travel, they are exploring different ways to see the world. Some of these ways are:

   • ecotourism, which aims to educate visitors about natural resources;

   • cultural tourism, where visitors study a region's culture and lifestyle;

   • health tourism, where travelers go to another country to obtain medical care; and

   • culinary tourism, where participants learn about food and cooking in other countries.

   Have you heard about any of these types of travel experiences? Would you like to travel in any of these ways? Why or why not?

VOCABULARY

Nouns	Verbs	Adjectives
challenge*	blossom	amazed
confidence	enable*	conventional*
determination	expose*	frantic
discomfort	sharpen	fundamental*
exhaustion		indelible
impact*		life-changing
insight*		overwhelming
meditation		remarkable
motivation*		rewarding
perspective*		sensitive
renewal		speechless
self-reflection		unknown
simplicity		
uncertainty		

* = AWL (Academic Word List) item

SELF-ASSESSMENT

In this chapter you learned to:

- ○ Skim a text to get an overview
- ○ Preview a text using visuals
- ○ Predict main ideas by writing questions
- ○ Understand and use synonyms, suffixes, definitions, and word forms
- ○ Guess the meaning of words from the context
- ○ Use a graphic organizer
- ○ Organize notes in columns

What can you do well? ☑

What do you need to practice more? ☑

CHAPTER 2

MULTICULTURAL LITERATURE:
Writing about Cultural Identity

MULTICULTURAL LITERATURE: written work by authors from a variety of racial, ethnic, or language backgrounds. Multicultural literature often explores the topic of cultural identity.

OBJECTIVES

To read academic texts, you need to master certain skills.

In this chapter, you will:

- Visualize images to understand a story

- Identify poetic devices

- Scan a text for specific information

- Guess the meaning of words from the context

- Use dictionary entries to learn different meanings of words

- Understand and use expressions and synonyms

- Identify the basic parts of a story and highlight the basic elements of a book review

Consider This Information

1   Look at the pie charts. With a partner, guess which percentage corresponds to which pie chart. Write the letters on the lines. Then check your answers at the bottom of the page.

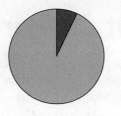  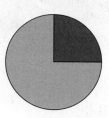

Chart 1: 7% _____   **Chart 2:** 12% _____   **Chart 3:** 20% _____   **Chart 4:** 25% _____

   a. the percentage of population that will be of mixed backgrounds in 2050

   b. the percentage of interracial marriages

   c. the percentage of population that speaks a language other than English at home

   d. the percentage of population born in another country

2   Discuss the questions in a small group.

   1. Do you think cultural identity is an interesting topic? Why or why not?

   2. Have you read any literature by writers of mixed racial, ethnic, or language backgrounds? If so, what? What was your opinion of the literature?

   3. What topics do you think writers of mixed backgrounds might find important? Why?

ANSWERS
1. b, 2. d, 3. c, 4. a

A Warm-Up

1 Read the e-mails.

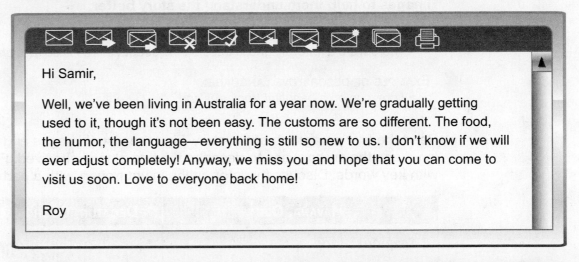

Hi Samir,

Well, we've been living in Australia for a year now. We're gradually getting used to it, though it's not been easy. The customs are so different. The food, the humor, the language—everything is still so new to us. I don't know if we will ever adjust completely! Anyway, we miss you and hope that you can come to visit us soon. Love to everyone back home!

Roy

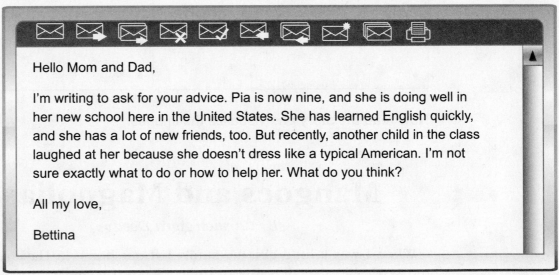

Hello Mom and Dad,

I'm writing to ask for your advice. Pia is now nine, and she is doing well in her new school here in the United States. She has learned English quickly, and she has a lot of new friends, too. But recently, another child in the class laughed at her because she doesn't dress like a typical American. I'm not sure exactly what to do or how to help her. What do you think?

All my love,

Bettina

2 With a partner, write responses to the e-mails.

E-mail 1

_____

_____

_____

E-mail 2

_____

_____

_____

Visualizing Images

Stories often include **strong visual images and descriptive language** that paint a picture for the reader. Good readers use this information to **create mental images to help them understand the story better**.

EXAMPLE OF A STRONG VISUAL IMAGE:
  • *There were a lot of magnolia trees on the street where I lived as a child.*

EXAMPLE OF DESCRIPTIVE LANGUAGE:
  • *I grew up on a beautiful tropical island.*

Read the first paragraph of the story. Find the visual images and descriptive language the author uses to describe the two places she lived. Fill in the chart with key words. Discuss the information in your chart with a partner.

HAVANA, CUBA	DECATUR, GEORGIA, UNITED STATES
• tropical island	• small southern town
•	•
•	•
•	•

Now read the story and visualize the images.

Mangoes and Magnolias

By Carmen Agra Deedy

1   When I was a little girl, my family left our home in Havana, Cuba, and **settled** in a small southern United States town—Decatur, Georgia. With its magnolia trees, changing seasons, and English-speaking southerners, it was a big change from our tropical island. In Cuba, fruit trees grow along the side of the road, it is summer all year long, and everyone speaks Spanish.

2   In time, though, I started to like my new home, and I even learned enough English to make a best friend. An American friend.

3   Then one day we had a really stupid fight over whose turn it was to ride a bike we shared. First we shouted at each other. Then it got really ugly. "Spic![1]" she **hissed**.

4   *Spic* is an ugly name for someone who speaks Spanish. I was twelve years old, and I didn't like it any more then than I do now.

5   "I am not—I'm an American!"

---
[1] This kind of word is called a *slur*, which is a highly unacceptable way to refer to people of different racial or ethnic backgrounds.

6   "Spic!" came the swift reply.
Ashamed and **furious**, I left the bike on the driveway and went back to the garden **in search of** my father. I found him kneeling[2] in the red Georgia clay.[3]

7   Angry tears unleashed[4] years of frustration that most, if not all, immigrant children go through. It ended in a **torrent** of angry words.

8   "And, Papi, I'm not really Cuban because I'm growing up in Decatur. And I'm not an American because I don't look like them and I don't talk like them. . . ." I trailed off as my neck and face grew hot.

9   My father, the gardener, looked at me **intently** for a few moments, then asked, "Do you remember what grafting is?"

10 "Why, um—sure, that's when you take a branch from one tree and stick it into another tree and they grow together, right?"

11 "That's right," he said. "When we took you from Cuba, Carmita, you were like a young mango tree, **torn up by the roots**. You could have withered[5] and died. Instead, you have been grafted into this small southern town, and you don't know it yet, but you are an amazing hybrid: a tree that gives forth both mangoes and magnolias."

12 My friend and I made up,[6] but I never forgot that story.

13 It's really hard to be a kid and be new or different—to leave a home, state, or country that's familiar and feel as if you'll never fit in. And you know what? I still feel that way sometimes. When I do, I remember Papi's story about mangoes and magnolias, and it always **reminds** me that I am Cuban and a southerner. And I don't have to stop eating the fruit . . . to smell the flowers.

---

[2] *kneeling:* on his knees

[3] *clay:* a type of soil

[4] *unleashed:* released, freed

[5] *withered:* become unhealthy

[6] *made up:* became friends again

COMPREHENSION

Ⓐ Main Ideas

Read each statement. Decide if it is *True* or *False* according to the reading. Check (✓) the appropriate box. If it is false, change it to make it true. Discuss your answers with a partner.

	TRUE	FALSE
1. The author's family moved to Cuba when she was a little girl.	☐	☐
2. She didn't speak English at first.	☐	☐
3. She and her friend fought over a bicycle.	☐	☐
4. Her father made her feel better by working in the garden with her.	☐	☐

Ⓑ Close Reading

Read the text again. Then circle the answer that best completes each statement. Share your answers with a partner.

1. Georgia, where the story takes place, is _____.

   a. a small town in Cuba

   b. in the northern part of the United States

   c. in the southern part of the United States

2. According to the reading, the author _____.

   a. grew to like her new home

   b. was not happy in Cuba

   c. was not happy in the United States

3. The author liked that her new friend _____.

   a. was Cuban

   b. was American

   c. spoke some Spanish

4. When the author's friend called her "an ugly name," she felt _____.

   a. angry and frustrated

   b. proud and happy

   c. ugly and afraid

5. She said she did not feel American because of _____.

    a. the way she acted

    b. the way she looked

    c. the family relationships she had

6. The author's father compared her to _____.

    a. a tropical island

    b. a hybrid tree

    c. a southern town

VOCABULARY

A **Guessing from Context**

Read the quotes from the reading. Guess the meanings of the words in bold from the context. Then circle the word or phrase that best explains the meaning of each word.

1. "First we shouted at each other. Then it got really ugly. 'Spic!' she **hissed**." (*paragraph 3*)

    a. said angrily

    b. said loudly

2. "Ashamed and **furious**, I left the bike on the driveway and went back to the garden." (*paragraph 7*)

    a. sad

    b. angry

3. "It ended in a **torrent** of angry words." (*paragraph 8*)

    a. small number

    b. strong flow

4. "My father, the gardener, looked at me **intently** for a few moments." (*paragraph 10*)

    a. with attention

    b. with confusion

5. "Papi's story . . . always **reminds** me that I am a Cuban and a southerner." (*paragraph 14*)

    a. makes me remember

    b. makes me believe

B Expressions with *torn*

Read the dictionary entries for the expressions with *torn*. Then complete the sentences with the correct expressions.

> **(to feel) torn between (two things)** *v.* to be uncertain about which thing you are more committed to
>
> **(to feel) torn apart** *v.* to be very upset about something
>
> **(to be) torn away from (a person or a place)** *v.* to have to leave, even though you have a strong desire to stay
>
> **(to be) torn up by the roots** *v.* to be removed from your origins

1. When I left my country, Peru, I was very sad. I felt _____ and couldn't stop crying for days.

2. I felt as if I had lost my origins. I had left everything important behind me. I felt as if I had been _____.

3. I felt so alone. I had been _____ my friends, my family, and my home.

4. After 20 years, I am used to life in my new country, the United States. But if people ask me: "Where are you from?" I feel _____ the two. I ask myself: Am I American, Peruvian, or both?

C Synonyms

Complete each sentence with a word or phrase from the box. Use the synonym in parentheses to help you select the correct word or phrase. Compare answers with a partner.

ashamed	roots	in search of	settled	torn away from

1. When I was in middle school, my family moved to the United States from China, _____*in search of*_____ a better life.
   (looking for)

2. We _____ in Los Angeles, where there is a large
   (went to live)
   Chinese population.

3. My mother wanted to make sure that my brother and I did not forget our

   _____.
   (origins)

4. Often, I was very homesick. I felt I had been _____

   my country.
   (removed by force from)

5. When my classmates made fun of my accent, I felt

   _____ that I could not speak English well.
   (embarrassed and guilty)

NOTE-TAKING: Identifying the Basic Parts of a Story

> Modern storytelling often includes **three basic parts**: (1) an **introduction**, which provides the context; (2) a **confrontation**, which describes a problem; and (3) a **resolution**, which brings the story to a conclusion.

Go back to the reading and read it again. Identify the paragraphs that correspond to each part of the story. Write the paragraph numbers on the lines. Compare answers with a partner.

INTRODUCTION: Paragraphs _____–_____

CONFRONTATION: Paragraphs _____–_____

RESOLUTION: Paragraphs _____–_____

CRITICAL THINKING

Discuss the questions in a small group. Be prepared to share your answers with the class.

1. Carmita says that she had "years of frustration." Why do you think she experienced this feeling?

2. Why was Carmita hurt when her friend called her an ugly word? What feelings did it bring out in her?

3. Why do you think Carmita's father used the idea of grafting to make her feel better?

4. What do you think mangoes and magnolias represent? Explain.

A **Warm-Up**

1   How did your family teach you important lessons about your culture? Check (✓) all that apply.

☐ food

☐ music and dance

☐ language

☐ traditional customs

☐ stories

☐ lessons from older people

☐ your own idea: _____

2   Share your thoughts with a partner.

B **Reading Strategy**

Identifying Poetic Devices

Poetic devices can produce a "feeling" in a work of poetry. Identifying these devices can help you better understand the meaning of a poem. Some common poetic devices are **alliteration**, **imagery**, and **repetition**.

alliteration: the repetition of initial consonant sounds
   EXAMPLE: *(I was) born into this **continent** at a **crossroads**.*

imagery: the use of words that appeal to the senses (taste, touch, sight, hearing, smell)
   EXAMPLE: *I speak English with passion: it's the **tongue** of my consciousness, a **flashing** knife blade of crystal.*

repetition: the repeating of words, phrases, or lines
   EXAMPLE: *spilling **water** into **water***

Preview the poems. Find at least one example of each poetic device. Write the examples on the lines. Share your answers with a partner.

1. alliteration: _____

2. imagery: _____

3. repetition: _____

Now read the poems and identify the poetic devices.

Li-Young Lee is an Asian American poet, who was born in Indonesia to Chinese parents. He often writes about his memories.

I Ask My Mother to Sing

By Li-Young Lee

1   She begins, and my grandmother joins her.
    Mother and daughter sing like young girls.
    If my father were alive, he would play
    his accordion and **sway** like a boat.

2   I've never been in Peking,[1] or the Summer Palace,
    nor stood on the great Stone Boat to watch
    the rain begin on Kuen Ming Lake, the picnickers
    running away in the grass.

3   But I love to hear it sung;
    how the waterlilies fill with rain until
    they **overturn, spilling** water into water,
    then rock back, and fill with more.

4   Both women have begun to cry,
    But neither stops her song.

---
[1] *Peking:* the capital of China, usually called "Beijing" in English

(continued on next page)

Aurora Levins Morales is a Puerto Rican Jewish poet. Both her mother, a Puerto Rican, and her father, a Ukrainian, were born in New York. She frequently writes about identity.

Child of the Americas

By Aurora Levins Morales

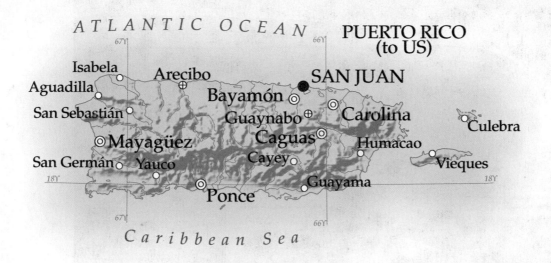

5 I am a child of the Americas,
    a light-skinned mestiza[2] of the Caribbean,
    a child of many diaspora,[3] born into this continent at a crossroads.

6 I am a U.S. Puerto Rican Jew,
    a product of the ghettos[4] of New York I have never known.
    An immigrant and the daughter and granddaughter of immigrants.
    I speak English with passion: it's the tongue of my **consciousness**,
    a flashing knife blade of **crystal**, my **tool**, my **craft**.

7 I am Caribeña,[5] island grown. Spanish is in my flesh,
    ripples from my tongue, lodges in my **hips**:
    the language of garlic and mangoes,
    the singing in my poetry, the flying gestures of my hands.
    I am of Latinoamerica, rooted in the history of my continent:
    I speak from that body.

---

[2]*mestiza:* a woman of mixed race, particularly Spanish and American Indian

[3]*diaspora:* a group migration from a country or region

[4]*ghetto:* a densely populated, poor area

[5]*Caribeña:* (Spanish) a woman from the Caribbean

8 I am not african. Africa is in me, but I cannot return.
   I am not taina.[6] Taino is in me, but there is no way back.
   I am not european. Europe lives in me, but I have no home there.

9 I am new. History made me. My first language was spanglish.[7]
   I was born at the crossroads
   and I am whole.

   ───────────────
   [6] *taina:* belonging to an American Indian tribe; the native inhabitants of Puerto Rico
   [7] *spanglish:* a mix of Spanish and English

COMPREHENSION

Main Ideas

Complete the sentences with a phrase from the box. Write the letter of the correct answer on the line. Check your answers with a partner.

> **a.** were immigrants
> **b** sang about a rainy afternoon in a park
> **c.** was a mixture of English and Spanish
> **d.** is no longer alive
> **e.** has made her the person that she is
> **f.** makes his mother and grandmother cry
> **g.** has never been to China
> **h.** has a complex racial, ethnic, and language background

"I Ask My Mother to Sing"

1. Li-Young Lee __g__.

2. His mother and grandmother ____.

3. The song ____.

4. Li-Young Lee's father ____.

"Child of the Americas"

5. Aurora Levins Morales ____.

6. Her parents and grandparents ____.

7. Morales's first language ____.

8. She feels that history ____.

Multicultural Literature: *Writing about Cultural Identity* **37**

B Close Reading

Read the quotes from the reading. Circle the statement that best explains each quote. Share your answers with a partner.

"I Ask My Mother to Sing"

1. "Mother and daughter sing like young girls. / If my father were alive, he would play / his accordion and sway like a boat."

   a. The poet's mother and grandmother don't like to sing.

   b. The poet believes his father would have liked the music.

   c. The poet's father did not play the accordion.

2. "But I love to hear it sung; / how the waterlilies fill with rain until / they overturn, spilling water into water, / then rock back, and fill with more."

   a. The poet is walking in a rainstorm.

   b. The poet enjoys the imagery in the song.

   c. The poet is remembering a rainy day.

"Child of the Americas"

3. "Spanish is in my flesh, / ripples from my tongue, lodges in my hips: / the language of garlic and mangoes, / the singing in my poetry, the flying gestures of my hands."

   a. The poet cannot speak Spanish fluently.

   b. Spanish is less effective than English for writing poetry.

   c. Spanish is an important part of the way the poet expresses herself.

4. "I was born at the crossroads / and I am whole."

   a. The poet is comfortable with her mixed background.

   b. The poet cannot accept her mixed background.

   c. The poet thinks that she will change.

VOCABULARY

A Definitions

Match each word with its definition. Use a dictionary if necessary.

___i___ 1. **consciousness**

_____ 2. **craft**

_____ 3. **crystal**

_____ 4. **hips**

_____ 5. **overturn**

_____ 6. **ripple**

_____ 7. **spilling**

_____ 8. **sway**

_____ 9. **tool**

a. causing or allowing something to flow over the edge of a container

b. move from side to side

c. something that helps people do a particular job

d. form small waves on the surface of the water

e. glass-like stone

f. part of the body above the legs

g. turn upside down

h. skill in making things

i. the state of being aware of yourself and the world

B Guessing from Context

Read the paragraphs. Complete each paragraph with words from the box. Use the context of the paragraphs to help you select the correct words.

consciousness	hips	ripples	sway
crystal	overturns	spills	tools

CHINESE CULTURE AND ARTS FESTIVALS

Like other ethnic groups, many Chinese Americans have a strong

_____consciousness_____ of their language and culture. If you want to
                    1.

learn more about this group, go to a culture and arts festival. You can see

people buying traditional crafts and enjoying theatrical events, which pass

down timeless lessons. One popular story is about a family whose wagon

is on such a bad road that it _____ and all the grain
                                            2.

_____ out of the wagon onto the road. The story teaches
        3.

us that we should not follow a path we know to be dangerous.

(continued on next page)

PUERTO RICO, AN ENCHANTED ISLAND

Puerto Rico is a popular tourist attraction. With its oceans as clear as

_____ and its water that _____
　　　　　　　4.　　　　　　　　　　　　　　　　　　　　　　　　　　　　　5.

along the shore, it is hard to find a more beautiful environment.

The culture, too, is fascinating. For example, in *salsa* music, dancers

_____ to the rhythms of drums. The dance, which
　　　　　　　6.

includes movement of the _____ and complex steps and
　　　　　　　　　　　　　　　　　　　　　　7.

turns, is famous worldwide.

The island also has a fascinating history. Its people are a blend of African,

Taino, and European ancestry. We know about the Tainos, the first inhabitants

of the island, from pre-Columbian artifacts and _____
　　　　　　　　　　　　　　　　　　　　　　　　　　　　　　　　　8.

discovered in Puerto Rico.

C **Using the Dictionary**

1 Read the dictionary entries for *rock* and *sway*. Notice that the words are very similar in meaning. However, they are used in slightly different ways.

> **rock** *v.* to move backwards and forwards or from side to side, or to make something else move this way, often in a repetitive movement: *The waves rocked the boat from side to side.*
>
> **sway** *v.* to move slowly from one side to another, where the base of the object is usually fixed and the top of the object moves: *The trees swayed gently in the breeze.*

2 Complete the sentences with the correct form of *rock* or *sway*.

1. I used to cry a lot when I was a baby. My mother would _____ me in her arms until I fell asleep.

2. I come from a beautiful island where there are a lot of palm trees. They

    _____ in the wind at the edge of the ocean.

3. My father has a favorite chair. He sits and _____ back and forth all day.

4. I don't like traveling by boat. When the ocean is rough, the waves

    _____ the boat so hard that I don't feel well.

CRITICAL THINKING

Both Aurora Levins Morales and Li-Young Lee have complex backgrounds, which they express through poetry. In what ways are the poets similar? How are they different? With a partner, complete the chart. Be prepared to share your ideas with the class.

SIMILARITIES	DIFFERENCES
Both authors are proud of their roots.	Aurora Levins Morales's parents are from different ethnic backgrounds; both of Li-Young Lee's parents are Chinese.

LINKING READINGS ONE AND TWO

Read the ideas expressed in Reading One. Then with a partner, decide if Reading Two expresses similar or different ideas.

	IDEAS IN READING ONE	IDEAS IN READING TWO
a.	Many immigrants experience years of frustration. They find it really hard to be new or different.	
b.	Children of immigrants sometimes face difficulties.	
c.	Parents should teach children about the cultural background of their families.	

A **Warm-Up**

1 If you wrote a story about your identity, which of these details would you include? Check (✓) all that apply.

☐ your appearance

☐ your first language

☐ your culture

☐ your family

☐ your own idea: _____

2 Share your thoughts with a partner.

B **Reading Strategy**

Scanning for Specific Information

Scanning is reading a text quickly to locate specific information. When you scan, you try to find only **the most important points** of a reading.

1 Read the questions. Then scan the first paragraph of the book review and find the answers. Share your answers with a partner.

1. How does the reviewer describe the United States?

2. Is identity a common topic of discussion?

3. What is *Mixed* about?

2 Now read the entire book review to find out more about identity.

Book Review of *Mixed: An Anthology of Short Fiction about the Multiracial Experience*

1 **A**merica has always prided itself on being a melting pot, a country where people of different ethnic and racial backgrounds live together, interact, and intermarry. However, even though there is a **vast** multiracial population in the United States, Americans do not always **confront** the issue of belonging and identity. In the collection *Mixed*, editor Chandra Prasad[1] opens up this discussion. She brings together eighteen stories by both new and published writers about the experience of coming from a multiracial background. The contributors all come from blended[2] families, and in their stories, they describe what it is like to have **complex** identities. The selections in *Mixed* are followed by notes from the authors.

2 In "My Elizabeth" by Diana Abu-Jaber, a young Palestinian girl moves to live with her aunt on a Native American reservation, where she meets a friend, Elizabeth. The girls are from different cultural backgrounds. However, they share a sense of **displacement** that brings them together. Their friendship is **profound** and sometimes **painful**.

3 In Neela Vaswani's "Bing-Chen," a young man of Chinese and Anglo-Saxon descent gets a haircut. This simple experience leads him to reevaluate[3] his sense of identity.

4 In "Minotaur," Peter Ho Davies uses an unusual metaphor[4] to express his feelings about the multiracial experience. He becomes a teenage minotaur (an animal who is half man, half bull).

5 The protagonist[5] of Lucinda Roy's "Effigies" is a powerful African American academic. He questions his identity when his white, Irish mother comes back into his life. She is like a ghost from his past and leaves him with questions and **doubts** about his **roots**.

6 The fiction in *Mixed* is fresh, **engaging**, **vital**, and above all exciting. It miraculously does the impossible: it provides a sense of unity and **togetherness** while confronting a wide variety of difficult questions.

---

[1] Chandra Prasad herself is part Italian, English, Swedish, and Indian.

[2] *blended:* from mixed backgrounds

[3] *reevaluate:* rethink

[4] *metaphor:* something that represents or symbolizes something else

[5] *protagonist:* the main character in a work of literature

COMPREHENSION

A **Main Ideas**

Complete the sentences based on the main ideas of the reading. Share your answers with a partner.

1. *Mixed* is an anthology of *short fiction about the multiracial experience* .

2. In bringing together these stories, Chandra Prasad is trying to open the discussion of _____.

3. _____ have contributed to the anthology.

4. The stories describe _____.

5. The reviewer thinks that *Mixed* _____.

B **Close Reading**

Read each question. Circle the correct answer.

1. According to the review, which is not part of the definition of a "melting pot"?
   a. people from different backgrounds marrying each other
   b. people from different racial backgrounds living together
   c. people following their own cultures, independent from others

2. In the reviewer's description of the United States, what does the reader learn?
   a. It is common for people from different groups to discuss their problems.
   b. There is a very large multiracial population in the United States.
   c. Immigration is an important national issue.

3. Which statement about writer Diana Abu-Jaber is not correct?
   a. The reader learns about her background.
   b. She is Native American.
   c. She tells a story about a friendship between two girls.

4. What brings the girls together in the story "My Elizabeth"?
   a. their similar experiences
   b. their anger
   c. the fact that they live near each other

5. What is interesting about the protagonist's experience in "Bing-Chen"?

   a. His parents have had the same experience as he has.

   b. A simple event creates a complex question.

   c. Nobody helps him.

6. What is one of the main similarities between the characters in "Minotaur" and "Effigies"?

   a. They are the same age.

   b. They have similar cultural roots.

   c. They both have "mixed" backgrounds.

7. What is probably true of the writers who appear in *Mixed*?

   a. They are from the same racial backgrounds.

   b. They want their readers to understand their experiences.

   c. They are all about the same age.

8. What is the reviewer's opinion of *Mixed*?

   a. It is impossible to fully understand.

   b. It performs a difficult task successfully.

   c. It does not always discuss issues of belonging and identity.

VOCABULARY

 Synonyms

Cross out the word that is NOT a synonym for the word in bold. Use a dictionary if necessary. Compare answers with a partner.

1. **confront**	face	~~avoid~~	deal with
2. **displacement**	removal	departure	acceptance
3. **doubts**	uncertainties	beliefs	questions
4. **engaging**	interesting	boring	exciting
5. **painful**	unpleasant	changing	sad
6. **profound**	deep	light	intense
7. **roots**	origins	birthplace	workplace
8. **togetherness**	closeness	harmony	disagreement
9. **vast**	small	large	enormous
10. **vital**	important	fundamental	unnecessary

B Guessing from Context

Read the book reviews. Complete each review with words from the box.
Use the context of the paragraphs to help you select the correct words.
Compare answers with a partner.

confront	displacement	engaging	profound	vital
complex	doubts	painful	togetherness	

Wei, the main character in *Acceptance*, has a _____*painful*_____

1.

experience as a teenager. His mother is Chinese, and his father is

Irish American, and when his girlfriend's family asks him about his

background, it is difficult for him to explain. This important novel is

_____ reading for all young people and is a deep and

2.

_____ examination of interracial relationships today.

3.

The protagonist of *A New Life in Australia* is a young girl called Champei,

who was born in Cambodia. When her family immigrated, her father gave her

a new, English name. He felt that "Champei" was hard for English speakers

to pronounce correctly, and he did not want her to _____

4.

any difficulties. The story gets interesting when Champei's father rethinks

his decision and begins to have _____. In discussing the

5.

situation, father and daughter develop a relationship of understanding and

_____.

6.

The United States's vast multicultural population is growing every day.

Metaphors for Today's U.S.A. is an interesting and _____

7.

new text that examines the term "melting pot," a metaphor that was popular

in the 19th century. The _____ of this term by other

8.

images, such as "salad bowl" or "patchwork quilt," demonstrates a better

understanding of the complicated and _____ situation in

9.

21st-century America.

NOTE-TAKING: Highlighting the Basic Elements of a Book Review

Book reviews generally contain certain ***basic elements:***
- the title and author or editor of the book,
- a summary of the book's contents, and
- the reviewer's opinion of the book.

Highlighting these elements is helpful in identifying the author's purpose for writing the review. It also helps you summarize the review.

EXAMPLE:

A Book of Luminous Things: An International Anthology of Poetry, edited by Czeslaw Milosz, is a collection of short poems by authors from all over the world. The reviewer thinks it is "a refreshing and wise anthology."

Go back to the reading and read it again. Highlight the basic elements. With a partner, use the elements to summarize the review.

CRITICAL THINKING

Read the statements. Decide how much you agree or disagree with each. Circle your answer on the scale. Explain your opinions in a small group.

1. The story "My Elizabeth" is unusual because there are probably very few Palestinian girls living on an American Indian reservation. However, most people can still understand the protagonist because of the friendship she develops with Elizabeth.

Strongly agree	Agree	Not sure	Disagree	Strongly disagree

2. In the story "Bing-Chen," the protagonist gets a haircut. Young people are very concerned about their personal appearance, which is probably why the experience makes him examine his sense of identity.

Strongly agree	Agree	Not sure	Disagree	Strongly disagree

3. The story "Minotaur" can be better appreciated by teenage readers because the Minotaur is a teenager.

Strongly agree	Agree	Not sure	Disagree	Strongly disagree

4. It is unlikely that a highly educated adult, like the one in "Effigies," would find it difficult to accept his background.

Strongly agree	Agree	Not sure	Disagree	Strongly disagree

BRINGING IT ALL TOGETHER

1 Choose one of the topics to discuss. Form three groups: *a*, *b*, and *c*. Use the questions to get you started. Use some of the vocabulary you studied in the chapter (for a complete list, go to page 49).

  a. *Facing stereotypes*
  - What kind of stereotypes do people of mixed origin face?
  - What comments and attitudes do they often need to deal with?

  b. *Finding a positive response*
  - What are some positive ways to react to discrimination?
  - How can writing about your experience help you deal with difficulties in life?

  c. *Passing on family lessons*
  - What should parents teach their children about their culture, and how?
  - When children grow up in a different country from their parents', what issues might they face?

2 Form new groups of three people. Be sure to include one person from Groups *a*, *b*, and *c*. Discuss the topics in new groups.

WRITING ACTIVITY

Choose one of the topics and write two paragraphs. Use at least five words you studied in the chapter. Try to use strong visual images and descriptive language.

1. a difficult moment you experienced as a child

2. an important lesson you learned from a parent or other adult

3. your background

4. fitting in

DISCUSSION AND WRITING TOPICS

Discuss these questions in a small group. Be prepared to share your answers with the class. Choose one of them and write a paragraph or two about it. Use the vocabulary from the chapter.

1. When people immigrate to another country, they often face difficulties adjusting to their new environment. How are the experiences of children, young adults, and adults different? How are they similar?

2. The word "culture" is very difficult to define. People sharing a culture often also share similar customs, values, and traditions. How would you define your own culture? What customs, values, and traditions are important to you? Why?

VOCABULARY

Nouns	Verbs	Adjectives	Adverb
consciousness	confront	ashamed	intently
craft	hiss	complex*	
crystal	overturn	engaging	**Phrases and Idioms**
displacement*	remind	furious	in search of
doubts	ripple	painful	tear up by the roots
hips	settle	profound	
roots	sway	vast	
togetherness	spill	vital	
tool			
torrent			

* = AWL (Academic Word List) item

SELF-ASSESSMENT

In this chapter you learned to:

○ Visualize images to understand a story

○ Identify poetic devices

○ Scan a text for specific information

○ Guess the meaning of words from the context

○ Use dictionary entries to learn different meanings of words

○ Understand and use expressions and synonyms

○ Identify the basic parts of a story and highlight the basic elements of a book review

What can you do well? ☑

What do you need to practice more? ☑

HEALTH SCIENCE:
High Tech, Low Tech, No Tech

HEALTH SCIENCE: a multidisciplinary field applying the science of technology to health care. Health care scientists are involved in the diagnosis, treatment, care, and support of patients.

OBJECTIVES

To read academic texts, you need to master certain skills.

In this chapter, you will:

- Predict the content of a text from its title

- Predict the content of a text from its first paragraph

- Skim a text to confirm the main idea

- Guess the meaning of words from the context

- Understand and use synonyms and word forms

- Use an outline

- Use a flowchart

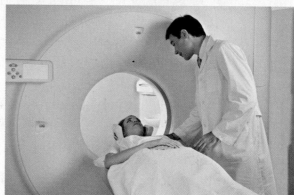

Consider This Information

1 Survey the class to find out what you know about different health problems. Then match the problems with a fact from the box. Check your answers at the bottom of the page.

__b__ 1. heart attack   ____ 5. hepatitis

____ 2. pneumonia   ____ 6. diabetes

____ 3. malaria   ____ 7. obesity

____ 4. loss of mobility

---

a. It is spread by mosquitoes and kills many people in Africa, Asia, and South America.

b. It is the main cause of death for people worldwide.

c. It is a condition that can often be prevented through proper diet and exercise. It can lead to many serious illnesses.

d. It is a group of conditions related to blood sugar.

e. It affects older people worldwide and can also be caused by accidents.

f. It affects the liver and is sometimes caused by infection.

g. It affects the lungs. It can be treated by medicines but is one of the main causes of death in poor countries.

---

2 In recent years, technology has begun to play a bigger role in health care. Decide how much technology is needed for the following activities. Write the numbers on the scale.

No Technology   A Lot of Technology

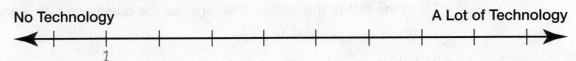

1. taking aspirin every day
2. exercising regularly
3. having knee surgery
4. practicing yoga
5. taking cholesterol medication

6. having a blood test
7. using an electric wheelchair
8. eating healthful food
9. having a kidney transplant
10. sleeping eight hours a night

3 Share your scale with a partner. Compare your responses.

A Warm-Up

1 Read the descriptions of robots used for health care. Check (✓) any that you are familiar with.

☐ **1.** The *Teddy Bear Robotic Pillow* is designed to help people sleep better. If you snore, the teddy bear will gently stroke your face until you stop snoring.

☐ **2.** *Robo-Doc* is a robot that moves around hospitals. It has a screen for a face, and the screen shows a doctor that patients can talk to if they want. The doctor can see the patient, ask questions, and read patients' records.

☐ **3.** *Robotic pets* are technological inventions that keep elderly people company. They have been shown to reduce stress, loneliness, and depression.

2 Discuss your reactions to the robots with a partner or in a small group. Do you know of any other ways that robots are used for health care? If so, what are they?

B Reading Strategy

Predicting Content from Title

You can usually **predict** (guess) **the content of a text by reading its title**. The title of a text often communicates the writer's main idea.

Read the title of the article. Then answer the questions with a partner.

1. What will the article discuss?

2. Which people can you expect the article to refer to?

Now read the article to find out if your prediction was correct.

Robots Improve Health Care, Helping Doctors, Nurses, and Patients

1 The term "robot" was first used in the 1920s, and today there are millions of robots in use throughout the world, according to the International Federation of Robotics. In the health industry, robots are being used more each day.

2 Increasingly,[1] surgeons use robots for remote surgery, also called *telesurgery*. In other words, they **operate** on patients without having to be in the same physical location: in fact, they may be far away. Although it might seem scary to have a robot performing an operation on you, robotic surgery has many **benefits**. Robots do not get **distracted** or become bored by **repetitive** tasks. In addition, they are much more precise. Consequently, a patient may feel less pain during an operation and **recover** more quickly.

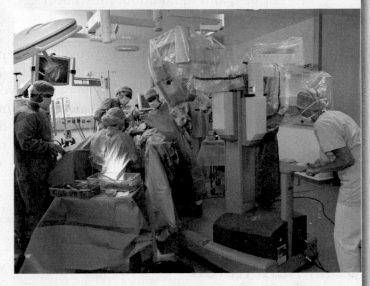

3 Medical students also use robots to learn about the human body. They practice on *human simulators*, mannequins equipped with the latest technology. These pieces of equipment not only **resemble** real people, but they also act like them. They can cry, sweat, produce saliva, and open and close their eyes. They can make breathing and heartbeat sounds, and they can **bleed** and respond to drugs. There are many varieties of these mannequins: male and female versions, teenage versions, and even pregnant and baby versions. Because they are so lifelike, these robotic patients can prepare future doctors for the real-life **scenarios** they might face in their careers. They can "suffer" from almost any emergency situation possible, like a heart attack or epileptic seizure.[2] This exposure to realistic "emergencies" may help prevent medical errors, which unfortunately are all too common.

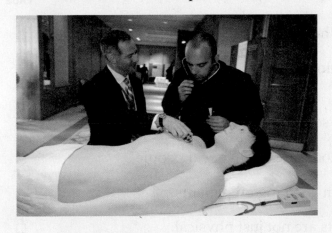

(continued on next page)

---

[1] *increasingly:* more and more

[2] *epileptic seizure:* sudden lack of consciousness, and dramatic movements of the body

4 Robots can help nurses, too. A common problem in hospitals is that nurses constantly have to move people from one bed to another, pick them up, or put them into a wheelchair. Robots are strong, so they can help with **tiring** tasks like these. Because they do not get tired, they can help prevent **injury**, and in addition, they never get angry, bored, or **frustrated**.

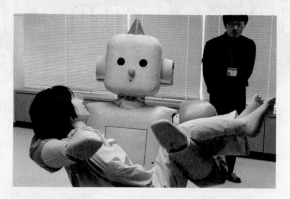

5 Finally, robots can also improve life for people who have lost mobility. Robotic pants allow paralyzed patients to move around independently instead of being confined to a wheelchair. The pants have advantages that are not only physical. One patient commented: "I never dreamed I would walk again. I forgot what it's like." He continued: "I have a 3-year-old daughter. The first time she saw me walking, she was silent for the first few minutes and then she said: 'Daddy, you are tall.' It made me feel so good, like I was soaring.[3]"

---

[3] *soaring:* flying

COMPREHENSION

A Main Ideas

Read each statement. Decide if it is *True* or *False* according to the reading. Check (✓) the appropriate box. If it is false, change it to make it true. Discuss your answers with a partner.

	TRUE	FALSE
1. Robots offer a lot of help to nurses.	✓	☐
2. Telesurgery allows doctors to talk with patients on the telephone.	☐	☐
3. Robots can perform some operations better than humans.	☐	☐
4. Human simulators look and act like real people.	☐	☐
5. Robots get tired from working on patients.	☐	☐
6. The benefits of robots are not just physical.	☐	☐

Read the quotes from the reading. Circle the statement that best explains each quote. Share your answers with a partner.

1. "Although it might seem scary to have a robot performing an operation on you, robotic surgery has many benefits." (*paragraph 2*)

    a. Most people are convinced that robots can perform operations successfully.

    b. There are many positive things about robotic surgery despite people's fears.

    c. People should not be scared of robots.

2. "Medical students also use robots to learn about the human body. They practice on *human simulators*, mannequins equipped with the latest technology." (*paragraph 3*)

    a. It is much better for medical students to work with real patients than with robots.

    b. Human simulators allow future doctors to learn about the human body.

    c. Technology is changing so quickly that mannequins are not useful for medical students.

3. "Because they are so lifelike, these robotic patients can prepare future doctors for the real-life scenarios they might face in their careers." (*paragraph 3*)

    a. It is likely that medical students will face emergencies, and robots can help students prepare for them.

    b. The robots that medical students use do not seem real, so they help the students overcome their fears.

    c. Working with robots is becoming widespread in medical training.

4. "Robotic pants allow paralyzed patients to move around independently instead of being confined to a wheelchair. The pants have advantages that are not only physical." (*paragraph 5*)

    a. Robotic pants help patients get in and out of a wheelchair.

    b. Patients who are paralyzed can move around in a wheelchair.

    c. Robotic pants give patients more physical and emotional freedom than a wheelchair does.

VOCABULARY

 Guessing from Context

Read the quotes from the reading. Guess the meanings of the words in bold from the context. Underline the words and phrases that help you understand. Then match the words with their meanings from the box.

1. "These pieces of equipment not only **resemble** real people, but they also act like them. They can cry, sweat, produce saliva, and open and close their eyes. They can make breathing sounds and heartbeats, and they can bleed and respond to drugs." (*paragraph 3*)

2. "Because they are so lifelike, these robotic patients can prepare future doctors for the real-life **scenarios** they might face in their careers. They can 'suffer' from almost any emergency situation possible, like a heart attack or epileptic seizure." (*paragraph 3*)

3. "A common problem in hospitals is that nurses constantly have to move people from one bed to another, pick them up, or put them into a wheelchair. Robots are strong, so they can help with **tiring** tasks like these." (*paragraph 4*)

situations	look like	takes away your energy

1. resemble _____

2. scenarios _____

3. tiring _____

B Synonyms

Circle the word or phrase that is a synonym for the word in bold. Compare answers with a partner.

1. **benefits**	(advantages)	problems	dangers
2. **bleed**	lose consciousness	lose hearing	lose blood
3. **recover**	become sick	get better	return
4. **resemble**	seem strange	look similar	act differently
5. **scenarios**	not real situations	possible situations	true situations

C Word Forms

1 Read each word and mark each **N** (noun), **V** (verb), or **A** (adjective). Use a dictionary if necessary.

1. operator _N_	operate _V_	operation _N_
2. distraction ___	distracted ___	distract ___
3. repetition ___	repeat ___	repetitive ___
4. blood ___	bleed ___	bloody ___
5. tire ___	tiring ___	tired ___
6. injury ___	injure ___	injured ___
7. recovered ___	recover ___	recovery ___
8. frustrated ___	frustrate ___	frustration ___

2 Complete the conversation between two nurses with the correct form of the words. Choose from the forms in parentheses.

JILL: Hi Andy! What are you doing?

ANDY: Oh, hi Jill. I'm trying to learn how to _____ operate _____ this
1. (operator / operate / operation)

new equipment. Do you know how it works?

JILL: Yes, that's a machine for lifting patients from one bed to another.

It's really helpful for patients who can't move around by themselves.

ANDY: That's great. Just this morning I was trying to help a poor lady with a

leg _____. She was a little heavy for me to lift,
2. (injury / injure / injured)

and I didn't want to hurt her.

JILL: Oh, yes, I saw her come in. She was _____ quite
3. (bloody / bleed / bleeding)

a lot. Is she OK?

ANDY: Yes. Luckily she's going to be fine. She's asleep now. She had a long

_____ early this afternoon, and I'm sure it was
4. (operator / operate / operation)

quite _____.
5. (tire / tiring / tired)

JILL: I'm so sorry. What happened?

ANDY: Well, she was working in a factory doing some _____
6. (repeat / repetition / repetitive)

tasks, and I guess she got _____. She dropped
7. (distract / distracting / distracted)

something heavy on her ankle and broke some bones. But the doctors

say she's going to make a full _____.
8. (recovery / recover / recovered)

JILL: Oh, that's good to hear!

NOTE-TAKING: Using an Outline

> **An outline helps you organize your notes**. An outline is a plan of the material in a text. It shows the **order** of the topics, the **importance** of the topics, and the **relationship** between the topics. Use Roman numerals (I, II, III, etc.) for main topics; use capital letters (A, B, C, etc.) for subtopics under main topics; and use numbers (1, 2, 3, etc.) for subtopics under those. Remember that you may not always need subtopics.

Go back to the reading and read it again. With a partner, take notes and complete the outline.

Title of article: _Robots Improve Health Care, Helping Doctors, Nurses,_
and Patients

I. Telesurgery

    A. Definition/Description: _use of robots by doctors to operate on patients_
without being in the same physical location

    B. Benefits

        1. _Robots do not get distracted or become bored._

        2. _____

        3. _____

II. Human simulators

    A. Definition/Description: _____

    B. _____

        1. _They not only look lifelike, but they act like real patients, too._

        2. _____

III. Robots in hospitals

    A. Help to doctors

        1. _____

        2. _____

(continued on next page)

B. Help to nurses

    1. _____

    2. _____

IV. _____

A. Physical advantage: _____

B. Another advantage: _____

CRITICAL THINKING

The reading mentions many benefits of robots in health care, but it does not discuss any disadvantages. With a partner, fill in the chart with possible disadvantages. Be prepared to share your ideas with the class.

INNOVATION	POSSIBLE DISADVANTAGES
Doctors use robots to perform operations on people, even if they are not in the same place as the patient.	Robots could break down.
Medical students learn about the human body on human simulators. They also learn to deal with emergency situations, like heart attacks and seizures.	
Robots are used in hospitals to move patients from one place to another.	
Robotic pants help people who have been paralyzed to move around instead of being confined to a wheelchair.	

A Warm-Up

1 Read the information.

A medical diagnosis is an attempt to find out what is making a person sick. A basic method doctors use to get information about a patient is a **SAMPLE** history. The letters are short for:

Symptoms
Allergies
Medications
Past medical history
Last thing the person ate or drank
Events that happened just before the illness

2 Discuss the questions with a partner.

1. Do you think a person needs many qualifications to get this basic information about a patient? Explain.

2. Can a person without medical training diagnose an illness? Explain.

B Reading Strategy

Predicting Content from First Paragraph

An important part of developing reading comprehension is identifying the overall idea of a text. The **main idea** is generally stated in **the first paragraph of a text**.

Read the first paragraph of the article. Decide what you think the text will be about. Write your ideas on the lines. Then compare ideas with a partner.

I think the text will be about _____

_____

_____

_____

_____

Now read the entire article to find out if your prediction was correct.

A SIMPLE DIAGNOSIS

1   Dr. George Whitesides, one of the world's leading chemists, is revolutionizing[1] the art of **diagnosing** illnesses as varied as liver failure, malaria, and AIDS. He and his team have invented a diagnostic system that is simple and inexpensive. It does not require electricity or any **specialized** equipment, and anybody can use it, whether or not they have advanced medical training. With Dr. Whitesides's **invention**, some of the world's most **devastating diseases** can be diagnosed quickly and accurately, for little or almost no cost.

2   The system involves using pieces of paper about the size of postage stamps. The paper looks normal, but it contains a medical laboratory that can conduct hundreds of tests. Like any paper, it can soak up a single drop of blood or urine, just as a tablecloth soaks up juice that is spilled on it. The paper changes color, allowing people with only basic training to make a diagnosis. Doctors do not have to be present, but they can **monitor** the test results if photos of the paper are e-mailed to them.

3   The paper diagnosis is especially **promising** for the developing world,[2] where most of the population does not live within easy access to modern hospitals. Since the paper is printed in only a few seconds and can be sent in large quantities, it is an inexpensive solution to a big challenge: the quick and **reliable** diagnosis of many serious health problems. In addition, once it has been used, the paper can be burned. In other words, it does not carry the same health risks as needles.

4   The small papers have many **potential** uses. In the future, they may also be used to detect liver damage, to see if milk has been infected with bacteria, or to find mold in food. This information can have a dramatic impact on people in remote regions of the world. "Information is so important in the health care system," says Dr. Whitesides. This **straightforward**, elegant[3] technology has many possible benefits.

Lab-on-a-chip devices, the size of postage stamps, offer enormous benefits.

---

[1] *revolutionizing:* making huge changes in

[2] *the developing world:* parts of the world that are not wealthy or very industrialized

[3] *elegant:* simple, effective

COMPREHENSION

A **Main Ideas**

Check (✓) the four statements that best express the main ideas in the reading. Discuss your answers with a partner.

☐ **1.** There is a new system for diagnosing diseases.

☐ **2.** Many people have criticized this system.

☐ **3.** The system is cheap and simple and does not require advanced training.

☐ **4.** In the developed world (advanced industrial and wealthy countries), people have access to technology.

☐ **5.** The system is especially important for the developing world.

☐ **6.** There are many potential uses of the system in the future.

B **Close Reading**

Read each statement. Decide if it is *True* or *False* according to the reading. Check (✓) the appropriate box. If it is false, change it to make it true. Discuss your answers with a partner.

	TRUE	FALSE
1. Dr. Whitesides is a highly qualified chemist.	☑	☐
2. Liver failure, malaria, and AIDS are serious diseases.	☐	☐
3. To use Dr. Whitesides's invention, local doctors must visit patients.	☐	☐
4. Plastic is used to soak up fluids.	☐	☐
5. Most people in the developing world have good health care.	☐	☐
6. The invention is a complex solution to a serious world problem.	☐	☐

A Synonyms

Work with a partner. Read the reading again and discuss the meanings of the words in bold. Then match each word with its synonym.

__e__ 1. devastating   a. uncomplicated

____ 2. diseases   b. possible

____ 3. monitor   c. check

____ 4. potential   d. illnesses

____ 5. straightforward   e. extremely harmful

B Word Forms

1 Fill in the chart with the correct word forms. Some categories can have more than one form. Use a dictionary if necessary.

	NOUN	VERB	ADJECTIVE
1.	diagnosis	diagnose	
2.			specialized
3.	inventor/		inventive
4.			promising
5.	reliability/		

2 Complete the pairs of sentences with the correct form of the words. Choose from the forms in the chart. Share your answers with a partner.

1. a. Dr. Whitesides wants to make it possible to _____ diagnose _____ illnesses even when the patient does not have access to a hospital.

   b. The technology he has invented has made it possible to make a correct _____ even in remote areas.

2. a. In the developing world, there are few doctors in rural areas, and even fewer _____.

   b. Currently, health care is a very _____ field.

3. a. Dr. Whitesides wanted to _____ a new way to diagnose serious diseases.

   b. Many people admire his _____.

4. a. Many doctors say that the paper diagnosis has a lot of

_____.

   b. The paper diagnosis is a _____ way to solve a

   complex problem.

5. a. Some critics are not sure we can _____ on

   Whitesides's tests.

   b. However, modern medical tests are very _____.

3 Complete the paragraph with the correct form of each word in parentheses. Compare answers with a partner.

Worldwide, health care is a very _____ *promising* _____
1. (promise)
field. However, in the developing world, few people have access

to _____ medicine. There are few medical
2. (reliability)
_____ in rural areas. Dr. Whitesides has come
3. (specialized)
up with a new system. He wants to make it possible for anyone to

_____ illnesses, even when patients do not have access to
4. (diagnosis)
hospitals. Whitesides has _____ a new way to diagnose
5. (invention)
serious diseases using small pieces of paper that change color according to

the illness. Some critics question the _____ of
6. (reliable)
Whitesides's invention, but many doctors believe the paper diagnosis is a

good way to solve a complex problem.

CRITICAL THINKING

Discuss the questions with a partner. Be prepared to share your ideas with the class.

1. Dr. Whitesides said: "My view of the health care worker of the future is not a doctor, but an 18-year-old . . . who has two things. He has a backpack full of these tests, and a way to occasionally take a blood sample." Do you see any problems with this vision? Do you think it is realistic? Explain.

2. How do you think the paper diagnosis can add to the SAMPLE history that deals with patients' symptoms when they get sick? Do you think it will improve health care? If so, how?

1 Robots and paper are changing the way we receive health care. Review the lists and choose items from the box to complete the chart.

> for training doctors
>
> for detecting liver damage
>
> for finding mold in food
>
> for helping nurses
>
> for helping patients with mobility problems
>
> for finding bacteria in milk

ROBOTS ARE BEING USED	PAPER WILL BE USED
• *for remote surgery*	• *for diagnosing illnesses*
• _____	• _____
• _____	• _____
• _____	• _____

2 With a partner, discuss how these groups of people might benefit from the innovations.

- farmers
- people in remote areas
- doctors and nurses
- patients
- older people
- poor people
- your own idea: _____

A Warm-Up

1 Nursery rhymes are traditional poems for young children that teach important lessons. Read the nursery rhyme aloud with the class.

> The best six doctors anywhere,
> And no one can deny it,
> Are sunshine, water, rest, and air,
> Exercise and diet.

2 What are the lessons this poem teaches about health? Discuss your answer with a partner.

B Reading Strategy

Skimming

Once you have identified **the overall idea of a text** by reading the first paragraph, you should **skim** (read quickly) the rest of the text to **check that your understanding is correct.**

1 Read the first paragraph of the reading. Check (✓) the statement that best expresses the main idea. Compare your answer with a partner's.

☐ **a.** The text is about an old wives' tale.

☐ **b.** The text is about a study.

☐ **c.** The text is about how to lose weight.

2 Confirm your decision by skimming the rest of the article. Check (✓) the two items that you see mentioned.

☐ **a.** advice that mothers give to children

☐ **b.** a description of an experiment

☐ **c.** traditional beliefs about water and health

☐ **d.** the results of an experiment

Now read the entire article. Did you have the correct overall idea?

Water Is Shown to Help People Lose Weight

1   Consume more water and you will become much healthier, goes an old wives' tale.[1] Drink a glass of water before meals and you will eat less, goes another. Such advice seems **sensible**, but it had little **rigorous** science to back it up. Until now, that is. A team led by Brenda Davy of Virginia Polytechnic Institute has run the first experiment studying the link between water **consumption** and **weight loss**. A report published earlier this year suggested that drinking water before meals does lead to weight loss. A yearlong follow-up study has confirmed and expanded those **findings**.

2   The **researchers** divided 48 **inactive** Americans, aged 55 to 75, into two groups. Members of one were told to drink about a pint (half a liter) of water before each of three daily meals. The others were given no instructions on what to drink. Before the trial, all participants had been consuming between 1,800 and 2,200 calories a day. When it began, the women's daily rations[2] were cut down to 1,200 calories, while the men were allowed 1,500. After three months the group that drank water before meals had lost about 15½ lb (7 kg) each, while those in the other group lost only about 11 lb (5 kg).

3   There is no selection bias,[3] Dr. Davy observes, since this is a **random** trial. It is possible that the water replaced sugary drinks in the group that drank water, but this does not explain the weight loss because the calories associated with any drinks consumed by the other group had to be within the daily limits.

4   Moreover, there seems to be a **long-lasting** effect. In the **subsequent** 12 months the participants have been allowed to eat and drink what they like. Those told to drink water during the trial have, however, stuck with the habit—apparently they like it. Surprisingly, they have continued to lose weight, whereas the others have put it back on.

5   Why this works is unclear. But work it does. It's cheap. It's simple. And unlike so much dietary advice, it seems to be enjoyable, too.

---

[1] *old wives' tale:* traditional belief

[2] *rations:* specified amounts of something, for example, food

[3] *bias:* unfairness

A Main Ideas

Read the main ideas from the reading. Put them in the correct order from 1 to 6. Discuss your answers with a partner.

_____ **a.** Researchers selected a random group of people for an experiment.

_____ **b.** A report suggested that the advice was true.

_____ **c.** The people who drank water before meals lost more weight than those who didn't.

__1__ **d.** An old wives' tale says that we should drink more water.

_____ **e.** A year later, the findings remained the same.

_____ **f.** They divided the people into two groups: those who drank water before meals and those who didn't.

B Close Reading

Read the quotes from the reading. Circle the statement that best explains each quote. Share your answers with a partner.

1. "Consume more water and you will become much healthier, goes an old wives' tale. . . . Such advice seems sensible, but it had little rigorous science to back it up. Until now, that is." (*paragraph 1*)

   a. An experiment has confirmed that an old wives' tale offers good advice.

   b. The advice that people usually give each other about weight loss is incorrect.

   c. Old wives' tales are not as good as scientific research.

2. "A report published earlier this year suggested that drinking water before meals does lead to weight loss. A yearlong follow-up study has confirmed and expanded those findings." (*paragraph 1*)

   a. The report and the study reached different conclusions.

   b. The report and the study reached the same conclusions.

   c. The report and the study were on different topics.

(continued on next page)

3. "It is possible that the water replaced sugary drinks in the group that drank water, but this does not explain the weight loss because the calories associated with any drinks consumed by the other group had to be within the daily limits." (*paragraph 3*)

    a. Neither of the groups had daily calorie limits for drinks.

    b. The group that drank sugary drinks was allowed to consume more calories than the other group.

    c. Both groups had calorie limits that included drinks.

4. "Those told to drink water during the trial have, however, stuck with the habit—apparently they like it." (*paragraph 4*)

    a. Drinking water is not very pleasant, in most people's opinion.

    b. The group that started drinking water continued to do so.

    c. Drinking water before meals is only enjoyable temporarily.

VOCABULARY

 Synonyms

Complete each sentence with a word from the box. Use the synonyms in parentheses to help you select the correct word. Compare answers with a partner.

findings	random	sensible
long-lasting	rigorous	subsequent

1. Doctors give their patients a lot of advice about how to remain healthy. For

    example, they tell them to follow a _____ *sensible* _____ diet.
                                           (good, wise)

2. Every culture has old wives' tales that contain advice. However, not all this

    advice is backed up by _____ research.
                                   (accurate, thorough)

3. The _____ of the Virginia Polytechnic Institute
        (results, conclusions)
    experiment were not surprising because most people think that drinking

    water is good for you.

4. The researchers used a _____ group of people to do
              (not specially selected or chosen)
    their experiment. They did not choose them for any special reason.

5. Once people begin to drink a lot of water, they seem to continue. It is a

    _____ habit.
    (enduring, continuing)

6. A report was published about the benefits of drinking water several years

ago. A _____ study reached the same conclusions.
(later, after)

B Word Forms

1 Fill in the chart with the correct word forms. Some categories can have more than one form. Use a dictionary if necessary. An *X* indicates there is no form in that category.

	NOUN	VERB	ADJECTIVE
1.	consumption/*consumer*	*consume*	/
2.	loss		
3.		weigh	X
4.	researcher/		X
5.	activity/		/

2 Read the conversations about weight loss. Complete the conversations with the correct form of the words. Choose from the forms in the chart.

CONVERSATION 1

A: I want to _____ *lose* _____ some weight before summer, but I
1.
don't know where to start.

B: Well, do you exercise regularly? Would you say you're generally

_____?
2.

A: Yes, I go jogging once a week. Last year I even went on a diet, and then I

lost 15 pounds. But I've put it all back on again. Do you know how much I

_____ now? I'm ashamed to tell you!
3.

B: I'm sorry to hear that. Well, what about your calorie intake? Is it high?

A: I don't know. I think it's about 2,000 calories a day. That's about average

for a woman, isn't it?

B: Yes, it is. But did you know that most people _____
4.
much more fat than they need? You should eat a lot of fruits

and vegetables and cut down on meat. There's been a lot of

_____ done on diets. You should read up on it.
5.

A: That's a good idea.

A: Did you hear about that new diet that's based on chocolate?

B: Chocolate? What are the _____ saying about that?

      6.
I mean, is this diet scientific?

A: Well, chocolate is supposed to lower your blood pressure. So, I suppose

that's good. And this diet involves a lot of exercise—you have to walk

thousands of steps every day for the diet to be effective.

B: I knew it! That's a lot of walking, and I really don't like physical

_____.

      7.

A: Well, everyone knows that weight _____ is linked

      8.
to exercise. I don't think you can avoid that. I think you should try this

chocolate diet. Listen to what it says: "Previous experiments suggested

that eating chocolate can help you lose _____.

      9.
Other studies have confirmed this theory."

B: Well, maybe I should check it out.

NOTE-TAKING: Using a Flowchart

A **flowchart** is a kind of diagram that **shows the steps in a process**. It is very helpful for taking notes on readings that describe experiments.

1   Go back to the reading and read it again. Then take notes on the flowchart.

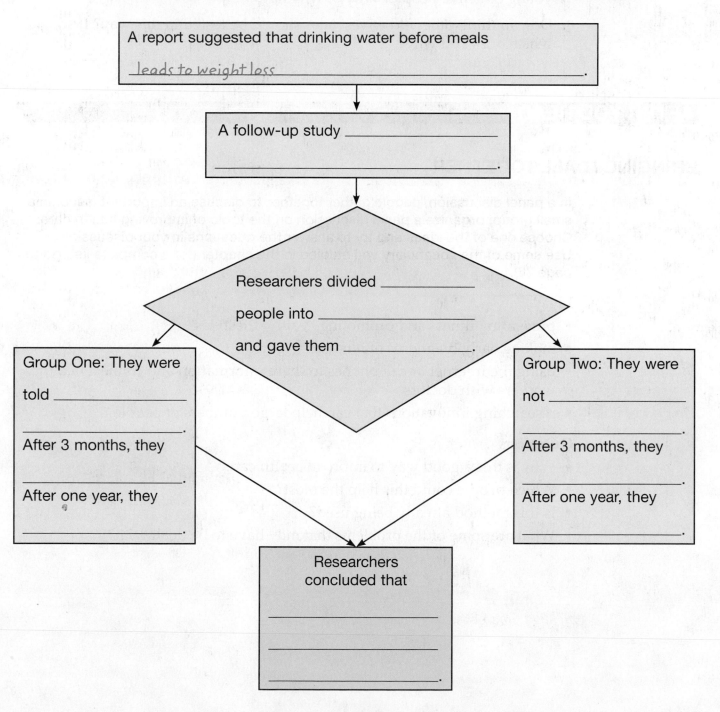

A report suggested that drinking water before meals _leads to weight loss_ _____.

A follow-up study _____.

Researchers divided _____ people into _____ and gave them _____.

Group One: They were told _____ _____. After 3 months, they _____. After one year, they _____.

Group Two: They were not _____ _____. After 3 months, they _____. After one year, they _____.

Researchers concluded that _____ _____ _____.

2   Use your notes to talk about the experiment with a partner. Begin like this:

"A report suggested that..."

CRITICAL THINKING

Discuss the questions in a small group. Be prepared to share your opinions with the class.

1. Do you think you consume enough water? Were you surprised by what you read? Explain.

2. Do you think that the findings would be different if the researchers used young or active people? Why or why not?

3. Do you think other old wives' tales should be tested in this way? If so, which ones and why?

AFTER YOU READ

BRINGING IT ALL TOGETHER

In a panel discussion, people gather together to discuss an important issue. In a small group, organize a panel discussion on the topic of improving health care. Choose one of the ideas and try to answer the questions in your discussion. Use some of the vocabulary you studied in the chapter (for a complete list, go to page 76).

Ideas

- preventing illness and promoting healthy lifestyles
- making early diagnoses of illnesses
- using the Internet or cell phones to share information and connect health workers with doctors
- researching innovations that can help large numbers of people

Questions

- Why is this a good way to improve health care?
- Which people could this help the most?
- Is this method already being used?
- What are some of the problems that may have to be dealt with?

WRITING ACTIVITY

Every culture has old wives' tales that give advice on health. Read the old wives' tales and choose one. Write a paragraph with your reaction to the advice. Use some of the vocabulary you studied in the chapter. Share your paragraph with a partner.

1. Eight glasses of water every day makes the doctor go away.

2. An apple a day keeps the doctor away.

3. Health is wealth.

4. An ounce of prevention is better than a pound of cure.

5. Say thumbs-up to hand hygiene.

6. The longer your waistline, the shorter your lifetime.

DISCUSSION AND WRITING TOPICS

Discuss these topics and questions in a small group. Choose one of them and write a paragraph or two about it. Use the vocabulary from the chapter.

1. Technology is becoming more and more important in every aspect of health care. What are the advantages and disadvantages of this trend? Do you think it is basically positive, or negative?

2. In Reading Two, you learned about one of the world's most important problems—the early diagnosis of serious diseases. What do you know about these diseases? Are you aware of any low-tech methods that are being used to help prevent, treat, or cure them?

3. Do you have a healthy lifestyle? Of the six "doctors" in the nursery rhyme on page 67, which do you think are most important? In what ways can you improve your lifestyle and live a healthier life?

VOCABULARY

Nouns	Verbs	Adjectives
benefit*	bleed	devastating
consumption*	diagnose	distracted
disease	monitor*	frustrated
finding	operate	inactive
injury*	recover	long-lasting
invention	resemble	potential*
weight loss		promising
researcher*		random*
scenario*		reliable*
		repetitive
		rigorous
		sensible
		specialized
		straightforward*
		subsequent*
		tiring

* = AWL (Academic Word List) item

SELF-ASSESSMENT

In this chapter you learned to:

○ Predict the content of a text from its title

○ Predict the content of a text from its first paragraph

○ Skim a text to confirm the main idea

○ Guess the meaning of words from the context

○ Understand and use synonyms and word forms

○ Use an outline

○ Use a flowchart

What can you do well? ☑

What do you need to practice more? ☑

CHAPTER 4

EDUCATION:
The Task of the Teacher

EDUCATION: the field of study that is concerned with teaching and learning; how a society passes its knowledge, skills, and values to the next generation

OBJECTIVES

To read academic texts, you need to master certain skills.

In this chapter, you will:

- Preview a text using visuals

- Predict the content of a text from its title and first paragraph

- Recognize the narrative structure of a text

- Guess the meaning of words from the context

- Use dictionary entries to learn different meanings of words

- Understand and use word forms, synonyms, suffixes, and literal and figurative meanings

- Use underlining to identify factual information and color coding to distinguish different types of information

Consider These Questions

1 Discuss the questions with a partner.

1. In your opinion, what is the difference between *learning* and *studying*?

2. How do you learn best: from others, from reading, from seeing something happen, or from doing it yourself?

3. Do you believe you have had a good education? Why or why not? What would you change about the education you've had in your life, if you could?

2 Read the quotes. Explain the meaning of each in your own words. Share your opinions with a partner.

1. "The mediocre teacher tells. The good teacher explains. The superior teacher demonstrates. The great teacher inspires."

   —*William Arthur Ward, American writer, 1921–1944*

2. "I cannot teach anyone anything. I can only make them think."

   —*Socrates, Greek philosopher, c. 469 B.C.–399 B.C.*

3. "Education is not the filling of a bucket, but the lighting of a fire."

   —*William Butler Yeats, Irish poet, 1865–1939*

READING ONE: Bloom's Taxonomy

 **Warm-Up**

Discuss the questions in a small group. Share your ideas with the class.

1. Is there something you can do well, such as singing, painting, or playing a sport? What steps did you take to learn it?

2. You will read an essay on Benjamin Bloom, a 20th-century educator who developed a list of educational goals. In your opinion, what are some important goals of education?

Previewing Using Visuals

Many informational texts include **visuals**. Visuals can be charts, graphs, photos, or illustrations. These can **help you understand the ideas the text presents**. Before you read an informational text, **examine all the charts** you see. This will help you understand what the text is about.

Look at Charts 1 and 2 in the text. With a partner, discuss what they show.

Now read the text to find out if you were correct.

BLOOM'S TAXONOMY[1]

1   Benjamin Bloom (1913–1999) was an American educational psychologist who did **extensive** research on the ways that teachers teach and students learn. In 1956, he and his colleagues presented their theory. It was a **classification** of educational goals and objectives called "Bloom's Taxonomy."

2   Bloom's Taxonomy showed how people learn—a process that he believed was very complex. As Chart 1 shows, learning begins on a basic level with *remembering* information (seen at the base of the pyramid). **However**, Bloom believed that students must also *understand* what they learn and *apply* it to other areas. **Furthermore**, he said that learners should not use only these "lower-order" levels of learning. Instead, he said they must practice the three "higher-order" skills of *analyzing, evaluating,* and *creating,* shown at the top of the pyramid.

3   *Remembering* is being able to **recall** what was learned. *Understanding* means that the meaning is clear. *Applying* refers to the ability to use the material in new situations. *Analyzing* includes **identifying** the different parts of ideas or things, discovering the relationship between the parts,

Chart 1: Bloom's Pyramid of Learning Skills

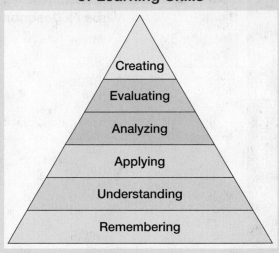

and recognizing how things are organized. *Evaluating* means being able to judge[2] the value of ideas or things. *Creating* means being able to put things together, to **synthesize** them, in order to arrive at a solution[3] or a new idea.

4   Bloom studied the different ways teachers **assessed** their students' learning. He found that over 95 percent of the questions on tests

(continued on next page)

---

[1] *taxonomy:* classification system

[2] *judge:* form an opinion or conclusion about something

[3] *solution:* way to deal with a problem

simply asked students to remember the information they had read. For example, teachers often asked students to name a historical figure or define some vocabulary. Bloom thought these tasks were good starting points, but that alone, they did not **encourage** students to learn. He thought that students should do more complex tasks, such as evaluating the information they had learned or comparing it with other information. Chart 2 shows higher- and lower-order skills, the verbs that describe them, and some typical tasks that Bloom thought teachers should assign at different levels of learning.

5   Bloom's Taxonomy was one of the most important studies on learning in the 20th century, and his ideas continue to **influence** our ideas about education. For example, many teachers today do not believe that students learn through the direct instruction of facts, which is a very traditional way of teaching. Instead, they often ask students to do more **creative** tasks so that they can develop higher-order skills.

CHART 2: TASKS TEACHERS CAN ASSIGN AT DIFFERENT LEVELS			
	Skills	**Verbs to Describe Skills**	**Tasks Teachers Can Assign**
HIGHER-ORDER SKILLS	Creating	Create Design Imagine	• find a solution to a problem • consider the consequences[4] of an action • come up with new ideas
	Evaluating	Evaluate Judge Criticize	• make judgments • debate different opinions • defend a point of view
	Analyzing	Analyze Classify Connect	• compare and contrast ideas • relate ideas to other ideas • organize information
LOWER-ORDER SKILLS	Applying	Apply Solve Experiment	• test ideas • apply what you know to another situation • find solutions to problems
	Understanding	Explain Summarize Describe	• retell information using your own words • explain something you read • summarize a reading
	Remembering	Remember List Define	• answer basic questions • define vocabulary • make lists

---

[4] *consequences:* results or outcome

COMPREHENSION

A Main Ideas

Read each statement. Decide if Bloom would agree or disagree. Check (✓) the appropriate box. Discuss your answers with a partner.

		BLOOM WOULD AGREE	BLOOM WOULD DISAGREE
1.	The process of learning is basically very simple.		
2.	Finding a solution to a problem requires a higher level of learning than identifying a problem.		
3.	Memorization, or simply remembering information, should be eliminated completely.		
4.	Being able to apply what we learn to a new situation is a more complex skill than being able to criticize an idea.		

B Close Reading

Read the quotes from the reading. Circle the statement that best explains each quote. Share your answers with a partner.

1. "Bloom studied the different ways teachers assessed their students' learning." (*paragraph 4*)

   a. Bloom never went into any classrooms.

   b. Bloom looked at what teachers did in their classrooms.

   c. Bloom gave many tests to students.

2. "He found that over 95 percent of the questions on tests simply asked students to remember the information they had read." (*paragraph 4*)

   a. Most test questions were too difficult for students.

   b. Most test questions were testing higher-order levels of learning.

   c. Most test questions did not help the students learn.

3. "Many teachers today do not believe that students learn through the direct instruction of facts, which is a very traditional way of teaching." (*paragraph 5*)

   a. Many teachers today agree with traditional teaching.

   b. Many teachers today disagree with Bloom.

   c. Many teachers today teach differently than teachers did in the past.

A Guessing from Context

Read each sentence and guess the meaning of the word in bold from the context. Then match the word with its meaning from the box.

1. I studied calculus when I was in high school, but now I've forgotten a lot. I really can't **recall** much of it. I should study it again.

2. I'm having a lot of difficulty reading this textbook. The syllabus says I'm supposed to **synthesize** Chapters 1 and 2, but they seem to be on totally different topics.

3. There's an exam in class next week. The teacher is going to **assess** our progress in class this semester.

4. I'm reading about Jean Piaget, a famous educator who did a lot of work with children. He did **extensive** research on the ways they learn.

5. The podcast of the class was pretty interesting, and **furthermore**, it's going to help me with my research paper.

6. I'm really not prepared for the exam next week. **However**, I do have the weekend to study.

a large amount of	but	combine	in addition	judge	remember

1. recall _____remember_____   4. extensive _____

2. synthesize _____   5. furthermore _____

3. assess _____   6. however _____

B Using the Dictionary

1 Read the dictionary entries for *assess*, *however*, and *recall*. Then read the quotes from the reading. Decide which definition explains the way each word is used. Share your answers with a partner.

assess *v.* **1** to make a judgment about a person or situation after thinking carefully about it: *The technique is being tried in classrooms to assess its effects.* **2** to calculate the value or cost of something: *The value of the business was assessed at $1.25 million.*

however *adv.* **1** used when you are adding a fact or piece of information that seems surprising, or seems very different from what you have just said [= but]: *This is a cheap and simple process. However, there are dangers.*
conj. **2** used to say that it does not matter how big, good, serious, etc., something is because it will not change a situation in any way [= no matter how]: *We have to finish, however long it takes.*

recall *v.* **1** to remember a particular fact, event, or situation from the past: *You don't happen to recall his name, do you?* **2** if a company recalls one of its products, it asks people who have bought it to return it because there may be something wrong with it: *The cars had to be recalled because of an engine fault.*

_____ **a.** "Bloom studied the different ways teachers **assessed** their students' learning." (*paragraph 4*)

_____ **b.** "Learning begins on a basic level with *remembering* information. . . . **However**, Bloom believed that students must also *understand* what they learn." (*paragraph 2*)

_____ **c.** "*Remembering* is being able to **recall** what was learned." (*paragraph 3*)

2 Complete each sentence with the correct form of *assess*, *however*, or *recall*. Compare answers with a partner.

1. He continued the experiment, _____*however*_____ tired he was.

2. In order to _____ whether we understood the text, our teacher assigned us summaries.

3. Our brand-new car was _____ because of an electrical problem.

4. I tried to _____ his name, but I just couldn't remember it.

5. The value of our family's house was _____ much higher than we'd thought it was worth.

6. I'd like to go out tonight. _____, I have to study for a test.

C Word Forms

1 Fill in the chart with the correct word forms. Use a dictionary if necessary.

	NOUN	VERB	ADJECTIVE
1.	extension		extensive/
2.	classification		
3.		identify	identified/
4.		assess	
5.		encourage	encouraged/
6.		influence	

2 Complete the conversation with the correct form of the words. Choose from the forms in parentheses.

LUCINDA: What are you reading?

CARLOS: It's an article about Benjamin Bloom. I didn't realize he was so

_____influential_____. Apparently, he had a big effect on
　　　　1. (influence / influential)

thousands of teachers.

LUCINDA: Why are you reading about him?

CARLOS: Well, you know that I'm in graduate school, right? I'm doing

an M.A. in child development. Look, it says here: "Bloom did

_____ research on the way children learn.
　　　2. (extensive / extend)

His _____ of skills is called 'Bloom's
　　　3. (classification / classify)

Taxonomy.' He _____ six levels of learning."
　　　4. (identification / identified)

LUCINDA: Will you stop reading the article to me! Can't you explain it in your

own words?

CARLOS: Lucinda, it's more difficult than you think. You're not being

very _____.
　　　5. (encouragement / encouraging)

LUCINDA: Sorry. I mean, tell me how this taxonomy will affect you personally.

CARLOS: Well, for example, teachers have to do a lot of

_____. They constantly have to test the

children they teach. Bloom's theory affects how teachers put those

tests together.

LUCINDA: Oh, I see. Actually, that sounds interesting.

NOTE-TAKING: Using Underlining to Identify Factual Information

> When you read academic texts in disciplines like education, history, and psychology, you should take notes on **factual information**. In order to be sure you have the facts correct, **underline information such as names, dates, and definitions**.

1 Go back to the reading and read it again. Underline the factual information that you need to remember.

EXAMPLE:

Benjamin Bloom (1913–1999) was an American educational psychologist who did extensive research on the ways that teachers teach and students learn. In 1956, he and his colleagues presented their theory. It was a classification of educational goals and objectives called "Bloom's Taxonomy."

2 Use the information you underlined to tell a partner what you have learned.

CRITICAL THINKING

1 Read the assignments given to elementary school students. Decide whether the tasks are examples of lower-order skills or higher-order skills, according to Bloom's Taxonomy.

	ASSIGNMENT	TASK	LOWER- OR HIGHER-ORDER SKILL
1.	The children read a story about a princess who falls in love with a frog.	The children tell the story in their own words.	☑ lower-order skill ☐ higher-order skill
2.	The children read a story about a bird who gets lost in the forest.	The children write a conversation between the lost bird and another bird he meets.	☐ lower-order skill ☐ higher-order skill
3.	The children sing a song about the planets and the sun.	The children list the planets in the correct order.	☐ lower-order skill ☐ higher-order skill
4.	The children study the multiplication tables.	They complete a page of multiplication exercises.	☐ lower-order skill ☐ higher-order skill
5.	The teacher tells a story.	The children listen to the story and then draw a picture about what they heard.	☐ lower-order skill ☐ higher-order skill

2 Discuss your answers with a partner. Take turns explaining why you think the tasks are examples of lower-order skills or higher-order skills.

EXAMPLE:

Student A: "The first assignment is an example of lower-order skills because the students have to repeat the story. That includes remembering and understanding, which are lower-order skills."

Student B: "Right. The second assignment . . ."

A **Warm-Up**

Discuss the questions in a small group.

1. What do you think someone needs to learn in order to make him or her a good teacher?

2. Do you think there is a place for humor in the classroom? If so, why or why not?

3. What might new teachers be able to learn from the illustration to the right?

B **Reading Strategy**

Predicting Content from Title and First Paragraph

In addition to reading the **title of a text**, you can **look at the first paragraph** to determine the content of the text and **predict what it will be about.** Like the title of a text, the first paragraph often communicates the writer's main idea.

Read the title and the first paragraph of the reading. Then answer the questions with a partner.

1. Where does this story take place?

2. What are some of the items the professor has?

3. Why do you think the professor doesn't explain what he is doing to the students?

4. How do you think the students in the class reacted?

Now read the rest of the story to find out what happens.

The Mayonnaise Jar and Two Cups of Coffee

1 A college professor walked into his child development class and looked at the faces of the students in the room. They were all future teachers, and they seemed quite nervous. The professor put some items down on the desk. He **wordlessly** picked up a very large and empty mayonnaise jar and **proceeded** to fill it with golf balls. Then he asked the students if the jar was full. They agreed that it was.

2 The professor picked up a box of pebbles and poured them into the jar. He shook the jar lightly, and the pebbles rolled into the open spaces between the golf balls. He asked the students again if the jar was full. They looked at each other, and then they said that it was.

3 Next, the professor picked up a box of sand and poured it into the jar. Of course, the sand filled everything else. He asked once more if the jar was full. The students **responded** with a **unanimous** "Yes!"

4 The professor took two cups of coffee from under the table and poured the entire contents into the jar, effectively filling the empty spaces between the sand. The students laughed.

5 "Now," said the professor as the laughter **subsided**, "I want you to recognize that this jar represents the mind of each student as he or she enters your classroom on the first day of school. The golf balls are the important things—family, friends, health, home, and the child's passions—and if everything else were lost and only they **remained**, his or her life would still be full.

6 "The pebbles represent the knowledge the children have **acquired** up until now. We are all different, so each child will probably have pebbles of different shapes and sizes in their jar.

7 "The sand is your responsibility! It is your job to fill your students' minds as tightly as you possibly can in the short time that you have them in your classes."

8 The professor paused.

9 One of the students raised her hand and **inquired** what the coffee represented. The professor smiled and said, "I'm glad you asked, because that's the most important question of all. The coffee is CARE and LOVE."

COMPREHENSION

A Main Ideas

Read the main ideas from the reading. Put them in the correct order from 1 to 6. Discuss your answers with a partner.

_____ a. He began filling the jar with golf balls.

_____ b. The professor filled the jar with several other items.

_____ c. The professor answered that it represented care and love.

__1__ d. A professor stood in front of his class with a jar.

_____ e. The professor explained what the jar and other items represented.

_____ f. A student asked what coffee represented.

B Close Reading

1 Fill in the chart. Write what each item from the text represents. Use your own words.

1. THE JAR	2. THE GOLF BALLS	3. THE PEBBLES	4. THE SAND	5. THE COFFEE
the students' minds on the first day of class				

2 Read the questions. Discuss your answers with a partner.

1. According to the reading, what is the responsibility of the teacher? Do you agree? Explain.

2. When a student asked what the coffee represented, the professor said that was the most important question of all. Why do you think he said that? Do you agree? Why or why not?

VOCABULARY

A Synonyms

Read each sentence. Circle the word or phrase closest in meaning to the word in bold. Compare answers with a partner.

1. **Wordlessly**, the professor wrote the math problem on the board.

   a. quickly   **b.** in silence   c. with gestures

2. After writing the problem on the board, she then **proceeded** to explain it.

   a. went on   b. stopped   c. interrupted

3. She asked if we understood. We were **unanimous**. We all said no.

   a. all in agreement   b. all of different opinions   c. not in agreement

4. The professor asked us some more questions. We wanted to **respond**, but the problem was very difficult.

   a. understand   b. not speak   c. answer

5. The professor left, but the teaching assistant **remained** after class had ended. He explained the problem slowly and carefully.

   a. got angry   b. stayed   c. helped

6. One of the students was really confused. He **inquired** about a particularly difficult part of the math problem.

   a. replied   b. asked   c. answered

7. Once our fears **subsided**, we relaxed. Then we could see how to solve the problem.

   a. began   b. became more   c. became less

8. When the assistant left the room, we realized that we had **acquired** a lot of confidence.

   a. gotten   b. lost   c. remembered

B Suffix: *-ly*

When you add **the suffix *-ly*** to an **adjective**, the word becomes an **adverb**. Many adjectives that end in *-less* are changed into adverbs by adding the suffix *-ly*.

EXAMPLE:
careless (adjective) + *-ly* = **carelessly** (adverb)
- She did her homework **carelessly**. She spent only a few minutes answering the questions.

1 Change the adjectives into adverbs by adding the suffix *-ly*.

1. careless _____*carelessly*_____

2. wordless _____

3. helpless _____

4. thoughtless _____

5. effortless _____

6. aimless _____

2 With a partner, guess the meaning of the adverbs from Exercise 1. Write the meanings. Use a dictionary, if necessary, to check your answers.

1. _____*without care, without paying attention*_____

2. _____

3. _____

4. _____

5. _____

6. _____

CRITICAL THINKING

Read the quotes from the reading. Decide whether you agree with the quote, disagree with the quote, or are not sure of your opinion. Check (✓) the appropriate box. Discuss your opinions with a partner.

	AGREE	DISAGREE	NOT SURE
1. "I want you to recognize that this jar represents the mind of each student as he or she enters your classroom on the first day of school." (*paragraph 5*)	☐	☐	☐
2. "The golf balls are the important things—family, friends, health, home, and the child's passions—and if everything else were lost and only they remained, his or her life would still be full." (*paragraph 5*)	☐	☐	☐
3. "It is your job to fill your students' minds as tightly as you possibly can in the short time that you have them in your classes." (*paragraph 7*)	☐	☐	☐

LINKING READINGS ONE AND TWO

Discuss the questions with a partner. Be prepared to share your answers with the class.

1. What levels of Bloom's Taxonomy did the professor's teaching achieve? Explain.

2. Look back at Yeats's quote on page 78. In your opinion, would Yeats like this professor's lesson? Why or why not?

3. Look back at Ward's quote on page 78. Which kind of teacher is the professor: mediocre, good, superior, or great? Explain.

A **Warm-Up**

Discuss the questions with a partner.

1. Who was the best teacher you had in elementary or middle school (when you were 5–13 years old)?

2. What did he or she teach you?

3. What made him or her special?

B **Reading Strategy**

Recognizing Narrative Structure

Reading Three is a **narrative**. Narratives are stories that often focus on **the author's personal experiences**. Narratives often include the use of:
- **the past tense:**   *I learned . . .*
- **transitions:**   *One time . . .*
- **dialogue or indirect speech:**   *She told us she made a tape . . .*

Look at the first two paragraphs of the reading. Then find examples in the text of these elements of a narrative structure. If there are no examples, write "none." Share your answers with a partner.

1. the past tense: *got, wrote*

2. transitions: _____

3. dialogue or indirect speech: _____

Working with clay, tie-dying, and putting taps in maple trees are common examples of elementary school activities.

Now read the whole story to find out about the author's teacher. Pay attention to the narrative structure.

A Teacher's Lasting Impression

By D. T. Max

1. If you are lucky, you get one great teacher in your life. I got mine in my first years of school. With Mrs. Monell, I wrote an essay about going to the Caribbean and a book about a monkey. With Mrs. Monell, I learned multiplication by solving pages of math problems she made up the night before. I tie-dyed. I took rubbings from fish skeletons. I put taps into maple trees and made maple syrup and cooked pancakes in an electric frying pan.[1]

2. One time Mrs. Monell brought in a tape for us to listen to. She was always **digging** things **up**. Twenty six-year-olds sat there listening to a soft symphony of strange noises playing on a tape. We tried guessing what we were hearing. A house? A factory? A store? She laughed and told us. She had made a tape at a dairy farm near her house. In all that time, none of the cows had mooed.

3. We all know education is more than filling a child with facts, but how does the child learn to think? It starts with **posing** questions: What does the world look like? What does the world sound like? Of course, I never thought about how Mrs. Monell did her job. How did she find those electric frying pans? She came from South Africa, and the children called her Mrs. Monell, although other teachers during that time were Michael and Joan and David.

4. I have one picture of Mrs. Monell, which I took in 1969 with an old camera. In the photo, she is standing next to a classmate of mine, Sarah, I think. Now it is hard to see her at all, but that seems **appropriate**. A great teacher is always in a sense invisible, leading the child into creative discovery.

5. Mrs. Monell took us away for a weekend once to a friend's house in the country. We hunted crayfish and stepped in cow patties. I accidentally broke a screen door. Robby broke a window sash,[2] Sarah cried. The lawn was getting chewed up by our kickball games. Mrs Monell's friend's house was **falling down** around her ears. I thought she was going to yell at us, but she didn't. Why did twenty **excited**, **bickering** children not affect her as they would other adults, including our parents?

6. Education is on the national **agenda** these days. It's clear there are things that can be done to make it more likely that more children will get an experience like the one I had. But my brother Eric, who attended the same school I did and had three teachers for those years, can't remember their names, suggesting that teaching when it succeeds is as much personal as structural.

7. I came to see years later that not every teacher would be like her: **caring**, **innovative**, ambitious[3] for us, and never bored. But we didn't know that then, and Mrs. Monell wouldn't have wanted us to know.

---

[1] *electric frying pan:* a pan used for cooking, which is heated by electricity

[2] *window sash:* the wooden frame that holds the glass in a window

[3] *ambitious:* having a strong wish for success

COMPREHENSION

A Main Ideas

Work with a partner. Answer the questions.

1. What six activities did the author do in Mrs. Monell's class?

   a. _He wrote an essay about going to the Caribbean._

   b. _____

   c. _____

   d. _____

   e. _____

   f. _____

2. What two experiences does the author remember having with Mrs. Monell and his classmates?

   a. _____

   b. _____

3. What four adjectives does the author use to describe Mrs. Monell?

   a. _____

   b. _____

   c. _____

   d. _____

Read each statement. Circle the item that correctly completes the statement. Underline the information in the text that helped you. Share your answers with a partner.

1. According to the information in paragraph 1, we can guess that the author ____.

   a. believes that everyone should have at least one great teacher in his or her life

   b. thinks that students should write more essays

   c. became a teacher himself

2. In the author's opinion, the most important thing a good education must include is ____.

   a. learning to listen to the teacher

   b. focusing mostly on basic skills: reading, writing, and math

   c. learning to think

3. The author believes that good teachers are not ____.

   a. bored

   b. caring

   c. great

4. Mrs. Monell was not ____.

   a. an elementary school teacher

   b. from the United States

   c. married

5. When the children went to the countryside, they ____.

   a. were very excited

   b. made the teacher angry

   c. didn't play much

6. From what we read in the text, Mrs. Monell ____.

   a. worked with the children's parents to improve their behavior

   b. seemed to love nature

   c. talked to her students about her own children

VOCABULARY

A **Guessing from Context**

Read each sentence and guess the meaning of the word in bold from the context. Then match the words with their meanings.

1. Teachers often see young children **bickering** and fighting during playtime and even in the classroom.

2. Teachers should not yell at children. Instead, they should learn **appropriate** strategies to help children behave well.

3. Teachers can't use the same old lessons all the time. They need to create **innovative** lessons that capture students' attention.

4. Educators around the world are constantly **posing** questions about the best way to teach students.

5. More training and better pay for teachers are issues on the educational **agenda** today.

_a_ 1. **bickering**	a. arguing
___ 2. **appropriate**	b. list of things that need to be done
___ 3. **innovative**	c. new and different
___ 4. **posing**	d. correct for the purpose
___ 5. **agenda**	e. asking

B Literal and Figurative Meanings

> Some words have a **literal, or exact, meaning** and a **figurative, or symbolic, meaning**. Use the context of the text or a dictionary to determine which meaning is being used.
>
> **EXAMPLE:** *falling down*
> **Literal:** We noticed that the window sash was **falling down**. (The window sash was coming off the window.)
>
> **Figurative:** The house was **falling down** around her ears. (The house wasn't in good shape.)

Read each sentence. Decide whether the word in bold has a **Literal** or **Figurative** meaning. Check (✓) the appropriate box. Share your answers with a partner.

	LITERAL	FIGURATIVE
1. a. Mrs. Monell was an innovative teacher. She was always **digging** things **up**.	☐	☐
b. The children were excited to be in the country. They spent hours **digging up** worms in the garden.	☐	☐
2. a. The school building was practically **invisible**. I couldn't see it through the fog and rain.	☐	☐
b. Good teachers are **invisible**, leading children into creative discovery.	☐	☐
3. a. Education is more than **filling** a child with facts.	☐	☐
b. He was filling the bucket with sap from the tree to make maple syrup.	☐	☐

C Word Forms

Complete the sentences with the correct form of the words. Choose from the forms in bold.

1. **innovation / innovate / innovative**

   a. Mrs. Monell was a very _____ innovative _____ teacher.

   b. She believed in the power of _____.

2. **care / careful / caring / carefully**

   a. She _____ designed lessons that would make her students love going to school.

   b. She was a very _____ person who loved seeing her students succeed.

3. **creation / creative / created / creativity**

    a. Mrs. Monell constantly _____ new lessons for her students.

    b. She was a very _____ person.

4. **excite / exciting / excited**

    a. When Mrs. Monell told her students that she was taking them on a trip, they were very _____.

    b. She was always coming up with new and _____ things for her students to do.

NOTE-TAKING: Using Color Coding to Distinguish Different Types of Information

> **Color coding a text** helps you to distinguish between different types of information. To use this method, decide on the types of information you need to identify. Then carefully read the text and **use highlighters of different colors to distinguish different types of information**.

1 Go back to the reading and read it again. As you read, try to find the author's opinions about education. Use one color to highlight this information. Use another color to highlight details about Mrs. Monell's teaching methods.

EXAMPLE:

If you are lucky, you get one great teacher in your life. I got mine in my first years of school. With Mrs. Monell, I wrote an essay about going to the Caribbean and a book about a monkey.

2 Share your color-coded text with a partner.

Work with a partner. Read Mrs. Monell's diary entries. Complete the entries. Think about this question: What was the educational purpose behind her lessons?

DIARY

September 12

I had a really good experience with my class today. I wanted the students to do rubbings of fish skeletons because __I wanted them to learn about science and small living creatures.__

November 2

It's late fall, so I decided to take the children on a trip to the country. We went to a forest of maple trees because _____

_____

January 9

The children worked on the math problems I made up last night. I gave them several pages of problems because _____

_____

February 6

I decided to have the children write their own books because _____

_____

March 14

I think it would be a good idea to do some cooking in the class because _____

_____

April 19

I'm tired because I took my class to the country last weekend. I did this because

_____

_____

BRINGING IT ALL TOGETHER

1 Form three groups, representing **Benjamin Bloom, the professor,** and **Mrs. Monell.** With the members of your group, think of two questions for each of the other groups.

   EXAMPLES:

   To Benjamin Bloom: What do you think tests should measure?

   To the professor: Why did you use a visual aid to teach your class?

   To Mrs. Monell: Don't you ever get frustrated or upset with your students?

2 Form new groups, with at least one person from each group, representing **Benjamin Bloom, the professor,** and **Mrs. Monell.** Ask the questions you prepared in Step 1, and answer the questions the other groups ask.

WRITING ACTIVITY

Write two paragraphs about a favorite teacher, or about a teacher you did not like. Use some of the vocabulary you studied in the chapter. Use these elements of a narrative structure to tell your story. In the first paragraph, write about your teacher and what he or she did in class. In the second paragraph, give your opinion about the teacher. Share your story with a partner.

• **the past tense:**	*I learned . . .*
• **transitions:**	*One time . . .*
• **dialogue or indirect speech:**	*She told us she made a tape . . .*

DISCUSSION AND WRITING TOPICS

Discuss these questions in a small group. Choose one of them and write a short essay about it. Use some of the vocabulary you studied in the chapter (for a complete list, go to page 102).

1. What advice would you give to someone who wants to be a teacher?

2. What are three qualities you think a teacher should have? Explain how these qualities can inspire students.

3. Tell about a time you learned to do something useful or interesting. What were the steps that helped you become better at doing it?

4. How do you get a young child "ready to learn" in elementary school? How do we get "ready to learn" in college?

VOCABULARY

Nouns	Verbs	Adjectives	Adverbs
agenda	acquire*	appropriate*	furthermore*
classification	assess*	bickering	however
	dig up	caring	wordlessly
	encourage	creative*	
	fall down	excited	
	identify*	extensive	
	influence	innovative*	
	inquire	invisible*	
	pose	unanimous	
	proceed		
	recall		
	remain		
	respond*		
	subside		
	synthesize		

* = AWL (Academic Word List) item

SELF-ASSESSMENT

In this chapter you learned to:

○ Preview a text using visuals

○ Predict the content of a text from its title and first paragraph

○ Recognize the narrative structure of a text

○ Guess the meaning of words from the context

○ Use dictionary entries to learn different meanings of words

○ Understand and use word forms, synonyms, suffixes, and literal and figurative meanings

○ Use underlining to identify factual information and color coding to distinguish different types of information

What can you do well? ☑

What do you need to practice more? ☑

PSYCHOLOGY:
Theories of Intelligence

PSYCHOLOGY: the study of the mind and behavior. A common topic in psychology is intelligence theory. Many psychologists have defined intelligence, but there is no agreement about what intelligence is and whether or not it can change.

OBJECTIVES

To read academic texts, you need to master certain skills.

In this chapter, you will:

- Understand and identify a text's purpose
- Use the KWL method to get the most out of a text
- Retell a text to monitor understanding
- Guess the meaning of words from the context
- Understand and use word forms
- Use dictionary entries to learn different meanings of words
- Fill in a chart and make triple entry notes

"We think he's showing an interest in banking and finance."

A Consider These Questions

There are many unanswered questions about intelligence, such as what it is and how to measure it. Read each debate. Then answer the question with a partner.

1.	The Intelligence Quotient Debate	Is there such a thing as "intelligence," and if so, can it be measured with tests? Explain.
2.	The Nature/Nurture Debate	Does intelligence come from what you learn (nurture), or are some people born with more intelligence than others (nature)? Explain.
3.	The Multiple Intelligences Debate	Is there just one way of being intelligent, or are there many different ways? Explain.
4.	The Emotional Intelligence Debate	Can people be "emotionally intelligent," and if so, how is this different from other types of intelligence?
5.	The Mozart Effect Debate	Can doing certain activities, like listening to music, make you smarter? Explain.
6.	The Flynn Effect Debate	Worldwide, IQ scores are increasing. Is this because people are smarter, or do they just take tests better? Explain.

B Your Opinion

Look at the cartoon on page 103. Discuss the questions with a partner.

1. Do you think the cartoon is funny? Why or why not?
2. What does the cartoon say about intelligence?

A Warm-Up

1 Read the information.

> Howard Gardner (1943–) is a psychologist who is best known for his theory of multiple intelligences. Gardner proposed that there are eight different ways of being intelligent.

Word Smart
(Linguistic and Verbal)

Number Smart
(Logical)

Picture Smart
(Spatial)

Body Smart
(Body/Movement)

Music Smart
(Musical)

People Smart
(Interpersonal)

Self Smart
(Intrapersonal)

Nature Smart
(Naturalist)

2 Look at the information in the chart.

IF YOU ARE GOOD AT . . .	YOU ARE LIKELY TO HAVE . . .
words, reading and writing, and foreign languages	linguistic and verbal intelligence
math and working out problems	logical intelligence
art, design, and understanding physical space	spatial intelligence
physical activities and sports	body/movement intelligence
instruments and rhythm	musical intelligence
communicating and understanding others	interpersonal intelligence
analyzing things and understanding yourself	intrapersonal intelligence
understanding nature, patterns, and your environment	naturalist intelligence

3 Discuss the questions with a partner.

1. Do you think that intelligence is something you're born with, or can you learn how to be more intelligent? Explain.

2. Do you think that certain types of intelligence are associated with success? Explain.

Understanding and Identifying Purpose

Texts can have different **purposes**, for example:

☐ to entertain the reader   ☐ to offer an opinion

☐ to give information   ☐ to make the reader think

☐ to persuade the reader   ☐ to tell a story

☐ to make a comment

Preview the reading. Read the different purposes again. Check (✓) the purpose(s) of the quiz. Then compare answers with a partner.

Now read the quiz to see if your answer was correct.

Types of Intelligence

1. What was your favorite subject in school?
   a. math
   b. music
   c. art
   d. physical education
   e. psychology
   f. biology
   g. reading
   h. speech and debate

2. During your free time, what do you like to do?
   a. listen to music
   b. draw and paint
   c. participate in sports
   d. spend time alone
   e. solve math equations
   f. camp, hike, or garden
   g. go to parties or visit with friends
   h. read

3. It's your day off, and it's a beautiful summer day. What are you most likely to do?
   a. curl up with a good book
   b. go to an art museum
   c. review your household **budget**
   d. hang out with your friends at the mall[1]
   e. enjoy a quiet day all to yourself
   f. invite your friends out for a game of soccer
   g. attend a local concert
   h. head to the nearest trail for a hike[2]

4. When you are trying to come up with ideas for a new project, what do you do to find inspiration?
   a. work in your garden
   b. list different alternatives and assign each a **score** based on various factors
   c. discuss your **options** with other people
   d. make a mind map exploring your different options
   e. listen to your favorite songs
   f. go for a jog through the neighborhood
   g. read articles related to the topic of your project
   h. reflect on the project quietly by yourself

---

[1] *mall:* building containing a group of stores

[2] *hike:* long walk in the country

5. At a party, what are you most likely to do?
- **a. browse** through the host's CD collection
- **b.** notice the architecture of the host's home
- **c.** get into a discussion about your favorite author
- **d.** challenge someone to a game of darts[3]
- **e.** spend the evening calculating how much the party cost
- **f. chat** with as many people as possible
- **g. keep to yourself** and observe[4] other people
- **h.** take a **stroll** through the host's garden

---

[3] *darts:* a game involving throwing a thin, pointed object at a target

[4] *observe:* watch

6. You have a big test tomorrow and need to review the material. What study method do you use?
- **a. get together** with classmates for a study session
- **b.** try to gain hands-on[5] experience
- **c.** focus on understanding the reasoning and **logic** behind the material
- **d.** lock yourself in your room to study quietly with no distractions[6]
- **e.** put concepts into different categories to make them easier to remember
- **f.** create visual diagrams and charts summarizing the material
- **g.** read over your notes and assigned readings
- **h.** make up songs to help you **memorize** different concepts

---

[5] *hands-on:* learned by doing it yourself

[6] *distractions:* interruptions, disturbances

COMPREHENSION

A Main Ideas

Read each statement. Decide if it is *True* or *False*. Check (✓) the appropriate box. If it is false, change it to make it true. Discuss your answers with a partner.

	TRUE	FALSE
1. The quiz focuses on activities most people can relate to.	✓	☐
2. There is only one correct answer for each of the questions.	☐	☐
3. The quiz gives you an idea of the sort of intelligence you may have.	☐	☐
4. The quiz asks readers to imagine themselves in different situations.	☐	☐
5. The eight possible responses to each question correspond to the same type of intelligence.	☐	☐

B Close Reading

1 Go back to the reading and read it again. Then review the information in the Warm-Up. With a partner, complete the chart with the answers to the questions that correspond to different types of intelligence.

Type of Intelligence	Question 1	Question 2	Question 3	Question 4	Question 5	Question 6
Linguistic and Verbal	g.					
Logical		e.				
Spatial			b.			
Body/Movement				f.		
Musical					a.	
Interpersonal						a.
Intrapersonal	h.					
Naturalist		f.				

2 Share your answers with the class.

VOCABULARY

A **Guessing from Context**

Read each sentence and guess the meaning of the word in bold from the context. Then match the word with its meaning from the box.

1. My husband often goes to bookstores and **browse** among the books. He doesn't always buy a book, but he likes to spend time looking around.

2. My daughter loves to **chat** on the phone with her friends. They don't seem to be saying anything important. They're just having a casual conversation.

3. Sometimes I take a **stroll** through the park on a bright sunny day. It's great to be able to take your time and relax as you walk along.

4. He's really a shy person. He likes to **keep to himself**. He doesn't get too involved with other people.

5. She's a very social person. She likes to **get together with** her friends every weekend and do something interesting, like seeing a movie or going to a restaurant.

meet friends informally	spend time alone	a slow walk
shop in a casual way	talk in a friendly way	

1. browse _____shop in a casual way_____

2. chat _____

3. stroll _____

4. keep to oneself _____

5. get together with _____

B **Word Forms**

1 Fill in the chart with the correct word forms. Use a dictionary if necessary. An *X* indicates that there is no form in that category.

	NOUN	VERB	ADJECTIVE
1.	budget	budget	
2.	logic	X	
3.		memorize	memorized /
4.	option		
5.	score		scored /

2 Complete the paragraph with the correct form of the words. Choose from the forms in the chart.

When Howard Gardner published his theory of multiple intelligences in 1983, many people were very excited. His claim that we are intelligent in different ways made sense: it seemed very _____logical_____. So it

1.

did not take long for people to start thinking about measuring intelligence in a different way, too.

Traditional IQ tests often give the impression that there is only one way to be smart. Gardner said that, in fact, there are many. Some people are musical, and some are good at sports. Some have a good _____

2.

and can learn new facts quickly and remember them easily. Others can handle mathematical concepts, like numbers and _____,

3.

but _____ low on language tests. It all depends on the

4.

individual.

Nobody wants to believe that they are not smart. Gardner's theory gives us a new possibility: the _____ of thinking that we can all

5.

be good at something. And who wouldn't want to believe that?

NOTE-TAKING: Filling in a Chart

> **Organizing notes in a chart** is one way to make sense of a text. Listing the topics discussed in a text and then filling in the chart with more information about those topics can help **expand your understanding of a text**.

Go back to the reading and read it again. With a partner, fill in the chart with activities people with each type of intelligence might enjoy.

TYPE OF INTELLIGENCE	ACTIVITIES PEOPLE MIGHT ENJOY
Linguistic and Verbal	*reading different types of books and articles*
Logical	
Spatial	
Body/Movement	
Musical	
Interpersonal	
Intrapersonal	
Naturalist	

CRITICAL THINKING

1 Take the quiz on pages 106 and 107. Circle the answer that corresponds to your opinion. Using the chart in the Close Reading exercise on page 108, count how many answers you have for each type of intelligence.

2 Discuss the questions with a partner. Be prepared to share your thoughts with the class.

   1. Were the results of the quiz accurate for you? Why or why not?

   2. Do you believe the quiz is a good way to measure a person's intelligence? Why or why not?

   3. Do you agree with Gardner that people are intelligent in different ways? Why or why not?

   4. Do you know anyone who is intelligent in one particular area? Tell your partner about him or her.

A Warm-Up

1 Read the conversations. Write responses to the questions.

CONVERSATION 1

A: My professor has assigned six chapters in the psychology text for next week's midterm. It seems like an awful lot of reading, and I don't want to spend so much time on it. I think I'm good at psych, though. If I focus hard enough during the exam, I'm pretty sure I will be able to pass. Do you think I should waste time doing so much reading?

B: _____

_____

_____

CONVERSATION 2

A: I'm taking elementary Mandarin in college, and I'm having a really hard time. The pronunciation is quite difficult for me, and I've never learned such a complex writing system before. I'm considering dropping the class, even though I'd love to know some of the language. What's your opinion: should I drop the class?

B: _____

_____

_____

CONVERSATION 3

A: I've been trying to write this essay all weekend, and I still don't think I'm making myself clear. I've looked at it for so long that I'm really sick and tired of the topic. It's a bit depressing. I feel like tearing it up and starting again. What do you think?

B: _____

_____

_____

2 With a partner, take turns role-playing the conversations.

Using the KWL Method

KWL is **a reading method** that helps you get the most out of a new text. This method activates prior knowledge about a topic, while guiding you through reading and understanding a text. The letters stand for:

KNOW Before you read, think about what you **know** about the topic.
WANT Before you read, think about what you **want** to learn.
LEARN After you read, think about what you have **learned**.

Apply the KWL method to the text. With a partner, answer the questions.

1. Read the title. What do you know about learning and motivation? What do you know about intelligence?

2. What do you want to learn from this reading?

Now read the text. Afterward, tell a partner what you learned.

TRANSFORMING STUDENTS' MOTIVATION TO LEARN

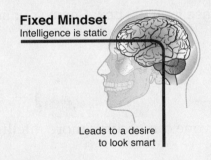

Fixed Mindset
Intelligence is static

Leads to a desire to look smart

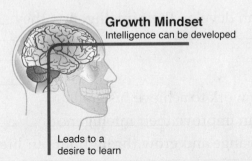

Growth Mindset
Intelligence can be developed

Leads to a desire to learn

1   Psychology professor Carol Dweck says this is an exciting time for our brains because these days there is an increasing amount of research into intelligence. Her own studies on the way our brains work have important **implications** for students' attitudes toward education.

2   According to Dweck, what students believe about their brains affects their motivation, and this, in turn, influences their academic **achievement**. Some students think that intelligence is something that's fixed and permanent. Others, however, see it as something that can grow and change. These different beliefs create different attitudes. On the one hand, you might be afraid of challenges and **devastated** by **setbacks**, while on the other, you relish[1] challenges and are resilient[2] in the face of setbacks.

3   If people believe that intelligence is fixed, they think that they possess only a certain amount of it. Dweck calls this belief a *fixed mindset*. She has shown that a fixed mindset makes challenges **threatening** for people because they believe that their fixed ability may not be up to[3] the

(continued on next page)

---

[1] *relish:* greatly enjoy
[2] *resilient:* able to recover from problems
[3] *be up to:* be capable of dealing with

task they are trying to accomplish. Furthermore, it makes errors and failures **demoralizing**, because people with this mindset believe that the mistakes they make indicate a low level of intelligence.

4   There is another, more positive attitude, which is to regard intelligence as something that can be **cultivated** through effort and education. Dweck calls this a *growth mindset*. Naturally, everyone has different abilities, and not everyone can be as smart as Einstein, but everyone can improve their abilities. And, as Dweck points out, Einstein didn't become Einstein until he put in years of focused hard work. As a result, confronting challenges, profiting from mistakes, and **persevering** in the face of setbacks help people to become smarter.

5   Dweck's work shows that if students believe that their intelligence can improve, they begin to love learning. A growth mindset makes students believe in the power of hard work. We all face setbacks in our lives, but it is preferable to react to them in a **constructive**, **determined** way.

COMPREHENSION

A Main Ideas

Complete the sentences with a phrase from the box. Share your answers with a partner.

1. Carol Dweck __e__.

2. Students with a *fixed mindset* ____.

3. Students who believe that everyone can become more intelligent ____.

4. Albert Einstein ____.

5. If students believe that they can develop their intelligence, they ____.

---

a. learn to love learning
b. have a *growth mindset*
c. put in many years of hard work to achieve his goals
d. do not believe that they can improve their intelligence
e. says that our brains can change and grow throughout our lifetime

---

B Close Reading

Circle the phrase that best completes each sentence. Share your answers with a partner.

1. Dweck says that this is an exciting time for our brains because _____.

   a. there is a lot of new research about intelligence

   b. students today are smarter than they were in the past

   c. we get smarter as we get older

2. Some students think that intelligence is fixed. They do not believe that _____.

   a. intelligence tests are accurate

   b. we are all equally intelligent

   c. intelligence can improve with practice

3. If people have a *fixed mindset*, and they are faced with a difficult challenge, they often _____.

   a. give up

   b. become competitive

   c. try harder than they did before

4. Students with a *growth mindset* _____.

   a. are smarter than others

   b. believe that hard work helps you improve your abilities

   c. do not have much motivation

5. If people believe that intelligence can grow and develop, they _____.

   a. never get angry

   b. can better deal with problems

   c. become frustrated

VOCABULARY

A Guessing from Context

Read the conversation and guess the meanings of the words in bold from the context. Then match the words with their meanings.

STEVE: Look at this! I only got a C+ on my midterm. I feel like giving up.

CHRISTINE: That attitude won't help you. It's not very **constructive**. Just try to do better on your next assignment.

STEVE: That's easy for you to say. You got an A–, right? But I'm **devastated**.

CHRISTINE: Look, I know how **demoralizing** it is when you get a bad grade. I'm sure you're disappointed, but you're a really good student. You probably just had a hard time with the topic.

STEVE: You're probably right. But you must admit, it's going to be pretty hard for me to get a good grade in the course. When you have a **setback** like this, it's difficult to recover.

CHRISTINE: Oh, I see. You're worried about the **implications** for your final grade. Well, look, I think you should just concentrate on doing your best over the next few weeks. You'll probably still manage to get a B+ overall.

STEVE: You're right. I feel a bit better. I'm **determined** to get the best grade I can.

_c_ 1. constructive	a. really upset
___ 2. devastated	b. something that delays your progress
___ 3. demoralizing	c. positive, helpful
___ 4. implications	d. possible effects
___ 5. setback	e. making you feel less confident
___ 6. determined	f. having a strong desire to do something

B Word Forms

1 Fill in the chart with the correct word forms. Some categories can have more than one form. Use a dictionary if necessary. An **X** indicates there is no form in that category.

	NOUN	VERB	ADJECTIVE
1.	achievement	*achieve*	X
2.		cultivate	
3.	X		demoralizing/*demoralized*
4.			determined
5.			devastating/
6.		persevere	X
7.			threatening/

2 Read each sentence. Cross out the one word in parentheses that does not complete the sentence correctly.

1. People often have to work very hard to (achieve, cultivate, ~~persevere~~) their goals.

2. My mother just graduated with her master's degree. We're all really proud of her (achievement, determination, devastation).

3. She says that it's important for students to (devastate, cultivate, achieve) good work habits.

4. My brother is feeling very (devastated, demoralized, cultivated) because he just failed an important exam.

5. Since I was very young, I've always had a lot of (determination, threat, perseverance). I knew I wanted to do well in school.

6. However, I faced difficulties, like my brother is facing now. I know that difficulties can be (devastating, determined, demoralizing).

7. I agree with my mother. (Devastation, Perseverance, Determination) is the key to success. You can't just give up if you run into a problem.

8. If people see failure as (threatening, determined, demoralizing), they often want to give up. But I think it's important to keep trying.

CRITICAL THINKING

Read the sayings about intelligence and success. Match each saying with a conversation. Compare answers with a partner.

SAYINGS	CONVERSATIONS
_____ **1.** Failure is not the worst thing in the world. The very worst is not to try.	**a. ANN:** "I'm really good at tests. I don't think I need to review anything before next week's midterm." **BEN:** "You shouldn't talk like that. You might be smart, but you need to work hard or you might not pass the test."
_____ **2.** Genius is one percent inspiration and ninety-nine percent perspiration.	**b. SUE:** "I don't know how to swim. I tried once, but I got scared and gave up." **TED:** "Well, you can't learn to swim if you're scared of it. You should give it another chance."
_____ **3.** If at first you don't succeed, then try and try again.	**c. BILL:** "I don't think I'm very good at languages, so I don't want to take French in college." **JOE:** "I understand how you feel, but why don't you take a class and see if you like it?"

Read each statement and the two possible responses. Decide who is more likely to give each response, a parent who believes in Gardner's theory of multiple intelligences, or a parent who believes in Dweck's theory of fixed and growth mindsets. Write *Gardner* or *Dweck* on the line. Compare answers with a partner.

1. I'm not going to take music. I don't think I'm very good at it.

    _____ a. Perhaps you should spend a little more time studying. You're probably going to get better at it if you do.

    _____ b. Well, that's OK. Why don't you take something you like better, such as dance?

2. I've never had the chance to study languages, but my school is offering elementary Japanese, and I might take it.

    _____ a. You should try it out. You like words and systems, so you might be good at Japanese.

    _____ b. You should try Japanese. But remember, it might be difficult at first. You will have to work hard to master the different scripts it uses.

3. I love art class. I've been practicing the techniques my teacher showed me.

    _____ a. That's great! The more you practice, the better you'll get.

    _____ b. That's great! I wish I were good at art, but I really prefer math.

A **Warm-Up**

1 **Read the information.**

- *Autism* affects 1–2 people per 1,000 worldwide. People with autism often make repetitive movements, need to follow precise rules, and are uncomfortable with change. Sometimes they find it difficult to interact with other people. Many autistics have strong visual skills.

- *Savant syndrome* is not well understood. A savant is a person with incredible mental abilities. A small number of autistics have savant abilities. Savants have incredible memories and are often superior artists and musicians. However, like people with autism, they may suffer many mental, emotional, or physical problems.

- *Synesthesia* involves making connections between senses. It is unconscious and

A B C D E F G H I J K L M N O P Q R S T U V W X Y Z

unplanned. People with synesthesia may be able to remember a lot of information by associating words with colors, sounds with colors, numbers with colors, or words with tastes. Most people with this condition say it is not unpleasant, although they may have right-left hand confusion and difficulty with mathematical and spatial abilities.

2 **Work with a partner. Fill in the information you have learned from the Warm-Up.**

1. Names of conditions   **a.** _autism_____

                                           b. _____

                                           c. _____

2. Special abilities people may have   **a.** _strong visual skills_____

                                           b. _____

                                           c. _____

3. Problems people may face   **a.** _need to follow precise rules_

                                              _____

                                           b. _____

                                              _____

                                           c. _____

                                              _____

Retelling to Monitor Understanding

Retelling a text is a way for readers **to monitor their understanding**. To retell, follow these steps: (1) read a text, or part of a text; (2) without looking at the text, tell another person what you have read, using your own words.

Now read the text. Then, with a partner, retell the text in your own words.

The Extraordinary Abilities of Daniel Tammet

1   Daniel Tammet is very different from most people. He has recited pi (π)[1] to 22,514 digits. He speaks ten languages: English, Spanish, French, German, Finnish, Lithuanian, Romanian, Icelandic, Welsh, and Esperanto. He has invented his own language, Mänti. He learned conversational Icelandic in one week and was interviewed in Icelandic on live television.

2   Tammet is an autistic savant. His extraordinary abilities **stem** from a combination of autism and a condition known as synesthesia. Tammet experiences things through a mixture of senses that the rest of us can't imagine. For instance, when he does math, he says: "I see landscapes in my mind. The numbers turn into shapes. They knit together in a way that forms almost like hills and mountains in my mind, full of color and full of shape and full of movement."

3   For all his remarkable **gifts**, Tammet has some everyday difficulties stemming from his autism. For instance, he doesn't like to go to a beach just a few minutes from his home because it is made up of pebbles—too many even for him to count. That makes him uncomfortable. Tammet can't drive or do many other things that require basic **coordination**. Even walking is something he had to learn to do through an effort of **will**.

4   However, after years of effort, Tammet has **overcome** many of his autistic disabilities. Unlike most autistic savants, he can describe what the experience of autism is like from the inside. He loves silence, for instance, and says: "I experience it as like a silvery texture[2] around my head, like condensation[3] running down a window." "If there's a sudden noise, it's like **shattering** that feeling." Tammet's **eloquence** may be his most remarkable gift, and it makes him a **prime** subject for autism researchers.

5   In a way, you could say that Tammet has come back from the country of autism, which is a very difficult place for researchers and for parents to reach. "I come from a place where I've felt so lonely, and so **unwanted** in a way," Tammet said. "But now I've come along this road, and I've found this bridge, and I've come across it. And I don't know how, I don't know why, but I'm here and I'm able to talk to you today. And, for me, that's amazing."

---

[1] *pi:* a mathematical number, approximately 3.14159

[2] *texture:* the way that a surface feels when you touch it

[3] *condensation:* water that collects on a cold surface

COMPREHENSION

(A) Main Ideas

Write the number of the paragraph that contains each main idea from the reading.

_4_ **a.** Tammet is able to relate to others and explain what it is like to be autistic.

_____ **b.** Tammet is very unusual. He is able to do things that other people cannot do.

_____ **c.** Tammet experiences difficulties because of his autism.

_____ **d.** Tammet feels less lonely because he can explain himself to others.

_____ **e.** Tammet has extraordinary abilities because of his medical condition.

(B) Close Reading

Read the quotes from the reading. Circle the statement that best explains each quote. Share your answers with a partner.

1. "For all his remarkable gifts, Tammet has some everyday difficulties stemming from his autism." (*paragraph 3*)

   a. Tammet has so many everyday problems that he finds it hard to appreciate his gifts.

   b. Tammet is very talented, and he shows it every day.

   c. Although Tammet is very talented, he also deals with daily problems.

2. "Tammet can't drive or do many other things that require basic coordination. Even walking is something he had to learn to do through an effort of will." (*paragraph 3*)

   a. Tammet learned to walk by being determined.

   b. Tammet has not been able to learn to move around on foot or in a car.

   c. There are some basic skills that Tammet will never acquire.

3. "After years of effort, Tammet has overcome many of his autistic disabilities. Unlike most autistic savants, he can describe what the experience of autism is like from the inside." (*paragraph 4*)

   a. Tammet cannot relate to other people or explain how he feels.

   b. Tammet is able to talk about what it is like to have autism.

   c. Tammet has not been able to overcome his disabilities.

4. "In a way, you could say that Tammet has come back from the country of autism, which is a very difficult place for researchers and for parents to reach." (*paragraph 5*)

    a. It is difficult for Tammet to travel to other countries.

    b. Tammet has been able to help people understand autism better.

    c. Parents and researchers are unable to understand Tammet.

VOCABULARY

Ⓐ Definitions

1 Match each word with its definition. Use a dictionary if necessary.

_h_	1. coordination	**a.**	ability to decide on something and take action
___	2. eloquence	**b.**	not desired or wished for
___	3. gifts	**c.**	come, originate
___	4. overcome	**d.**	destroying, breaking
___	5. shattering	**e.**	successfully deal with a problem
___	6. stem	**f.**	natural abilities or talents
___	7. unwanted	**g.**	fluent speaking or writing
___	8. will	**h.**	ability to use parts of your body together

2 Complete the paragraph with the words from Exercise 1. Compare answers with a partner.

In recent years, there has been new interest in savants. These people have changed our idea of intelligence, _____*shattering*_____ our ideas about

                                            1.
what makes a person intelligent. Here are some dramatic examples:

- Derek Paravicini is called the *human iPod*. He can play thousands of musical

  pieces by heart and mix them together in complex forms. His memory and

  hand _____ is remarkable, especially because Derek is

                  2.
  blind and cannot read music.

- Alonzo Clemons makes animal sculptures in perfect detail. He can

  transform any picture into a 3-D figure. He has never had any artistic

  training, but his talents seem to _____ from a bad fall

                                 3.
  when he was a baby.

(continued on next page)

- Stephen Wiltshire did not speak until he was nine. Now his remarkable artistic _____ 4. are recognized worldwide. He has been called *the living camera*. He draws large panoramic pictures of cities,

Stephen Wiltshire's art has become popular all over the world.

such as London, New York, and Tokyo, after seeing them only once from a helicopter.

- Ellen Bourdreaux has _____ 5. many of the challenges caused by her blindness by using two amazing abilities. She uses sounds to "see" around her, so she never has difficulty walking into things. She also knows exactly how many seconds and minutes are passing, although she has never seen a clock.

- Kim Peek, the world's most famous savant, memorized more than 9,000 books during his lifetime, including the complete works of William Shakespeare. He read two pages at a time, one with each eye. Although Peek had difficulty with many everyday tasks, before his death, he spoke with great _____ 6. of the need to treat all people equally.

- Leslie Lemke was extremely disabled when he was born and was given up for adoption. A nurse, Mary Lemke, was sad to see an _____ 7. baby, so she decided to adopt him. With a strong _____ 8. , she helped him to learn how to eat and how to walk. When Leslie was 16, he woke up his parents in the middle of the night, playing Tchaikovsky's Piano Concerto No. 1 on the family piano. He had no training and had heard the piece only once on television.

B Using the Dictionary

1 Read the dictionary entries for *gift*, *prime*, *stem*, and *will*.

> **gift** *n.* **1** a present that you give to someone **2** a natural ability to do something
>
> **prime** *adj.* **1** very important, very good **2** describes a number that can only be divided by itself and one
>
> **stem** *v.* **1** to develop or originate from something else **2** to stop something from spreading or growing
>
> **will** *n.* **1** the determination to do what you have decided to do **2** a legal document that shows what to do with your money and possessions when you die

2 Now read each sentence. Mark which entry, *1* or *2*, explains the way the word in bold is used.

1. _____ **a.** Many savants have serious disabilities, but they also have remarkable **gifts**.

    _____ **b.** Perhaps their greatest **gift** to the world is making people think differently about unusual people.

2. _____ **a.** Daniel Tammet has such advanced math abilities that he can tell if a number is **prime** within seconds.

    _____ **b.** The reason Tammet is such a **prime** subject for researchers is that he can explain his condition.

3. _____ **a.** Tammet's abilities seem to **stem** from a combination of factors.

    _____ **b.** Researchers are trying to **stem** the apparent increase in autism worldwide.

4. _____ **a.** When she dies, my mother wants to leave some of her savings for autism research in her **will**.

    _____ **b.** Many autistic children have a very strong **will** and are determined to have their way.

NOTE-TAKING: Making Triple Entry Notes

> **Making triple entry notes** can help you work out the meaning of passages in a text, as well as think about your reactions. To make triple entry notes, divide a sheet of paper into three vertical columns. In the left column, **copy exact quotes** (sentences or short passages) from the text that you think are important. In the middle column, **explain what you think they mean**. In the right column, **explain your reactions**.

Copy short passages from the text and make triple entry notes to explain and react to them.

EXACT QUOTES	WHAT THEY MEAN	YOUR REACTIONS
"I see landscapes in my mind. The numbers turn into shapes."	Tammet has a visual image of numbers in his mind.	I think this is an interesting way to talk about numbers. I've never thought about numbers having shapes.

CRITICAL THINKING

Discuss the questions with a partner. Be prepared to share your thoughts with the class.

1. Do you know of anyone with autism, savant syndrome, or synesthesia? Does he or she face any difficulties or have any special abilities? Explain.

2. What other learning difficulties do you know of? What are some of the challenges facing people with those difficulties?

3. People with autism often prefer not to be "labeled" as "autistic" but rather referred to as "people with autism." What effect does the language we choose have on our reaction to people with autism and other learning difficulties?

BRINGING IT ALL TOGETHER

1 Review what you have learned in the three readings. Make notes in the chart. Use some of the vocabulary you studied in the chapter (for a complete list, go to page 129). Compare notes with a partner.

READING ONE: TYPES OF INTELLIGENCE	READING TWO: TRANSFORMING STUDENTS' MOTIVATION TO LEARN	READING THREE: THE EXTRAORDINARY ABILITIES OF DANIEL TAMMET
The answers to certain questions can explain your type of intelligence. For example, . . .	New research shows that our brains are . . .	Daniel Tammet has some amazing gifts, despite the fact that he is . . .

2 With a partner, read the three quotes below. Which of the three readings does each relate to most? Share your ideas with the class.

1. "It's not that I'm so smart: it's just that I stay with problems longer."

   —*Albert Einstein*, *German physicist, 1879–1955*

2. "Genius is essentially creative; it bears the stamp of the individual who possesses it."

   —*Madame de Stael*, *Swiss author, 1766–1817*

3. "I believe that every person is born with talent."

   —*Maya Angelou*, *American author, 1928–*

WRITING ACTIVITY

Write a paragraph in response to one of the questions. Share your paragraph with a partner.

1. After reading this chapter, how would you define "intelligence"?

2. Who is the most intelligent person you have ever met? What makes that person intelligent?

3. Do you consider yourself intelligent? In what ways?

DISCUSSION AND WRITING TOPICS

Discuss these questions in a small group. Choose one of them and write one or two paragraphs answering it. Use the vocabulary from the chapter.

1. In this chapter, you have read about some remarkable people. However, on an everyday level, many people are particularly talented in some ways and not in others. How do you think intelligence should be tested, if at all?

2. Most people take an intelligence test at some time in their lives, either when they are children or young adults. Have you ever taken one? How did you feel about it? What did it show about your abilities? Do you think it was accurate?

3. For centuries, people have debated what intelligence is and whether it can be measured. Why do you think intelligence is such a fascinating subject for researchers?

4. This chapter is about human intelligence, but animal intelligence and artificial intelligence are also very interesting subjects. What do you know or think about these topics?

VOCABULARY

Nouns	Verbs	Adjectives	Phrases and Idioms
achievement*	browse	constructive*	get together
budget	chat	demoralizing	keep to oneself
coordination*	cultivate	determined	
eloquence	memorize	devastated	
gift	overcome	prime*	
implication*	persevere	threatening	
logic*	shatter	unwanted	
option*	stem		
score			
setback			
stroll			
will			

* = AWL (Academic Word List) item

SELF-ASSESSMENT

In this chapter you learned to:

○ Understand and identify a text's purpose

○ Use the KWL method to get the most out of a text

○ Retell a text to monitor understanding

○ Guess the meaning of words from the context

○ Understand and use word forms

○ Use dictionary entries to learn different meanings of words

○ Fill in a chart and make triple entry notes

What can you do well? ☑

What do you need to practice more? ☑

CHAPTER 6

BUSINESS:
The Changing Workplace

BUSINESS: the academic study of economics and management

OBJECTIVES

To read academic texts, you need to master certain skills.

In this chapter, you will:

- Preview a text by reading section headings

- Use the 3-2-1 strategy to review a text

- Deal with difficult words or expressions

- Guess the meaning of words from the context

- Understand and use word forms, synonyms, word usage, and prefixes

- Label paragraphs

- Write margin notes

Consider These Questions

1 Discuss the questions with a partner.

  1. What careers interest you?

  2. What is your ideal workplace?

  3. What do you want from a job?

2 Psychologist Dr. John L. Holland established six categories to match people with careers. Check the three categories that best represent your personality. Share your responses with a partner.

  ☐ **Realistic:** You are athletic or mechanical. You like working with machines and being outdoors.

  ☐ **Investigative:** You like to learn and to solve problems.

  ☐ **Artistic:** You like to use your imagination and work in unstructured environments.

  ☐ **Social:** You like to work with people, especially to help them.

  ☐ **Enterprising:** You are a good leader and like being in charge of situations.

  ☐ **Conventional:** You are good at numbers and can follow instructions well.

The Holland Code

A Warm-Up

When 26-year-old Sean Aiken graduated from college, he could not decide what career path to follow. He came up with the idea of doing a different job every week for one year, and donated his salary to a charity. He called this experience the *One Week Job*. Sean did a variety of one-week jobs, working as a dairy farmer, florist, exterminator, astronomer, firefighter, and cowboy.

Discuss the questions in a small group. Share your ideas with the class.

1. Why do you think Sean made the decision to do what he did?

2. What do you think of Sean's idea? Would you like to do something similar? Why or why not?

B Reading Strategy

Previewing by Reading Section Headings

Understanding the way a reading is organized can help you read more efficiently. If a reading is organized by section, **read the heading in each section**.

Look at the headings in the reading (in this case, the interviewer's questions). With a partner, discuss what the interviewer is asking, and imagine what the answers might be.

EXAMPLE:

"*In question 1, the interviewer is asking why Sean made the decision to do what he did.*"

Now read the interview with Sean Aiken to see his answers.

The One Week Job: 52 Jobs in 52 Weeks

1 Why 52 jobs in 52 weeks?

I didn't know what I wanted to do with my life. I finished my college degree in business administration, and because business is so general, it allowed me to **put off** my decision further. I was sitting around the dinner table and talking to my family about what I should be doing, and my dad said, "It doesn't matter, as long as it's something you're **passionate** about." I wanted to learn about what I was looking for in a career, and take a year to **figure** it **out.**

2 What jobs have you liked the best? Which were the worst?

They've all been so different. I liked being a cancer fundraiser,[1] a fashion buyer, working at the Georgia Aquarium, and being a yoga instructor—that was challenging. By the end of the week, I was teaching a class. I didn't realize how tiring yoga could be. As for the worst, I really don't like office jobs and doing the same thing day after day.

3 What skills can you take away from all the jobs you've performed this year?

The biggest skill would be **dealing with** uncertainty. For the project, every week I have no idea what's going on next week. I know how to adapt to changing environments, and I'm open to learning new things and new skills. With my business degree, I did a lot of presentations, but now I'm learning the practical aspects of my education. I remember being in school and hearing that you learn all you need to know on the job, and that's true. The most important thing is not what I learned in school; it's learning how to learn.

4 The current generation goes through more jobs in a lifetime than their parents did. Why do you think this is the case?

I think our generation is having difficulty finding a career path, and we're looking for more than just a career. We've seen our parents do a job for 30 years and not necessarily enjoy it. But we have different **expectations** of the workforce. Our parents value job security and a paycheck, but we place more importance on a **balanced** lifestyle and satisfaction. Maybe it's our sense of entitlement[2]—because our parents are working harder, that gives us more freedom. I hope it's not just that we're lazy.

5 Has the One Week Job project brought you any closer to figuring out what you want to do?

I want changing tasks, something with **flexibility**. Whatever it is, I want to see **the bigger picture** and see how I'm contributing to something greater than myself and not just the bottom line.[3] I believe it when people say that if you do what you love, the money will come. I'm very **idealistic**.

---

[1] *fundraiser:* someone who tries to get money for a special cause

[2] *entitlement:* privilege or benefit

[3] *the bottom line:* money (informal)

COMPREHENSION

(A) Main Ideas

Complete the summary of the reading. Underline the correct word or phrase in parentheses. Compare answers with a partner.

Sean Aiken came up with the innovative idea of doing a different job every

week for a year _____*after he graduated from college*_____. His family
                  1. (while he was in college / after he graduated from college)

_____ his plan.
            2. (agreed to / was against)

Most of the jobs he took were _____, and
                          3. (quite similar / very different)

they taught him a lot. For example, from being a _____,
                                  4. (yoga teacher / cancer fundraiser)

he learned that what you think a job will be isn't always what you think after you

actually do it. He also learned what he, personally, wanted from a job, and stated

that he values _____.
              5. (doing what he loves / making a lot of money)

Young people today change jobs a lot, partly because they

_____ than their parents, and because they
        6. (are lazier / have more freedom)

value different things, such as _____. Sean is
                         7. (comfort / satisfaction)

_____ other young people in this way.
       8. (similar to / different from)

He says he wants to contribute to _____.
                      9. (something greater than himself / the bottom line)

B Close Reading

With a partner, complete the outline of the reading with details from the box. Compare answers with another partner.

> He doesn't know what he wants to do.
> He wants to find something he is passionate about.
> They want balance.
> He wants flexibility.
> He can deal with uncertainty.
> He likes challenging jobs, like fundraising and yoga instruction.
> They want job satisfaction.
> He doesn't like repetitive jobs.
> He has learned how to learn.
> He wants to contribute to others.

I. Reasons for Sean's project (*paragraph 1*)

   A. _He doesn't know what he wants to do._

   B. _____

II. Examples of jobs Sean liked best and least (*paragraph 2*)

   A. _____

   B. _____

III. Skills Sean has learned (*paragraph 3*)

   A. _____

   B. _____

IV. Reasons the current generation has many jobs (*paragraph 4*)

   A. _____

   B. _____

V. Results of Sean's project (*paragraph 5*)

   A. _____

   B. _____

VOCABULARY

A Guessing from Context

Read the paragraph and guess the meaning of the words in bold from the context. Then match each word with its meaning from the box.

When I graduated from college, I couldn't make a decision about what to do. So I **put** it **off** for a month . . . and another month . . . and then another. Finally, my mother asked me what was wrong. I burst into tears, and that's when I realized that I needed some help. She said that I shouldn't worry and told me that we would **figure** it **out** together. She said I couldn't see the forest for the trees—meaning that I was only concerned about my immediate problems, and not thinking about **the bigger picture**. She also said that, basically, I should try to find a job that I was **passionate** about. Her advice made me feel much better. I've decided to calm down, **deal with** my stress, and look for something that is really going to make me happy.

feeling strongly	solve	the overall view or perspective
not do	take care of	

1. put off   _not do_

2. figure out   _____

3. the bigger picture _____

4. passionate   _____

5. deal with   _____

B Word Forms

1 Fill in the chart with the correct word forms. Some categories can have more than one form. Use a dictionary if necessary. An *X* indicates there is no form in that category.

	NOUN	VERB	ADJECTIVE
1.	balance		balanced
2.	expectation		
3.	flexibility	X	
4.		X	idealistic/
5.		X	passionate

2 Complete the conversation with the correct form of the words. Choose from the forms in the chart.

ELLIE: My life is so crazy. I have too many responsibilities at home and at work, and it's difficult to _____balance_____ everything.
 1.

NATHANIEL: I understand. It's the same for me. My boss has very high

_____ of me at work. Sometimes I think he
 2.

_____ too much of his employees.
 3.

ELLIE: Mine too! He talks about being _____ all the
 4.

time, but he's actually really strict. The other day I asked if I could

leave half an hour early, and he said no.

NATHANIEL: Really? I'm surprised that he wouldn't help you. I mean, it's hard

to find an employee that is more dedicated than you. You're really

_____ about what you do.
 5.

ELLIE: It's true. I love my job, but I need more _____.
 6.

Every Tuesday, I have to pick my son up from school, and leaving

early is becoming a real problem at work.

NATHANIEL: Can't your husband help you with that?

ELLIE: He has a 9 to 5 schedule, and I don't think he can change that.

But, you know, I've been thinking of looking for another job.

My _____ job would be something that
 7.

allows me to leave early sometimes. Of course, I'd make up the

time—I could come in early or skip my lunch.

NATHANIEL: Well, you've got to find _____ in life.
 8.

That's really important.

> One of the most helpful ways to find the main ideas in a reading is to **label the paragraphs** on the side of the page. You should **limit these labels to a few words**.

1 Go back to the reading and read each question and the author's answer again. Label each paragraph with a few words in the margin.

EXAMPLE:

Why 52 jobs in 52 weeks?   Label: reasons for author's decision

2 Compare labels with a partner.

CRITICAL THINKING

Read the statements. Decide whether you think they are likely or unlikely. Find statements from the interview that support your opinions. Check (✓) the appropriate box. Share your opinions with a partner.

	LIKELY	UNLIKELY
1. In Sean's experience, a business administration major is not very focused.	☑	☐
2. Sean doesn't really like tiring jobs.	☐	☐
3. Sean would enjoy answering phones in an office.	☐	☐
4. Sean did mostly theoretical work while he was in college.	☐	☐
5. Sean values the lessons he has learned in the workplace.	☐	☐
6. Sean is very grateful to his parents.	☐	☐

A **Warm-Up**

1 Look at the photos and read the captions.

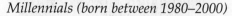

Millennials (born between 1980–2000)

Baby Boomers (born between 1946–1965)

2 Do you think these descriptions apply mostly to Baby Boomers or to Millennials? Check (✓) the boxes that apply, and compare responses with a partner.

Which group . . . ?	Baby Boomers	Millennials	Both
is excellent at technology	☐	☐	☐
likes to work in teams	☐	☐	☐
expects to have job satisfaction	☐	☐	☐
is willing to have many jobs in lifetime	☐	☐	☐
wants a balanced lifestyle	☐	☐	☐

B **Reading Strategy**

Using the 3-2-1 Strategy

3-2-1 is a reading strategy that asks you to write down **3 things you learned, 2 things you found interesting, and 1 question you have about a text.** It is a useful and fun way to review information from a text you have read.

Now read the article and respond to the questions. Then discuss your responses with a partner.

1. What are three things you have learned about the topic? _____

_____

2. What two ideas did you find most interesting? _____

_____

3. What question do you have about the text? _____

_____

FLIP FLOPS AND FACEBOOK BREAKS: MILLENNIALS ENTER THE WORKPLACE

By Reena Nadler

1 In our recent book *Millennials in the Workplace*, Neil Howe and I argue that today's rising youth workforce is not a liability[1] and a challenge, but an **asset** and an opportunity. We analyze how the Millennials are transforming workplaces, and how employers can **recruit** them, retain them, and maximize their productivity.

2 Perhaps it's no surprise that managers often **misinterpret** the Millennials. Data consistently show that today's young adults are nothing like the Boomers who **preceded** them. They are pressured and programmed. They are **bonded** to their parents and **networked** to their friends. They want structure and instant **feedback**. They work well in teams and have complete confidence in their future. They fear risk and **dread** failure. They want the system to work.

3 So what will tomorrow's Millennial-friendly workplace look like? We found that the Millennial Magnets (companies that attract Millennials) share five basic best practices:

4 **Personal-Touch Recruiting** Millennials think of themselves as "special" and want to work for an employer who does too. Millennial Magnet companies take an active and personal role in the recruitment of young employees, matching recruits with current employees who can share their experience, or sending new employees a handwritten welcome note.

5 **Work-Life Balance.** Millennials look at workaholic[2] Boomers and want a more well-rounded and balanced life. Millennial-friendly companies offer employees flexible schedules and the ability to bring their personal life (like phone calls with parents) into the office occasionally.

6 **Group Socializing.** Millennial Magnet companies understand that this generation enjoys working and socializing in groups. They are moving away from individual competition and toward teamwork, team compensation,[3] and communal office spaces.[4]

7 **Recognition.** These companies know how to motivate Millennials through positive feedback, instituting programs where managers can give out small **rewards** (like a $5 gift card) for any job well done.

8 **Casual but Professional Environment.** Many Millennial Magnets are crafting a corporate environment that is friendly and comfortable, complete with couches, cafes, and gathering spaces.

9 The Millennials will continue to flood into the workplace over the next fifteen years, and employers who get them right will have an important advantage. Maybe it's time to stop **complaining** about their flip flops—and start harnessing[5] their energy.

---

[1] *liability:* something that puts you at a disadvantage

[2] *workaholic:* working long hours

[3] *compensation:* payment

[4] *communal office spaces:* work areas that people share

[5] *harnessing:* making use of

COMPREHENSION

(A) **Main Ideas**

Read each statement. Decide if it is *True* or *False* according to the reading. Check (✓) the appropriate box. Discuss your answers with a partner.

According to a recent book, Millennials _____.

	TRUE	FALSE
1. are likely to grow in number	☑	☐
2. have similar values to earlier generations	☐	☐
3. appreciate having a colleague to work with	☐	☐
4. are close to their parents	☐	☐

The workplace environment that Millennials prefer probably has _____.

	TRUE	FALSE
5. private areas to work in	☐	☐
6. an area to share coffee with others	☐	☐
7. strict rules that are followed at all times	☐	☐
8. a friendly atmosphere	☐	☐

(B) **Close Reading**

Write answers to the questions. Then discuss your answers in a small group.

1. Many employers think hiring young people today is challenging because they have different values from other generations. What is the opinion of the authors of the book *Millennials in the Workplace*? (*paragraph 1*)

   Millennials are not a challenge, but an opportunity.

2. The reading offers advice to employers about how they can do three things. What are they? (*paragraph 1*) _____

   _____

(continued on next page)

3. What are four characteristics of the Millennial generation? (*paragraph 2*)

_____

_____

4. Why would Millennials appreciate a handwritten note when they start a new job? (*paragraph 4*) _____

_____

5. What would be the effect of giving a Millennial worker a gift card? (*paragraph 7*) _____

_____

6. Why might Millennials enjoy a comfortable corporate environment? (*paragraph 8*) _____

_____

7. Why is it so important for employers to understand the particular needs of the Millennial generation? (*paragraph 9*) _____

_____

VOCABULARY

Ⓐ Synonyms

1 Complete the sentences with the words from the box. Use the synonym in parentheses to help you select the correct word.

asset	dread	complaining	misinterpret	networked	rewards

1. Millennials are not a liability and a challenge, but an _____*asset*_____
   (benefit)
   and an opportunity.

2. Managers often _____ Millennials. They are nothing
   (don't understand)
   like the Boomers who preceded them.

3. They are _____ to their friends through Facebook
   (connected)
   and e-mail.

4. They fear risk and _____ failure.
   (are afraid of)

5. Managers give out small _____, like a $5 gift card,
(gifts)

for doing good work.

6. Maybe it's time to stop _____ about Millennials.
(expressing frustration)

2 Read the paragraphs. Complete each paragraph with the words from Exercise 1.
Compare answers with a partner.

The book *Millennials in the Workplace* is essential reading for

employers today. According to Nadler and Howe, older people

frequently _____*misinterpret*_____ young workers. They spend time
                                    1.

_____ about how Millenials dress and how they are
              2.

_____ to their friends. In fact, many older people
              3.

probably _____ having to supervise Millennials, because
                              4.

they are so different from previous generations.

However, the book makes the point that Millennial workers can be a real

_____ to a company. Because they are so good with
              5.

technology, they can do many tasks more efficiently than older workers, who

tend to be less familiar with computers. And if from time to time, Millennials

receive small _____ for doing a job well, they feel very
                                6.

appreciated and are likely to have a great attitude about their work.

B Word Usage

Complete the conversations with the correct word from the box. Compare answers with a partner.

asset	bonded	complain	feedback

CONVERSATION 1

JADE: Hi, Ethan. I heard about your promotion! I just wanted to

congratulate you. Well done! You're a real _____asset_____
                                                            1.
to the company!

ETHAN: Oh, thanks, Jade. I have to say I was very happy about it. Sometimes

you do a lot of work and get no _____, so you're
                                                2.
not sure whether you are doing things right or not.

JADE: Well, we have a great supervisor. I can't _____
                                                                          3.
about her at all.

ETHAN: Yes, and I think we have a great team, too. We've really

_____ , and we work well together.
              4.

dread	misinterpret	preceded	recruit

CONVERSATION 2

REBECCA: Oh, no! Is it five o'clock already? I'm feeling stressed because I have

to get this report in before tomorrow morning.

EMILY: Poor you. I _____ those tight deadlines.
                                          5.

REBECCA: Me too. But I have to try to get this done. I heard that the team that

_____ ours got a big reward.
              6.

EMILY: Really? Well, if you need to _____ an
                                                            7.
additional member, just give me a call!

REBECCA: Thanks for the offer. But please don't _____
                                                                        8.
what I said. I'm doing this work because I like it, not just because I

want to win the prize!

NOTE-TAKING: Wr...

... s a useful reading technique. You can **comment**
... esents or **write a question** about something
... an use your notes to organize a response to
... w up on vocabulary or expressions you do

P. 135

...ge, but
...ortunity.

That's interesting. I think the author believes that employers should hire young workers, because they bring the company a lot of benefits.

What do the words "asset" and "liability" mean?

1 Read the reading again and make notes in the margin with your comments and questions.

2 Then share your comments and questions with a partner. Make sure you check on any items you did not understand.

CRITICAL THINKING

Discuss the questions in a small group. Use information from the reading to support your answers.

1. How is today's workplace changing, and what is likely to happen in the future?

2. How are younger workers generally different from their older colleagues?

3. What is the best way for employers to react to the changing workplace?

Read the quotes. How might Sean Aiken and Reena Nadler react to each quote? What is your reaction? Discuss your answers with a partner.

1. "Find a job you like and you add five days to every week."

   —*H. Jackson Brown, Jr., author, 1940–*

2. "If you put all your strength and faith and vigor* into a job and try to do the best you can, the money will come."

   —*Lawrence Welk, musician, 1903–1992*

3. "Laziness may appear attractive, but work gives satisfaction."

   —*Anne Frank, author and victim of the Holocaust, 1929–1945*

4. "The best way to appreciate your job is to imagine yourself without one."

   —*Oscar Wilde, author and poet, 1854–1900*

5. "The only place where success comes before work is in the dictionary."

   —*Donald Kendall, business executive, 1921–*

   _____

   * *vigor:* force or effort

Statue of Anne Frank in Amsterdam

Oscar Wilde in 1882

(A) Warm-Up

Most employers value similar skills in their employees. Check (✓) the three main skills that you consider important or add others of your own. Use a dictionary if necessary. Share your ideas with a partner.

- ☐ discipline
- ☐ honesty
- ☐ maturity
- ☐ motivation
- ☐ optimism
- ☐ patience
- ☐ responsibility
- ☐ your own idea(s): _____

(B) Reading Strategy

Dealing with Difficult Words or Expressions

In texts you read, you will often have to **deal with difficult words or expressions**. Don't worry about the meaning of each word. As you read, try to get the overall meaning of the text. Later, after you have finished reading and have gotten a general idea of the text, you can think about the words or expressions whose meanings you weren't sure of, and then look them up in a dictionary.

Read the paragraph. With a partner, decide which sentence expresses the overall meaning. Check (✓) the correct sentence.

A valued worker is honest. She has good relationships with her peers, and she tries to work with them toward the same goal. A valued worker is too meticulous to let any detail slip by her. She is always interested in learning more about her job and is committed to the organization.

- ☐ 1. A valued worker usually is happy at her job.
- ☐ 2. There are many qualities of a valued worker.
- ☐ 3. A valued worker makes a lot of money.

Now read the flyer and try to get the overall meaning of the text, without looking up difficult words or expressions in the dictionary.

Eight Keys to Employability[1]

1. Personal Values

Valued workers are honest and have good **self-esteem** and a positive self-image. They have personal and career goals, demonstrate emotional stability, exhibit a good attitude, are **self-motivated**, and do not **limit** themselves.

2. Problem-Solving and Decision-Making Skills

Valued workers are flexible, creative, and innovative, can adapt to the changing demands of a job, can plan and organize work, can make **objective** judgments, and keep their mind on several parts of a job at a time.

3. Task-Related Skills

Valued workers complete work on time, can follow oral, visual, written, and multistep directions, work neatly, stick with a task and keep busy, are precise and meticulous,[2] care for tools and materials, are accurate, and constantly improve their performance.

4. Communication Skills

Valued workers ask questions, seek[3] help when needed, notify supervisors of absences and the reasons for absences, clearly express themselves orally, and listen well.

5. Relations with Other People

Valued workers are team members and are friendly, **cooperative**, and **tactful**. They have leadership qualities, respect the rights and property of others, and accept authority, supervision, and constructive criticism. They respect diversity.

6. Maturity

Valued workers work well without supervision, are reliable and dependable, accept responsibility, don't let their personal problems interfere with their work, are willing to perform extra work and work overtime, are always prepared for work, show pride in their work, show initiative, remain calm and self-controlled, accept responsibility for their own behavior, demonstrate **maturity** in thoughts and deeds,[4] evaluate their own work, are patient, use time wisely, are **assertive** when necessary, and show self-confidence.

7. Health and Safety Habits

Valued workers observe safety rules, maintain a good work pace and production rate, practice good grooming[5] and personal hygiene, dress appropriately, perform well under stress and tension, have appropriate physical stamina[6] and **tolerance** for the kind of work they're doing, and are in good health.

8. Commitment to Job

Valued workers are punctual and have good attendance records, observe all organizational policies, and consider their work more than a job. They are interested and enthusiastic, want to learn more, exhibit **loyalty** to the organization and its employees, give their best efforts consistently, strive[7] to please, and show concern for their future career with the organization.

---

[1] *employability:* your chances of finding the job you want

[2] *precise and meticulous:* showing attention to detail

[3] *seek:* ask or look for

[4] *deeds:* actions or behavior

[5] *grooming:* appearance

[6] *stamina:* strength

[7] *strive:* try hard

COMPREHENSION

A **Main Ideas**

Read each comment. Check (✓) the behaviors that correspond to valued workers according to your understanding of the reading.

☑ **1.** "I'm a little tired today because I went to bed late, but you can be sure I'll get my work done on time."

☐ **2.** "You told me to send the letter before I made the phone call, but now you seem to be telling me the opposite."

☐ **3.** "I finished the weekly report by the deadline, but next time I'm going to be more organized so that I can get it done even faster."

☐ **4.** "Excuse me, could you help me with something? I'm not sure I understand exactly what you wanted me to do."

☐ **5.** "Let's work together on this report. I don't mind writing the first draft."

☐ **6.** "I can't concentrate today. My husband and I had a big fight this morning, and I can't seem to settle down."

☐ **7.** "I think I'll wear jeans to work tomorrow."

☐ **8.** "I'll be 10 or 15 minutes late to the office, but that won't matter too much."

B **Close Reading**

Read the descriptions of Amy and Ben, who are excellent employees. Underline the phrases in the reading that explain their work habits.

Amy

1. Amy is usually in a good mood. (*Key 1*) exhibit a good attitude

2. She never wastes time. (*Key 3*)

3. If she doesn't understand something, she talks to her boss. (*Key 4*)

4. If she feels sick and needs to miss work, she calls to let the office know. (*Key 4*)

5. If her boss tells her that she made a mistake, she tries to improve her work. (*Key 5*)

Ben

6. Ben treats everyone the same, no matter where they come from or what they believe. (*Key 5*)

7. He always finishes his projects on time. (*Key 6*)

8. He never acts silly or childish. (*Key 6*)

9. He's clean and dresses very nicely. (*Key 7*)

10. He wants to stay with the company and work toward a more responsible position. (*Key 8*)

VOCABULARY

Ⓐ Word Forms

1 Fill in the chart with the correct word forms. Some categories can have more than one form. Use a dictionary if necessary. An *X* indicates there is no form in that category.

	NOUN	VERB	ADJECTIVE
1.	assertiveness		assertive
2.			cooperative
3.	maturity/		mature/
4.	tolerance		
5.	loyalty	X	
6.	limit		
7.		X	tactful
8.			objective

2 Read the conversation. Complete the conversation with the correct form of the words. Choose from the forms in the chart.

SUPERVISOR: Good morning, sir. You asked me to give you an evaluation of

Mr. Ben Peterson and Mr. Wilson Dacosta. I have tried to be as

_____*objective*_____ as possible and not take my personal
         1.

feelings into account. So let me see . . . Well, Ben is an extremely

good worker. You can count on his _____
                                                   2.

with his peers: he always supports his colleagues. And he's very

_____ of other people's opinions, even if he
                         3.

doesn't share them.

MANAGER: That's very good to hear. But I understand that you've been

having some trouble with Wilson Dacosta.

SUPERVISOR: Unfortunately, that's true. He's often very _____,

make jokes in meetings and things like that. And he hasn't

shown much _____ to the company. Just last

week, he said that he'd prefer to work somewhere else.

MANAGER: That's not very _____. In fact, it's

quite insensitive. In addition, in today's economy, there are

_____ opportunities in his field, so that was

not a smart comment. Have you spoken to him?

SUPERVISOR: No, but I'll set up a meeting with him.

MANAGER: I think you'll need to be quite _____.

He needs to know that he has to change his behavior at work.

B Prefix: *self-*

Study the noun and adjectives that use the prefix *self-*. Then complete the
sentences with the words.

• **self-esteem**	→	pride in your own abilities
• **self-motivated**	→	able to motivate yourself
• **self-controlled**	→	able to control your words and actions
• **self-confident**	→	confident of your own abilities

1. Peter is sure of his own abilities. He is quite _____.

2. When Elizabeth finishes a task, she just goes on to some other work.

   She's very _____.

3. Nigel knows that he has some extremely good qualities. He has very high

   _____.

4. Even if Shirley is tired or frustrated, she rarely shows it. She is a very

   _____ person.

C Negative Prefixes: *un-*, *in-*, *dis-*, *im-*, *ir-*

> Various prefixes are used to make adjectives negative. They include **un-**, **in-**, **dis-**, **im-**, and **ir-**.
>
> **EXAMPLE:**
>   Employers appreciate it when employees are cooperative. It is harder to deal with **uncooperative** people. (uncooperative: not cooperative)
>
> We often use **im-** or **ir-** for words beginning with the letter *m*, *p*, or *r*. However, there are many exceptions to this rule. To be sure of the form of a negative adjective, you should check a dictionary.
> * mature   →   **immature**, not acting in a reasonable, adult way
> * patient   →   **impatient**, not calm or able to deal with problems
> * responsible   →   **irresponsible**, not sensible or able to be trusted

1 Look at the list of words beginning with the prefixes *un-*, *in-*, *dis-*, *im-*, and *ir-*. Write the meaning of each. Use a dictionary if necessary.

MEANING

1. unafraid   _not afraid, brave_

2. inaccurate   _____

3. disrespectful   _____

4. imprecise   _____

5. irregular   _____

2 With a partner, fill in the chart with the antonym (opposite) of each word. Use prefixes to make the word negative. Then write the meaning of the antonym.

	ANTONYM	MEANING
1. cooperative	uncooperative	
2. acceptable		
3. tolerant		
4. loyal		
5. motivated		

CRITICAL THINKING

Discuss the questions with a partner.

1. The reading says that employees should ask for help when they need it. Do you think there are times when an employee should not ask for help, but just trust his or her own judgment? Give an example.

2. The reading says that employees should be good team members. When do people need to work alone, start a project on their own, or finish a task by themselves? Give examples.

3. The reading says that employees should be honest. Is it ever a good idea for an employee to lie? If so, give an example.

AFTER YOU READ

BRINGING IT ALL TOGETHER

1 Review your responses to the Holland Code, page 131. Read the career choices. With a partner, decide which career choices you think correspond to each personality type. Complete the chart with words from the box.

advertiser	manager
artist	medical records specialist
banker	nurse
computer engineer	police officer
consultant	psychologist
designer	salesperson
economist	travel agent
educator	urban planner

PERSONALITY TYPE	Realistic	Investigative	Artistic	Social	Enterprising	Conventional
CAREER CHOICES						

2 Discuss the questions in a small group.

1. Why did you choose the careers you did for the personality types?

2. Do your own personality types correspond to any of the careers that are listed? Explain.

3. Have you ever thought about working in one of the careers? Why?

4. Do you think that a person's personality type has an influence on career choice or how successful a person is in that career? Explain.

WRITING ACTIVITY

Write a paragraph about one of the topics below. Use some of the vocabulary you studied in the chapter (for a complete list, go to page 155). Share your paragraph with a partner.

1. Describe your ideal job. Include such things as location, hours, responsibilities, types of peers, and salary.

2. Write about a time you or someone you know had a conflict at work. What happened?

3. Describe a job you think you would hate, and explain why you feel this way.

DISCUSSION AND WRITING TOPICS

Discuss these topics in a small group. Choose one of them and write a paragraph or two about it. Use the vocabulary from the chapter.

1. What would you do if you loved your job but didn't like your boss?

2. Do you think that new college graduates should try to work right away, or should they take some time off before entering the workforce? Explain.

3. Do you think it's better to have fewer jobs over your lifetime, or to have many? Explain.

4. What views does your parents' generation have about employment? How do their views compare to your generation's views?

VOCABULARY

Nouns	Verbs	Adjectives	Idiom
asset	complain	assertive	the bigger
expectation	deal with	balanced	picture
feedback	dread	bonded*	
flexibility*	figure out	cooperative*	
loyalty	limit	idealistic	
maturity*	misinterpret*	networked*	
reward	precede*	objective	
self-esteem	put off	passionate	
tolerance	recruit	self-motivated	
		tactful	

* = AWL (Academic Word List) item

SELF-ASSESSMENT

In this chapter you learned to:

○ Preview a text by reading section headings

○ Use the 3-2-1 strategy to review a text

○ Deal with difficult words or expressions

○ Guess the meaning of words from the context

○ Understand and use word forms, synonyms, word usage, and prefixes

○ Label paragraphs

○ Write margin notes

What can you do well? ✓

What do you need to practice more? ✓

CHAPTER 7

MATH: Developing a Love of the "Language of Science"

MATHEMATICS: the study of quantity, shape, and change, using numbers and symbols

OBJECTIVES

To read academic texts, you need to master certain skills.

In this chapter, you will:

- Understand an author's viewpoint

- Understand an author's purpose

- Scan a text for time markers to understand the sequence of events

- Understand and use definitions, word forms, and word usage

- Guess the meaning of words from the context

- Identify topic sentences

- Paraphrase

Psychedelic art contains many mathematical patterns.

Consider This Information

1 Look at the chart comparing different countries of the world based on students' scores in math and science. A rank of 1 is the highest, and 10 is the lowest. Discuss your reactions with a partner.

COUNTRY	MATH RANK	SCIENCE RANK
Taiwan	1	2
South Korea	2	4
Singapore	3	1
Japan	4	3
Hungary	5	6
United Kingdom	6	5
Russia	7	9
United States	8	10
Czech Republic	9	7
Slovenia	10	8

2 Discuss the questions in a small group.

1. Did you find any of the information surprising? If yes, how so?

2. In your opinion, what should teachers do to help their students do well in math and science?

A Warm-Up

1 Read the comments.

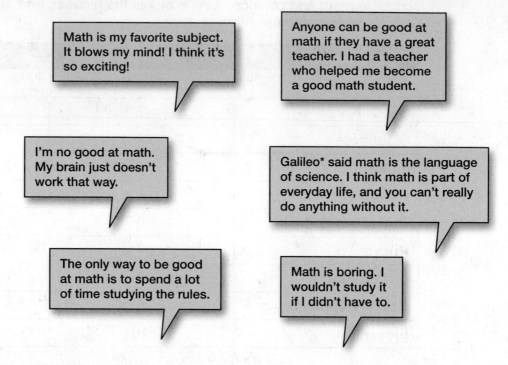

> Math is my favorite subject. It blows my mind! I think it's so exciting!

> Anyone can be good at math if they have a great teacher. I had a teacher who helped me become a good math student.

> I'm no good at math. My brain just doesn't work that way.

> Galileo* said math is the language of science. I think math is part of everyday life, and you can't really do anything without it.

> The only way to be good at math is to spend a lot of time studying the rules.

> Math is boring. I wouldn't study it if I didn't have to.

2 Discuss the questions with a partner.

1. Which comment or comments best describe your feelings about math? Why?

2. If you were in a conversation with the people making the comments, how would you respond?

B Reading Strategy

Understanding Author's Viewpoint

Some texts communicate information or tell a story, but others **express a viewpoint**. In order to understand an author's viewpoint, ask yourself these questions when you read a text: Who is the author? What is he or she saying? How strongly does he or she feel?

1 Scan the reading. With a partner, answer the questions.

1. A *lament* is an expression of disappointment or complaint. What is the author disappointed and complaining about?

2. Who else expresses an opinion on the subject?

2 Now read the essay to learn more about the author's viewpoint.

---

*Galileo Galilei (1564–1642) was an Italian mathematician.

A Mathematician's Lament

By Paul Lockhart

1   If I had to design a mechanism for the express purpose of destroying a child's natural **curiosity** and love of pattern-making, I couldn't possibly do as good a job as is currently being done—I simply wouldn't have the imagination to come up with the kind of **senseless**, soul-crushing[1] ideas that constitute[2] **contemporary** mathematics education.

How many triangles are there in the picture?

2   Everyone knows that something is wrong. The politicians say, "We need higher standards." The schools say, "We need more money and equipment." Educators say one thing, and teachers say another. They are all wrong. The only people who understand what is going on are the ones most often **blamed** and least often heard: the students. They say, "Math class is stupid and boring," and they are right.

3   Mathematics is an art. The difference between math and the other arts, such as music and painting, is that our culture does not recognize it as such. Everyone understands that poets, painters, and musicians create works of art, and are expressing themselves in word, image, and sound. In fact, our society is rather generous when it comes to creative expression; architects, chefs, and even television directors are considered to be working artists. So why not mathematicians?

4   Part of the problem is that nobody has the faintest idea[3] what it is that mathematicians do. The common **perception** seems to be that mathematicians are somehow connected with science—perhaps they help the scientists with their formulas, or feed big numbers into computers for some reason or other.

5   Nevertheless, the fact is that there is nothing as **dreamy** and poetic, nothing as radical,[4] **subversive**, and **psychedelic**, as mathematics. It is every bit as **mind blowing** as cosmology[5] or physics (mathematicians conceived of black holes long before astronomers actually found any), and allows more freedom of expression than poetry, art, or music (which depend heavily on properties of the physical universe). Mathematics is the purest of the arts, as well as the most **misunderstood**.

---

[1] *soul-crushing:* destroying the soul

[2] *constitute:* make up, form

[3] *has the faintest idea:* not know or understand

[4] *radical:* extreme, intense

[5] *cosmology:* the science of the origin of the universe

COMPREHENSION

Ⓐ Main Ideas

Read the questions. Choose the correct answer. Discuss your answers with a partner.

1. According to the essay, what is the main problem with math education?

   a. It destroys students' interest in math.

   b. It is not challenging enough.

2. When students complain about math education, what do other people do?

   a. They say the students are to blame.

   b. They provide more money for math education.

3. What does Lockhart say about math?

   a. It is not an art.

   b. It is misunderstood by most people.

4. What is Lockhart's opinion of math?

   a. It is exciting and creative.

   b. It is systematic but hard to learn.

Ⓑ Close Reading

Read each statement. Decide if it is *True* or *False* according to the reading. Check (✓) the appropriate box. If it is false, change it to make it true. Discuss your answers with a partner.

	TRUE	FALSE
1. It is normal for children to like making patterns.	☑	☐
2. Math classes are exciting and meaningful.	☐	☐
3. Politicians, schools, and teachers all agree that there is a problem.	☐	☐
4. Like painting, music, and cooking, math is usually considered a form of creative expression.	☐	☐
5. People don't really understand what mathematicians do.	☐	☐
6. Mathematics restricts freedom of expression.	☐	☐

VOCABULARY

A Definitions

1 Match each adjective with its definition. Choose a word from the box.
Use a dictionary if necessary.

contemporary	mind blowing	psychedelic	subversive
dreamy	misunderstood	senseless	

1. incredibly impressive   *mind blowing*

2. without any meaning   _____

3. showing intense, vivid patterns   _____

4. opposed to traditional ideas   _____

5. magical, mysterious   _____

6. belonging to the present   _____

7. having the wrong idea   _____

2 Go back to the reading and read it again. Write the adjective or adjectives that
describe the nouns from the reading.

1. mathematics: *dreamy,* _____

2. ideas that math education is based on: _____

3. math education: _____

B Word Forms

1 Fill in the chart with the correct word forms. Some categories can have more than one form. Use a dictionary if necessary. An **X** indicates there is no form in that category.

	NOUN	VERB	ADJECTIVE
1.	blame		blamed
2.	curiosity	X	
3.			misunderstood
4.	perception		perceptive/
5.			senseless

2 Complete the conversation with the correct form of the words. Choose from the forms in the chart.

NATALIE: Look at this assignment. We're supposed to write something about these questions: "Why are there 24 hours in a day? Why are there 60 seconds in a minute? Why are there 360 degrees in a circle?" I don't _____understand_____ what our professor wants us to
1.
do. It's an absolutely _____ assignment.
2.

SHEILA: Don't be silly. I think that's a great assignment. Aren't you

_____ about those questions?
3.

NATALIE: Well, I don't have the faintest idea how to answer them.

SHEILA: Look, there's a common _____ that everything
4.
is based on 10, or the decimal system. But actually that's not true. The ancient Egyptians used 12 as their base, and that's why there are 24 hours in a day.

NATALIE: Oh, OK, that makes more _____.
5.

SHEILA: Yeah, not everything is based on 10. That's a _____.
6.
I mean, they sell eggs in dozens, not tens. And there are 16 ounces in a pound. Why is that?

NATALIE: I get it! At first, I _____ the assignment.
                              7.

But now I see that the professor is just trying to stimulate our

_____. I guess it is really interesting, after all.
                    8.

SHEILA: I'm glad you said that. I don't think you should

_____ the professor if a subject seems boring
                    9.

to you.

NOTE-TAKING: Identifying Topic Sentences

> Most good writers use **topic sentences** to help readers understand
> the focus of each paragraph. A topic sentence **summarizes the main
> idea in the paragraph**. It is usually found at or near the beginning of a
> paragraph or at the end of a paragraph.

Go back to the reading and read it again. Underline the topic sentences in
paragraphs 3, 4, and 5.

EXAMPLE: PARAGRAPH 2

Everyone knows that something is wrong. The politicians say, "We need
higher standards." The schools say, "We need more money and equipment."
Educators say one thing, and teachers say another. They are all wrong. The
only people who understand what is going on are the ones most often blamed
and least often heard: the students. They say, "Math class is stupid and boring,"
and they are right.

CRITICAL THINKING

Discuss the questions with a partner. Be prepared to share your answers with
the class.

1. Lockhart says that many students think math class is stupid and boring.
   Do you think this is true? Explain your opinion.

2. Lockhart dismisses the opinions of educators and teachers, although he
   himself is a math teacher. How do you think other teachers might react to
   his opinion?

3. Lockhart says that math is "the purest of the arts" and that it "allows more
   freedom of expression than poetry, art, or music." Have you heard anyone
   express this opinion before? What's your opinion?

4. Look at the picture of the triangle in the reading. Can you answer the
   question in the caption? What's the best way to figure out the answer?
   Do you think it's fun trying?

A Warm-Up

Read each statement. Mark your opinion on the scale. Share your opinions with a partner.

1. When you learn math, you have to memorize many formulas. Once you learn the basics and feel more confident, you can apply what you know.

Strongly agree	Agree	Not sure	Disagree	Strongly disagree

2. Unless you understand the rules learned in math class, math is meaningless.

Strongly agree	Agree	Not sure	Disagree	Strongly disagree

3. Whatever subject you are studying, you should be able to apply what you have learned to real life.

Strongly agree	Agree	Not sure	Disagree	Strongly disagree

4. If students learn math formulas and become good at math, they will automatically enjoy it.

Strongly agree	Agree	Not sure	Disagree	Strongly disagree

B Reading Strategy

Understanding Author's Purpose

When you read a text, you should always **determine the author's purpose**. Some common purposes are **(a) to entertain, (b) to tell a story, (c) to ask a question, (d) to complain, (e) to convince someone of something,** and **(f) to express an opinion**. Authors may have more than one purpose.

Scan the comments about math education. Which of the purposes listed above do you think corresponds to the comments? Check (✓) the appropriate box(es). Discuss your answers with a partner.

1. Comment 1:　　☐ a.　　☐ b.　　☑ c.　　☐ d.　　☑ e.　　☑ f.

2. Comment 2:　　☐ a.　　☐ b.　　☐ c.　　☐ d.　　☐ e.　　☐ f.

3. Comment 3:　　☐ a.　　☐ b.　　☐ c.　　☐ d.　　☐ e.　　☐ f.

4. Comment 4:　　☐ a.　　☐ b.　　☐ c.　　☐ d.　　☐ e.　　☐ f.

5. Comment 5:　　☐ a.　　☐ b.　　☐ c.　　☐ d.　　☐ e.　　☐ f.

Now read the comments to check your answers.

What's Wrong with Math Education?

Comment 1

Math and science education seem to have gone badly wrong in the United States. What is going on? Perhaps teachers should be more **strict**. Perhaps they should be more **inspiring**. There doesn't seem to be any clear solution to the problem, but meanwhile, we are **lagging behind** the rest of the world.

Comment 2

I don't think teachers should just tell students to memorize math rules in the hope that they'll **internalize** them. Instead, math education should be more practical. Classes should **link** math to everyday problems. Students who are good at math become engineers and scientists, architects and software designers, and if they understand that, they automatically become more interested in math.

Comment 3

You do not study mathematics because it helps you build a bridge. You study mathematics because it is the poetry of the universe.

Comment 4

Since when did **practicality** become the only goal of our educational system? Should English classes **dispense with** classic literature in favor of company annual reports? Should music and art be jettisoned[1] to make way for classes in accounting and taxes?

Comment 5

Mathematics, like literature, music, science, and any other subject worth studying, should be taught and learned for its own sake.[2] Just as we teach students the beauty of poetry, we should teach students the beauty of mathematics. If we try to make math **curriculums** "relevant" to daily life, we will end up teaching students a series of **disconnected** formulas.

---

[1] *jettisoned:* gotten rid of, thrown out

[2] *for its own sake:* as an end in itself, for no other reason

COMPREHENSION

A **Main Ideas**

Read each statement. Decide if it is *True* or *False* according to the comment.
Check (✓) the appropriate box. If it is false, change it to make it true. Discuss
your answers with a partner.

	TRUE	FALSE
1. Comment 1: There ~~is~~ *isn't* a clear solution to the crisis in math education.	☐	☑
2. Comment 2: Teachers need to have students memorize math rules.	☐	☐
3. Comment 2: Studying math can help you get a better job.	☐	☐
4. Comment 3: Mathematics is beautiful.	☐	☐
5. Comment 4: Education should be made more practical.	☐	☐
6. Comment 5: Math curriculums should be linked to daily life.	☐	☐

B **Close Reading**

Read the quotes from the reading. Circle the statement that best explains each
quote. Share your answers with a partner.

1. "You do not study mathematics because it helps you build a bridge.
   You study math because it is the poetry of the universe." *(Comment 3)*

   a. You should study math because it helps explain the world in a
      beautiful way.

   b. You should study math because it will help you get a better job.

2. "Since when did practicality become the only goal of our educational
   system?" *(Comment 4)*

   a. We should have clear goals when we study something.

   b. We should not only think about the end result when we study
      something.

3. "Mathematics, like literature, music, science, and any other subject worth
   studying, should be taught and learned for its own sake." *(Comment 5)*

   a. Literature, music, and science are practical subjects to study.

   b. We should study subjects not because they will help us, but because
      they are interesting.

VOCABULARY

A **Guessing from Context**

Read the sentences and guess the meanings of the words in bold from the context. Then match the words with their meanings.

1. My twin brother was great at math, but I was never much good at it. I was always **lagging behind** on the homework.

2. I'm tutoring some middle school students, and I'm trying to emphasize the **practicality** of math. They need to understand that once they know some basic rules, they can use math for all kinds of different purposes.

3. I think math classes should be organized around interesting questions, and teachers should **dispense with** all the complicated explanations and formulas. They aren't necessary or helpful.

4. You have to memorize math rules. Once you **internalize** them, you don't need to think about them any more.

5. If teachers **link** math to things that children like, such as games and puzzles, then children begin to like math more.

_b_ 1. **lagging behind**	**a.** connect
___ 2. **practicality**	**b.** unable to keep up
___ 3. **dispense with**	**c.** get rid of
___ 4. **internalize**	**d.** a situation when you do something rather than just think about it
___ 5. **link**	**e.** make part of what you know

B **Word Usage**

1 Complete the conversations with the correct word or phrase from the box. Compare answers with a partner.

disconnected	dispense with	internalized	practicality	relevant

CONVERSATION 1

BEATRICE: I really love my math course. I could _____ *dispense with* _____

                                                                                    1.

all my other subjects!

PETER: I know you're joking, Beatrice. But honestly, I think you're a bit

unusual. Most people don't feel that passionate about math.

(continued on next page)

BEATRICE: Well, it's the _____ of math that appeals to me.
2.
Without math, we couldn't build skyscrapers or have computers or

do pretty much anything.

PETER: A lot of people don't like math, and they've _____
3.
the idea that math has nothing to do with our daily lives. I know I've

always felt that way. That's why I couldn't stand math in school.

BEATRICE: Yes, it's a real problem in schools. I think school administrators

should make math more interesting. Most people feel

_____ from math, and that's too bad. Math
4.
is _____ to everyone's daily life!
5.

| curriculum | inspiring | lagging behind | link | strict |

CONVERSATION 2

NANCY: Look at this study. It says that the United States is

_____ other countries in math and science.
6.
ARTHUR: Let me see that. Mmm, well, it doesn't surprise me. The

_____ that they use in schools is far too
7.
disconnected. They should _____ math to other
8.
subjects to show students how practical math is.

NANCY: Don't you think teachers should make the students work harder,

they should be more _____? I mean, don't you
9.
think they should give more homework and more tests?

ARTHUR: Not really. I think that math teachers need to be more

_____. They should make students feel more
10.
passionate about math. Math is fun! Haven't you ever tried to learn

the digits in pi? Or studied what Leonardo Da Vinci said about the

golden ratio?

NANCY: Not really. Maybe I should! I would like to be good at math.

> **Paraphrasing** means **expressing ideas in your own words**. Whenever you write about a text, you should paraphrase the ideas, not copy them directly.

With a partner, paraphrase the main idea of each of the comments. Share your answers with the class.

According to the author,

1. *there is a serious problem with math education in the United States.*
2. _____
3. _____
4. _____
5. _____

CRITICAL THINKING

Discuss the questions with a partner. Be prepared to share your ideas with the class.

1. The writer of Comment 1 thinks that math teachers in the United States should be either more strict or more inspiring. What do you think?

2. The writer of Comment 2 thinks that math education should be very practical, and that students should realize that they have to be good at math if they want to become engineers, architects, or software designers. Do you agree? Explain.

3. The writer of Comment 3 believes that people study math because it is interesting and beautiful, not because of any practical purpose. Do you think that is true? Why or why not?

4. The writer of Comment 4 says that contemporary education is limited to what is practical. Is that true, in your experience? Explain.

5. The writer of Comment 5 thinks that if math education is linked to daily life, math will end up seeming more disconnected, not more connected. Do you agree? If so, how might that be possible?

LINKING READINGS ONE AND TWO

1 The readings comment on problems in math education and their solutions. Review the readings and fill in the chart with the ideas you find.

	PROBLEMS WITH MATH EDUCATION	SOLUTIONS TO THE PROBLEMS
READING ONE	• Math classes are boring. • •	• Schools should make math classes more interesting. • •
READING TWO	• • •	• • •

2 Compare your chart with a partner's. Which of your partner's ideas do you agree with? Which do you disagree with?

READING THREE: Angels on a Pin

A Warm-Up

A student saw this question on a physics test:

How can you calculate the height of a tall building using a barometer?

The student suggested tying a rope to the end of the barometer, lowering the barometer from the top of the building to the street, and measuring the length of the rope. His professor (Professor 1) failed him because his answer did not show any knowledge of physics.

This story is about what happened when another professor, Professor 2, gave the student a second chance to answer the question.

A barometer

Discuss the questions in a small group.

1. Why do you think Professor 1 failed the student?

2. What answer do you think the professor expected?

3. If you were Professor 1, would you have failed the student?

Scanning for Time Markers

Narratives are often arranged in **chronological order**, telling events in the order they occur. **Time markers help the reader to follow the story.**

Scan the reading and underline the time markers.

EXAMPLE:

<u>At the end of five minutes</u>, he had not written anything.

Now read the rest of the story, written by Professor 2, to see what happens.

Angels on a Pin
By Alexander Callandra

1 I gave the student six minutes to answer the question with the **warning** that the answer should show some knowledge of physics. At the end of five minutes, he had not written anything. I asked if he wished to give up, but he said no. He had many answers to this problem; he was just thinking of the best one. I excused myself for interrupting him and asked him to please go on. In the next minute he **dashed off** his answer, which read:

2 "Take the barometer to the top of the building and lean over the edge of the roof. Drop that barometer, timing its fall with a stopwatch.[1] Then using the formula $S = \frac{1}{2}at^2$,[2] **calculate** the height of the building."

3 At this point I asked my colleague if he would give up. He **conceded**, and gave the student almost full credit.

4 In leaving my colleague's office, I recalled that the student had said

---

[1] *stopwatch:* a special watch used to time tests or races

[2] This is an advanced mathematical formula that measures acceleration, or speed.

he had many other answers to the problem, so I asked him what they were. "Oh, yes," said the student. "There are a great many ways of getting the height of a tall building with a barometer. For example, you could take the barometer out on a sunny day and measure the height of the barometer and the **length** of its shadow, and the length of the shadow of the building and by the use of a simple **proportion**, determine the **height** of the building."

5 "Fine," I asked. "And the others?"

6 "Yes," said the student. "There is a very basic **measurement** method that you will like. In this method you take the barometer and begin to walk up the stairs. As you climb the stairs, you mark off the length of the barometer along the wall. You then count the number of marks, and this will give you the height of the building in barometer units. A very direct method.

7 "Of course, if you want a more **sophisticated** method, you can tie the barometer to the end of a string, swing

(continued on next page)

it as a pendulum, and determine the value of 'g'[3] at the street level and at the top of the building. From the difference of the two values of 'g', the height of the building can be calculated."

8 Finally, he concluded, there were many other ways of solving the problem. "Probably the best," he said, "is to take the barometer to the basement and knock on the superintendent's[4] door. When the superintendent answers, you speak to him as follows: "Mr. Superintendent, here I have a fine barometer. If you tell me the height of this building, I will give you this barometer."

---

[3] *"g"*: shorthand for "gravitational force"

[4] *superintendent*: a person who takes care of a building

COMPREHENSION

(A) Main Ideas

Read each statement. Decide if it is *True* or *False* according to the reading. Check (✓) the appropriate box. If it is false, change it to make it true. Discuss your answers with a partner.

	TRUE	FALSE
1. Professor 2 thought the student would need more time than he did to take the test.	✓	☐
2. The student wanted to give up after six minutes.	☐	☐
3. Professor 2 believed the student was good at physics, even though Professor 1 failed him.	☐	☐
4. The student had advanced knowledge of physics.	☐	☐
5. The student presented his solutions to the question from the easiest to the most difficult.	☐	☐

The student proposed six methods for answering the question. Put the methods in the order he gave them.

_____ **a.** You can walk up the stairs to the top of the building, using the barometer as a ruler.

_____ **b.** You can offer a worker in the building the barometer as a reward for telling you the height.

_____ **c.** You can drop the barometer, time its fall, and use a formula to calculate the height.

__1__ **d.** You can tie a rope to the barometer, lower it from the top of the building, and measure the length of the rope.

_____ **e.** You can use a proportion to figure the height from the lengths of the building's shadow and the barometer's shadow.

_____ **f.** You can swing the barometer, measure its gravitational force (*g*) at street level and at the top of the building, and calculate the difference.

VOCABULARY

A **Guessing from Context**

Read the sentences and guess the meanings of the words in bold from the context. Then match the words with their meanings.

1. When I did my math homework, I worked with a friend. We both got the answer wrong. My teacher gave me a **warning**. She said that it was OK to work together, but that if she saw we had copied homework from each other, we would both get an "F."

2. I have a friend who is brilliant at math. In the test, he just **dashed off** the answers to the questions, while I sat there for half an hour trying to figure out how to solve the problems.

3. My girlfriend is knitting a sweater that's really pretty. It's full of **sophisticated** patterns.

4. I just saw a great chess match between two champions at my college. After four hours, one of the players lost. The other player said that he had made some serious errors, and he **conceded**.

_____ **1. warning**   **a.** admitted defeat

_____ **2. dashed off**   **b.** piece of strong advice

_____ **3. sophisticated**   **c.** complex

_____ **4. conceded**   **d.** quickly wrote

B Word Forms

1 Fill in the chart with the correct word forms. Use a dictionary if necessary. An **X** indicates there is no form in that category.

	Noun	Verb	Adjective
1.	*calculation*	calculate	X
2.		concede	
3.	height	X	
4.	length	X	
5.	measurement		
6.	proportion	X	proportional/
7.		X	sophisticated

2 Complete the conversation between Professor 2 and Professor 1 with the correct form of the words. Choose from the forms in the chart.

PROFESSOR 2: So, what do you think of that student now?

PROFESSOR 1: Well, now that I've seen his performance on the test, I must admit that he is actually a very good physics student. I just didn't realize that at first.

PROFESSOR 2: Some of his methods were really funny, don't you think?

PROFESSOR 1: Yes. I liked the one where he wanted to

_____*measure*_____ the _____
          1.   **2.**

of the building by walking up the stairs with a pencil in

one hand and the barometer in the other! But he didn't

_____ how _____
          3.   **4.**

that would take. Hours, I would imagine!

PROFESSOR 2: Yes, I was laughing really hard when I read that. But

you know, the student had some very complex and

_____ methods, too. I especially liked
          5.

the solution that showed the length of the shadow as a

_____ of the height of the building.
          6.

PROFESSOR 1: Yes. I can't believe how many methods he came up with! I have to

_____ that he is a very creative young man!

7.

PROFESSOR 2: Yes, right? As soon as he began to dash off his answers, I knew

you would have to give up!

PROFESSOR 1: Well, I'm glad you convinced me to give him a second chance.

CRITICAL THINKING

1 The title of the story refers to a question from the Middle Ages about critical thought: How many angels can dance on the head of a pin? If you wanted to give the story a different title, what would it be? Share your title with the class.

EXAMPLES:

- Student Challenges Professor
- Math Problems Have Many Answers
- Many Tests Are Too Simple
- your own idea: _____

2 Discuss the questions in a small group. Be prepared to share your answers with the class.

1. What do you think of the student in the story? Have you ever met a person like that?

2. There is an expression *to think outside the box*, which is what the student did. What do you think that means? Are there times when it's important "to think outside the box"? Explain.

3. The question from the Middle Ages suggests that there are many answers to most problems. Do you agree? Explain.

BRINGING IT ALL TOGETHER

1 The readings emphasize that math is connected to many other areas of life. With a partner, discuss how math is related to the examples.

Poetry
William Wordsworth's famous poem "Daffodils" begins with this verse:

> I wandered lonely as a cloud
> That floats on high o'er vales and hills,
> When all at once I saw a crowd,
> A host, of golden daffodils;
> Beside the lake, beneath the trees,
> Fluttering and dancing in the breeze.

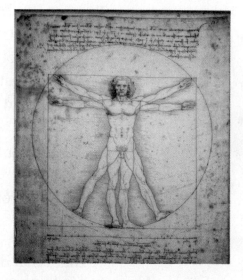

Visual Arts
One of the most famous drawings in the world is Leonardo da Vinci's *Vitruvian Man*.

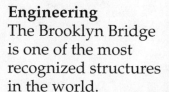

Music
Musical notes are used to express the rhythm and melodies of music.

Engineering
The Brooklyn Bridge is one of the most recognized structures in the world.

Carrot Cake with Icing

For the cake:
2 cups all purpose flour
1 cup sugar
2 teaspoons baking soda
1 teaspoon cinnamon
1 teaspoon salt
4 eggs
$1\frac{1}{2}$ cups vegetable oil
3 cups grated carrots

For the icing:
1 package cream cheese
1 stick of butter
$\frac{1}{2}$ box powdered sugar
2 teaspoons vanilla extract

Cooking
Carrot cake is a popular dessert for which there are many recipes.

2 In a small group, discuss how math is related to other academic disciplines or hobbies. Then share your group's ideas with the class. Use some of the vocabulary you studied in the chapter.

WRITING ACTIVITY

1 **"Freewriting"** means writing without focusing too much on what you are saying. It allows your thoughts to develop easily. Choose one of the questions and freewrite about it. Use some of the vocabulary from the chapter (for a complete list, see page 179).

1. Some people think that teachers should formally explain difficult concepts, making extensive use of the blackboard. This approach is called "chalk and talk." Do you think this method is effective for math education? Why or why not?

2. A recent piece of advice about teaching is that teachers should not be "the sage on the stage" (the expert who lectures students) but "the guide on the side" (the person who encourages students to explore concepts on their own). Which kind of teacher teaches math most effectively? Explain.

3. Some math educators believe that "practice makes perfect," and say that students should complete many exercises until they master the material. Others say that "when you drill you kill" (when you do repetitive exercises you kill interest in the subject). What do you think?

2 Share your writing with a partner.

DISCUSSION AND WRITING TOPICS

Discuss these topics in a small group. Choose one of them and write a three-paragraph essay about it. Use the vocabulary from the chapter.

1. Most young children enjoy math games and puzzles, but as they get older, some people begin to say that they do not understand math and that they are not good at it. This phenomenon is known as "math anxiety." Do you suffer from math anxiety? In your opinion, why do people feel this way about math? What makes them change their opinion?

2. Whether or not they are math students, most people enjoy math for leisure. For example, people play number puzzles, such as Sudoku; they enjoy origami or kirigami; they have fractals as screen savers. Are you interested in math for leisure? If so, which sorts of puzzles? What is enjoyable about them?

The art of origami is based on mathematical patterns.

3. Many numbers are interesting and mysterious, such as pi, square numbers, irrational numbers, imaginary numbers, triangular numbers, zero, and infinity. Do you know anything about these numbers? What other interesting numbers do you know about? Explain the numbers and why they are interesting to you.

VOCABULARY

Nouns	Verbs	Adjectives
curiosity	blame	contemporary*
curriculum	calculate	disconnected
height	concede	dreamy
length	dash off	inspiring
measurement	dispense with	mind blowing
perception*	internalize*	misunderstood
practicality	lag behind	psychedelic
proportion*	link*	relevant*
warning		senseless
		sophisticated
		strict
		subversive

* = AWL (Academic Word List) item

SELF-ASSESSMENT

In this chapter you learned to:

○ Understand an author's viewpoint

○ Understand an author's purpose

○ Scan a text for time markers to understand the sequence of events

○ Understand and use definitions, word forms, and word usage

○ Guess the meaning of words from the context

○ Identify topic sentences

○ Paraphrase

What can you do well? ✓

What do you need to practice more? ✓

CHAPTER 8

PUBLIC SPEAKING: Messages and Messengers

PUBLIC SPEAKING: speaking to a group of people in order to communicate ideas or opinions, influence the audience, or entertain people

OBJECTIVES

To read academic texts, you need to master certain skills.

In this chapter, you will:

- Skim by reading topic sentences
- Understand rhetorical modes
- Examine footnotes
- Guess the meaning of words from the context
- Understand and use word forms and word usage
- Use dictionary entries to learn different meanings of words
- Research a person or topic and use a chart to group ideas

Benjamin Franklin (1706–1790), one of the Founding Fathers of the United States, was also a noted public speaker.

Frederick Douglass (1818–1895), was a freed slave who became a skilled public speaker.

John F. Kennedy (1917–1963), the 35th president of the United States, was known for his passionate speeches.

Lee Iacocca (1924–), former president of Chrysler car company, gave many speeches in favor of U.S. business exports during the 1980s.

Barack Obama (1961–), the first African American president of the United States, has spoken with conviction about the need for social change.

A **Consider These Questions**

Discuss the questions with a partner. Check (✓) one answer. Share your answers with the class.

1. Where do you most often hear people speak before audiences?
   - ☐ at colleges or universities
   - ☐ on TV
   - ☐ in public meetings
   - ☐ your own idea: _____

2. What is the number one skill a public speaker should possess?
   - ☐ the ability to convince others
   - ☐ self-control
   - ☐ the ability to sound honest
   - ☐ a nice appearance
   - ☐ a strong voice
   - ☐ your own idea: _____

3. Which is the most important quality of a good speech?
   - ☐ It's "short and simple."
   - ☐ It's interesting.
   - ☐ It's emotional.
   - ☐ It's not too serious.
   - ☐ The speaker uses visual aids.
   - ☐ your own idea: _____

4. What makes a speech really bad?
   - ☐ It's boring.
   - ☐ The audience can't hear it.
   - ☐ The speaker reads from notes.
   - ☐ The speaker doesn't make eye contact.
   - ☐ The speaker doesn't pay enough attention to the audience.
   - ☐ It's too long.
   - ☐ your own idea: _____

B Your Opinion

Discuss the questions with a partner.

1. The comedian George Jessel said: "The human brain starts working the moment you are born and never stops until you stand up to speak in public." What do you think he meant?

2. Have you ever made a speech in public? Was it successful? Explain.

3. Do you have any of these reactions when speaking in public? Check (✓) all that apply.

   ☐ You feel extremely stressed.

   ☐ You have a dry mouth.

   ☐ You have "butterflies in your stomach." (Your stomach hurts.)

   ☐ Your legs feel like jelly. (You feel really weak.)

   ☐ You get tongue-tied. (You can't think of what to say.)

4. What advice would you give to people who are nervous about public speaking?

READING ONE: The Power of Public Speech

A Warm-Up

Read the quotes about public speaking. With a partner, discuss what you think they mean.

"Big things are best said, are almost always said, in small words."

—*Peggy Noonan, speechwriter, 1950–*

"Listening is the shortest route to the heart."

—*Dianna Booher, author and executive, 1948–*

"They may forget what you said, but they will never forget how you made them feel."

—*Carl W. Buehner, church member and government representative, 1898–1974*

B Reading Strategy

Skimming by Reading Topic Sentences

Skimming is a reading technique that is used to **get a quick "gist" of a text**. Reading the **topic sentence** (first sentence) of a paragraph and especially the **keyword** in it will help you get the gist, or main idea, of each paragraph in a text.

Look at Reading One. Underline the topic sentence in each paragraph. Then circle the keywords that preview the main ideas.

Now read the text to find out more about its main ideas.

The Power of Public Speech

1   History shows that public **addresses** can raise people's **awareness** about **critical** issues. The most famous speeches in U.S. history have to do with important causes—movements or goals—like securing independence or women's rights, ending child labor, or protecting the poor. Frederick Douglass, a Maryland slave who fought for the freedom of all slaves, is considered one of the country's greatest **orators**. He was never allowed to go to school, yet he understood that words were powerful forces for change, and he used them to communicate passionately about the **abolition** of slavery.

2   In addition to addressing important topics, some people seem to have the power to move people to tears or to action. Compelling[1] speeches inspire enthusiasm, but skilled speakers can connect with their audiences[2] on an even deeper level. They are **articulate**, inspiring, and **sincere**. They bring important questions into focus and possess eloquence, the power to persuade with forceful and fluent speech. Often their message is straightforward, but they use words that fill us with emotion. People fought to get an opportunity to hear lawyer Clarence Darrow speak against the death penalty. Beloved baseball player Lou Gehrig brought audiences to tears when he announced he had a disease that would eventually kill him. First Lady Eleanor Roosevelt reminded her listeners of the ideals that we all share when she chaired the committee that approved the Universal Declaration of Human Rights. Martin Luther King Jr.'s description of a more equal society, one in which his four children would "not be judged by the color of their skin but by the content of their character," has inspired millions of Americans to make his dream a reality.

3   In the United States, public speaking has a long history: Indeed, the Native Americans had a rich oral tradition and understood the power of speech to inform and entertain their audiences. Yet as technology has allowed elected leaders to reach growing audiences, oratory[3] has become even more important. The public's opinion can be shaped by an official's performance before an audience. In addition to the message they bring and the words they use, speakers also communicate personal qualities like self-confidence, determination, **compassion**, **conviction**, and **trustworthiness**.

Lawyer Clarence Darrow, a brilliant orator, argued passionately against the death penalty in the Leopold and Loeb case, 1924.

---

[1] *compelling:* very strong, interesting

[2] *connect with an audience:* communicate with listeners in a seemingly open way

---

[3] *oratory:* the art of formal public speaking

COMPREHENSION

A Main Ideas

Read each statement. Decide if it is *True* or *False*, or if there is *No Information* found in the reading. Check (✓) the appropriate box. Discuss your answers with a partner.

	TRUE	FALSE	NO INFORMATION
1. Most well-known American speeches deal with problems.	✓	☐	☐
2. Frederick Douglass learned public speaking from other slaves.	☐	☐	☐
3. Some people are particularly good public speakers.	☐	☐	☐
4. Elected leaders are the best public speakers.	☐	☐	☐
5. Public speaking is less important today than it used to be.	☐	☐	☐
6. Speakers communicate more than just ideas or opinions.	☐	☐	☐

B Close Reading

Answer the questions with information from the reading.

1. What are some important issues that are mentioned in the text?

   The text mentions independence, women's rights, and abolishing child labor.

2. What was so amazing about Frederick Douglass's command of speech?

   _____

3. What qualities do skilled speakers possess?

   _____

4. What examples of skilled speakers does the text give?

   _____

5. How is public speaking different today than it was in the past?

   _____

6. In addition to the message, what else do speakers communicate to their audiences?

   _____

VOCABULARY

A Guessing from Context

Read the conversation and guess the meanings of the words in bold from the context. Then match the words with their meanings.

ANDY: Hi! What are you doing later? Do you want to watch the president's State of the Union speech with me?

LOUISA: Not really. I think his public **addresses** are too long and involved.

ANDY: I can't believe you're saying that. It's **critical** for people to listen to their elected officials.

LOUISA: Look, I know that the president is a skilled **orator**. But I don't really understand a lot of the issues he's talking about.

ANDY: Well, that's one of the reasons you should watch the speech! I recently watched him talking about unemployment, and I thought he seemed very **sincere**.

LOUISA: Well, he definitely has **conviction**. It's clear he really believes in what he's saying. OK, I'll join you tonight.

_c_ 1. **addresses**	**a.**	genuine, honest
____ 2. **critical**	**b.**	very important
____ 3. **orator**	**c.**	speeches delivered in public
____ 4. **sincere**	**d.**	skilled public speaker
____ 5. **conviction**	**e.**	the feeling of being sure that what you say is true

B Word Forms

1 Fill in the chart with the correct word forms. Some categories can have more than one form. Use a dictionary if necessary. An *X* indicates there is no form in that category.

	NOUN	VERB	ADJECTIVE
1.	awareness	X	*aware*
2.	abolition/abolitionist		X
3.			articulate/
4.	compassion	X	
5.		X	sincere/
6.	trust		

2 Complete the biographies with the correct form of the words.

Sojourner Truth was a famous participant in the

_____*abolitionist*_____ movement, a movement to end
   1. (abolition/abolish/abolitionist)

slavery in the United States. As a person who was born into

slavery herself, she was uniquely _____
                        2. (aware/awareness)

of the need to fight for equality for all. She spoke with great

_____ and _____ about the rights of
   3. (sincerity/sincere)   4. (compassion/compassionate)

African Americans and women.

Abraham Lincoln was America's 16th president. He is best known for

leading his country through the Civil War and for ending slavery. He

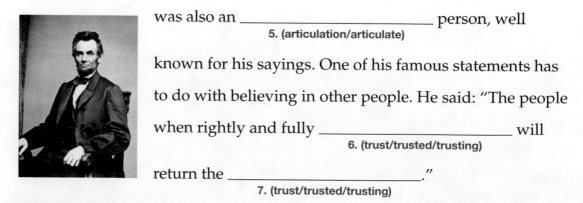

was also an _____ person, well
       5. (articulation/articulate)

known for his sayings. One of his famous statements has

to do with believing in other people. He said: "The people

when rightly and fully _____ will
       6. (trust/trusted/trusting)

return the _____."
       7. (trust/trusted/trusting)

C Using the Dictionary

1 Read the dictionary entries for *address*.

> **address** *n.* **1** the details of where someone works or lives, that you use to send him or her letters, packages, or e-mails **2** a series of words, letters, and numbers used to reach websites on the Internet **3** a formal speech
>
> **address** *v.* **1** to write a name or an address on an envelope or package **2** to speak directly to a person or group **3** to use a particular name or title when speaking or writing to someone

2 Read the sentences. Decide which part of speech is being used. Write **Noun** or **Verb**. Then determine which meaning (1, 2, or 3) is being used. Compare answers with a partner.

	PART OF SPEECH	MEANING
1. The president should be **addressed** as "Mr. President."	Verb	3
2. I didn't get my voting card. It was sent to the wrong **address**.		
3. The mayor **addressed** the city last night.		
4. I don't know why this package was sent back to me. I **addressed** it correctly.		
5. Several world leaders met to hear an **address** on human rights.		
6. Can't you find the right website? Type the **address** in the box at the top of the page.		

When you are reading a text with a lot of new factual information, it is a good idea to **make notes on what the text states** about a topic. You also should think about **questions to ask to help you expand your research on the topic**.

EXAMPLE:

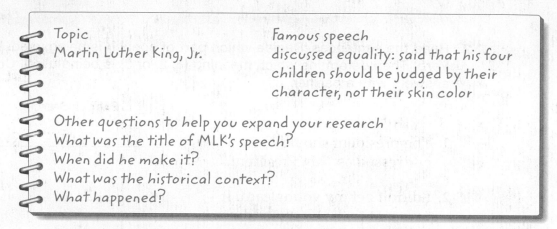

Topic
Martin Luther King, Jr.

Famous speech
discussed equality: said that his four
children should be judged by their
character, not their skin color

Other questions to help you expand your research
What was the title of MLK's speech?
When did he make it?
What was the historical context?
What happened?

Go back to the reading and find references to these people and topics. Make notes on what the text states. Then write questions to help you expand your research on each person or topic.

- Frederick Douglass
- Clarence Darrow
- Lou Gehrig
- Eleanor Roosevelt
- the death penalty
- the Universal Declaration of Human Rights

CRITICAL THINKING

Discuss the questions in a small group. Be prepared to share your ideas with the class.

1. What qualities, not mentioned in the text, do public speakers communicate?

2. The reading discusses important causes that speakers addressed in the past. What issues or topics do speakers address today? Which of these issues are you most interested in? Why?

3. The reading suggests that some people are particularly good at giving speeches in public, and it points out that Frederick Douglass, one of history's greatest orators, had no official training as a public speaker. Do you believe some people are naturally better at public speaking than others? Can public speaking be taught and learned? Explain.

A **Warm-Up**

Discuss the questions with a partner.

1. How is a good speech similar to and different from a good essay? Check (✓) all that apply.

	SPEECH	ESSAY	BOTH
• given orally	☐	☐	☐
• given in writing	☐	☐	☐
• has a clear message	☐	☐	☐
• uses clear vocabulary	☐	☐	☐
• can improve with practice	☐	☐	☐
• depends on speaker's/writer's personality	☐	☐	☐
• has a clear structure	☐	☐	☐

2. Can you think of any other similarities or differences?

B **Reading Strategy**

Understanding Rhetorical Modes

Texts often use specific **rhetorical modes**, or ways of organizing ideas. Some of these modes are:
- ☐ description (describing a person, place, or thing)
- ☐ definition (defining a concept or topic)
- ☐ narration (telling a story)
- ☐ comparison and contrast (showing similarities and differences)
- ☐ cause-and-effect analysis (explaining the relationship between two ideas)
- ☐ persuasion (trying to get someone to believe something)
- ☐ process analysis (explaining how to do something)

Read the title and the first paragraph of the reading. Check (✓) the rhetorical modes you think are used in the text. Compare answers with a partner.

Now read the website to find out if your prediction was correct.

The Best Way to Structure a Speech

By Professor Stephen E. Lucas

1 The main requirement for a successful speech is having something important to say. Lots of times people focus on **delivery**, personal appearance, **gestures**, eye contact, and the like.[1] Those things are certainly important. But the most important thing is the speaker's message. If you have a message that you're **committed** to, that you want to communicate to people, you will communicate better.

2 One basic structure for a speech falls into three parts: an introduction, a body, and a conclusion. Each part is designed to do something different. You need to have an introduction that gets the audience's attention and lets people know about the importance of the subject, why it's important for them to listen. It makes a first **impression**. In journalism they call it a *hook*: something that's going to pull your audience in to your speech. The introduction should also reveal the speech's topic and give the audience some idea of the main points to be discussed.

3 The body of the speech is where the speaker develops his or her main points—the big ideas of the speech. You should probably limit yourself to four or five main points in a speech, whether it's a 10-minute or a 60-minute speech. That will give you time to develop the points you're making. If you have too many main points, the audience will have trouble sorting them out[2], and you may find that you aren't able to develop them in enough **depth** to be clear and **convincing**.

4 The conclusion is important because it's where you leave your most lasting impression. It's the last chance to drive the ideas home[3] to the audience, and ideally the speaker will find a way to leave a lasting impression, both in terms of what he or she says and in terms of the delivery. Some famous speeches end with **stirring** conclusions. A **celebrated** one is Patrick Henry's **exhortation** "give me liberty—or give me death."

---

[1] *the like:* things of the same kind

[2] *sorting (an idea) out:* understanding the importance of something

[3] *drive (an idea) home:* make something clearly understood

COMPREHENSION

A Main Ideas

Work with a partner. Write answers to the questions.

1. According to Professor Lucas, what is the single most important component of a good speech?

   The most important component is having something important to say:
   something you are committed to.

2. What are the three main parts of a speech?

   _____

3. What feature do both good public speakers and journalists use?

   _____

4. How are long and short speeches similar?

   _____

5. What is the danger of having too many points in a speech?

   _____

6. Why is the conclusion so important?

   _____

B Close Reading

Read the quotes from the reading. Write a paraphrase for each quote. Discuss your answers with a partner.

1. "If you have a message that you're committed to, that you want to communicate to people, you will communicate better." (*paragraph 1*)

   _____

2. "You need to have an introduction that gets the audience's attention and lets people know about the importance of the subject, why it's important for them to listen." (*paragraph 2*)

   _____

3. "If you have too many main points, the audience will have trouble sorting them out, and you may find that you aren't able to develop them in enough depth to be clear and convincing." (*paragraph 3*)

   _____

4. "[The conclusion is] the last chance to drive the ideas home to the audience, and ideally the speaker will find a way to leave a lasting impression, both in terms of what he or she says, and in terms of the delivery." (*paragraph 4*)

   _____

VOCABULARY

Ⓐ Guessing from Context

Read the conversation and guess the meanings of the words in bold from the context. Then match the words with their meanings from the box.

A: What did you think about the speech the vice president gave on her end-of-year report?

B: Well, I'm not sure. She didn't sound too sure of her plans for next year. In fact, she didn't sound at all **convincing** to me.

A: Really? I thought she made a very good **impression** on the audience.

B: Well, she's definitely a good public speaker. I mean, she speaks loudly and uses a lot of **gestures**, so she's interesting to watch. But I just don't think she sounds all that sincere. She doesn't seem to be very **committed** to the company, in my opinion. And she makes too many jokes. That's too superficial.

A: Look, all good public speakers make jokes. That doesn't mean she has no **depth**.

B: You can't convince me. I've pretty much forgotten what she was saying, anyway. If she'd made a better speech, I think I would remember more.

> **a.** feeling given to people who see or hear you
> **b.** capable of making people believe what you are saying is true
> **c.** sincere ideas
> **d.** willing to work hard at something you value
> **e.** movements of the head, arms, or hands

__b__ 1. convincing

____ 2. impression

____ 3. gestures

____ 4. committed

____ 5. depth

B Synonyms

Read the paragraph. Match each word in bold with its synonym. Compare answers with a partner.

The **famous** social activist Jack Peterson gave a **speech** last Friday on climate change. He is a **celebrated** speaker, whose **stirring** words always leave his listeners inspired and ready to take action. He gives the **exhortation** "Think globally, act locally" new meaning. He is so **committed** to the cause that he has rebuilt his house to use 70 percent less energy than it did before! His **delivery** was strong and effective, and he left all of us in the room with the **impression** that the future of climate change was in our hands.

_b_	1. **famous**	a.	manner of speaking
____	2. **speech**	b.	well-known
____	3. **celebrated**	c.	formal talk
____	4. **stirring**	d.	effect
____	5. **exhortation**	e.	loyal
____	6. **committed**	f.	great
____	7. **delivery**	g.	emotionally moving
____	8. **impression**	h.	recognized phrase

Like texts, speeches can be organized according to rhetorical modes. Read the excerpts and decide which mode the speaker is using. Choose from the box. Share your answers with a partner.

> description
> definition
> narration
> comparison and contrast
> cause-and-effect analysis
> persuasion
> process analysis

___narration___ 1. "Childhood is a very important time in a person's life. When I was a child, I lived on a small farm with my parents and grandparents. We were surrounded by nature, and I used to help take care of the ducks and rabbits. That is where I learned how beautiful life is."

_____ 2. "There are three reasons why the minimum wage should be increased. First, it has been at the same level for many years. Second, more and more people depend on this money for the well-being of their families. Third, and most important, it's a question of equality. Let's make sure that people get what they deserve, and raise the minimum wage to a respectable level."

_____ 3. "What makes a good leader? A leader is someone who listens to others and is sensitive to their opinions. But a leader is also someone who knows how to take charge of a situation when it is necessary to do so."

_____ 4. "Let me paint the scene for you. There is a housing development in the background, with a school nearby. The streets are full of local residents on their way to work. But yards away is a factory spilling out black smoke and endangering everyone's health."

_____ 5. "Congratulations on buying your new electronic device. First, make sure you register it with the website listed on the package. You need to make sure that you have the right code, which you'll find on the material that came with it. Don't give this code to anyone else. After you register the item, restart it so that your transaction gets downloaded to the device."

_____ 6. "Rising temperatures across the globe have led to a massive reduction in the world's population of polar bears. Icebergs are floating farther and farther apart, so these creatures have to swim for miles. Sadly, many of them do not make it to safety."

_____ 7. "Unlike today, when there are laws protecting children from forced labor, children in the past were often made to work long hours in factories. Today, thanks to the efforts of many people, child labor has been greatly reduced. It was as high as 25% worldwide in the past, but now this figure has been brought down to about 10%."

LINKING READINGS ONE AND TWO

1 Go back to Readings One and Two and read them again. Take notes on what makes a speech effective.

READING ONE	READING TWO
• The speech raises awareness about important issues. • • •	• The speaker has something important to say. • • •

2 Use your notes to make a list of tips for public speakers. Use all the ideas from the readings and add ideas of your own.

DO	DON'T
• make eye contact • • •	• cover too many points • • •

A **Warm-Up**

Benjamin Franklin (1706–1790) was one of the Founding Fathers of the United States. Among his many talents was the ability to give advice in short statements. These have become some of the best-known sayings in the English language.

Work with a partner and read Franklin's ideas aloud. How many of these sayings have you heard before? Check (✓) all that apply.

☐ Remember that time is money.

☐ A place for everything, everything in its place.

☐ A penny saved is a penny earned.

☐ By failing to prepare, you are preparing to fail.

☐ God helps those who help themselves.

☐ Honesty is the best policy.

B **Reading Strategy**

Examining Footnotes

Many texts include **footnotes**, which can **provide either a reference or a comment on an idea in the text**. Be sure to review footnotes so that you understand the additional information they provide about the text.

Now read the excerpts from famous American speeches, paying attention to the footnotes.

FAMOUS AMERICAN SPEECHES

1 **Frederick Douglass, "If I Had a Country, I Should Be a Patriot," September 1847[1]**
Ours is a glorious land. . . . Yet the damning fact remains, there is not a rood of earth under the stars and the eagle on your flag, where a man of my **complexion** can stand free. There is no mountain so high, no plain so extensive, no spot so sacred, that it can **secure** to me the right of liberty.

2 **Sojourner Truth, "Ain't I a Woman?" May 1851**
I have as much muscle as any man, and can do as much work as any man. I have plowed and reaped and husked and chopped and mowed, and can any man do more than that? I have heard much about the sexes being equal. I can carry as much as any man, and can eat as much too, if I can get it. I am as strong as any man that is now.

3 **Abraham Lincoln, "Gettysburg Address," November 1863**
Four score and seven years ago our fathers brought forth on this continent a new nation, conceived in **liberty**, and **dedicated** to the proposition that all men are created equal.

4 **Susan B. Anthony, "Are Women Persons?" June 1873**
The preamble of the federal Constitution says: "We, the people of the United States. . . ." It was we, the people: not we, the white male citizens; nor yet we, the male citizens; but we, the whole people, who formed the Union. And we formed it not to give the blessings of liberty, but to secure them; not to the half of ourselves and the half of our **posterity**, but to the whole people—women as well as men.

5 **Florence Kelley, "Freeing the Children from Toil," June 1905[2]**
Tonight while we sleep, several thousand little girls will be working in textile mills, all the night through, in the deafening noise of the spindles and the looms spinning and weaving cotton and wool, silks and ribbons for us to buy.

Child labor in a factory in the early 20th century

6 **Clarence Darrow, "In Defense of Leopold and Loeb," August 1924[3]**
I am **pleading** for the future; I am pleading for a time when hatred and cruelty will not control the hearts of

(continued on next page)

---

[1] The United States was founded on July 4, 1776, on people's right to freedom and the pursuit of happiness. However, the country's ideals were limited because they did not recognize the basic rights of African Americans or women. Speeches 1–4 focus on the struggle to secure equality for these groups.

[2] Speech 5, made in the early 20th century, at the height of the Industrial Revolution, focuses on the campaign against child labor. The speaker here is specifically talking about children working in clothing factories. A national law passed in 1938 abolished child labor in the United States.

[3] Speech 6, also made in the early 20th century, focuses on ending the death penalty. The death penalty continues to be a controversial issue today. In the United States, some states have abolished it, but others have not.

men. When we can learn by reason and **judgment** and understanding and faith that all life is worth saving, and that mercy is the highest **attribute** of man.

7 **Franklin D. Roosevelt, "The Only Thing We Have to Fear Is Fear Itself," March 1933[4]**
The only thing we have to fear is fear itself—nameless, unreasoning,

---

[4] The use of public speaking as a way to inspire the public is evident in Roosevelt's speech. In the midst of the Great Depression, unemployment reached new heights. Roosevelt's words gave people new hope.

unjustified terror, which **paralyzes** needed efforts to **convert** retreat into advance.

8 **John F. Kennedy, "Ask What You Can Do for Your Country," January 1961[5]**
And so, my fellow Americans: ask not what your country can do for you— ask what you can do for your country.

---

[5] Kennedy had his speechwriter study Lincoln's "Gettysburg Address" for this speech.

COMPREHENSION

Ⓐ Main Ideas

Read each excerpt in the reading again. Decide whether *a* or *b* represents the main idea of the excerpt. Discuss your answers with a partner.

1. Excerpt 1 is about .

   a. values in the United States

   b. nation building

2. Excerpt 2 is about _____.

   a. poverty and wealth

   b. sexual equality

3. Excerpt 3 is about _____.

   a. equality among all people

   b. pride in one's country

4. Excerpt 4 is about _____.

   a. adults and children

   b. men and women

5. Excerpt 5 is about _____.

   a. children's rights

   b. workers' rights

6. Excerpt 6 is about _____.

    a. crime

    b. the right to live

7. Excerpt 7 is about _____.

    a. independence

    b. determination

8. Excerpt 8 is about _____.

    a. responsibility

    b. equality

B **Close Reading**

Read each quote from the reading. Then read the question. Circle the correct answer. Share your answers with a partner.

1. "Yet the damning fact remains, there is not a rood of earth under the stars and the eagle on your flag, where a man of my complexion can stand free." (*Excerpt 1*)

    What is the speaker saying?

    a. He is asking for a change in the Constitution.

    b. He is describing a situation that he disagrees with.

2. "I have plowed and reaped and husked and chopped and mowed, and can any man do more than that?" (*Excerpt 2*)

    What is the speaker saying?

    a. She can do as much work as any man.

    b. She regrets doing so much work.

3. "Four score and seven years ago our fathers brought forth on this continent a new nation." (*Excerpt 3*)

    When was the speech made?

    a. eighty-seven years after the American Revolution

    b. when the United States first became a country

4. "The preamble of the federal Constitution says: "We, the people of the United States. . . ." It was we, the people: not we, the white male citizens; nor yet we, the male citizens; but we, the whole people." (*Excerpt 4*)

    Why does the speaker mention the Constitution?

    a. to point out a mistake that it makes

    b. to explain what the Constitution is saying

(continued on next page)

5. "Tonight while we sleep, several thousand little girls will be working in textile mills." (*Excerpt 5*)

What is the speaker doing in this sentence?

a. She's explaining a process.

b. She's making a comparison.

6. "I am pleading for the future; I am pleading for a time when hatred and cruelty will not control the hearts of men." (*Excerpt 6*)

What is the speaker expressing?

a. a fact

b. a wish

7. "The only thing we have to fear is fear itself." (*Excerpt 7*)

Why does the speaker repeat the word "fear"?

a. He wants listeners to think about his ideas carefully.

b. He cannot think of a good synonym for the word "fear."

8. "And so, my fellow Americans . . ." (*Excerpt 8*)

What does the speaker want to point out?

a. He shares the audience's background.

b. He does not understand his audience.

VOCABULARY

A **Guessing from Context**

1 Read the comments on a political blog and guess the meanings of the words in bold from the context. Then match the words with their meanings.

What political issues concern you?

J. Wong said, July 14, at 10:06 A.M.

I think the most important issue today is racism. I really admire Martin Luther King, Jr. His "I Have a Dream" speech shows that people shouldn't pay any attention to a person's **complexion**. What's important is what is inside a person.

Flash-T said, July 14, at 10:38 A.M.

War is the most important concern on everyone's minds these days. I was happy to read about the new peace agreement. That will **secure** a safer world for us all.

Zuzana said, July 14, at 11:01 A.M.

In my opinion, we need to think about building a stronger economy. After all, economic structures that work are what we should be leaving for **posterity**.

SHG said, July 14, at 11:25 A.M.

As far as I'm concerned, **liberty** is the most important concern these days. If we don't have the ability to do what we think is right at any particular moment, we can't make any progress.

TooSmart said, July 14, at 12:03 P.M.

Corruption is my number one concern. Look at our political candidates these days! Where are the important **attributes** of honesty, sincerity, and discipline?

Poligirl said, July 14, at 12:10 P.M.

I agree! I'm **pleading** with our candidates to be more honest with voters.

_a_ 1. **complexion**

____ 2. **secure**

____ 3. **posterity**

____ 4. **liberty**

____ 5. **attributes**

____ 6. **pleading**

a. the natural color of a person's skin

b. future generations

c. qualities

d. achieve something important after a lot of effort

e. asking for something, in an urgent and emotional way

f. freedom

B Word Forms

1 Fill in the chart with the correct word forms. Use a dictionary if necessary.

	NOUN	VERB	ADJECTIVE
1.	conversion	convert	
2.		dedicate	
3.		paralyze	
4.	judgment		judgmental/

2 Complete the book review with the correct form of the words. Choose from the forms in the chart.

A new book, *Women and Their Voice*, documents women's right to vote, which became law in the United States in 1920. At that time, a woman's role began the slow but sure _____ from silent

1.

observer to participant in the political process. The author, Antonia Silvers,

_____ the book to her mother, a role model for her, who

2.

has been active in her local community all her life and still speaks widely about women's issues today. Even though she is now 95 years old, partly

_____ and in a wheelchair, Mrs. Silvers was still present

3.

at her daughter's book party and spoke before the assembled crowd. She said: "Even today, people are so _____ about others. That isn't

4.

right. Whether we are young or old, rich or poor, men or women, we all have a voice, which is what my daughter's book has tried to show."

NOTE-TAKING: Using a Chart to Group Ideas

When you are comparing different texts or parts of texts, **use a chart or organizer to group similar ideas together**.

Read the excerpts in the reading again. Check (✓) all the boxes you think apply. Share your ideas with a partner.

AUTHOR	USES REPETITION	USES MANY EXAMPLES	USES POWERFUL VOCABULARY	USES STRONG REASONING	USES EMOTIONAL APPEAL
1. Douglass	✓		✓		✓
2. Truth					
3. Lincoln					
4. Anthony					
5. Kelley					
6. Darrow					
7. Roosevelt					
8. Kennedy					

CRITICAL THINKING

Discuss the questions with a partner.

1. Do you know of any famous speeches? What were the circumstances when the speech was given, and how did it affect people? What do you think it was like to be present at the actual speech?

2. Have you ever had to give a speech? What was the rhetorical mode or modes you used? Was it effective?

3. Do you think that public speakers are not as skilled today as they were in the past? Explain.

BRINGING IT ALL TOGETHER

1 Watch a speech given by a politician on TV or on the Internet. Take notes on everything you see and hear. Then summarize your notes, using these questions as a guide:

- What issues did the person discuss?
- Did the person communicate self-confidence, conviction, trustworthiness, or other qualities? Explain.
- Would you say this speaker connected well with the audience? In what way?
- How did the speech make you feel? Were you affected by it in any way? Explain.
- What other comments can you make about the speech?

2 Share your opinions with a partner.

WRITING ACTIVITY

Most public speakers plan what they want to say in writing before they deliver a speech. Write a one-page speech on an issue you feel strongly about. Use some of the vocabulary you studied in the chapter (for a complete list, go to page 206). Follow these steps to write your speech:

1. Select an issue from the list or choose your own.
   - immigration
   - health care
   - taxes
   - marriage laws
   - the economy
   - environmental protection
   - animal rights
   - the death penalty

2. Find and read at least three articles about the issue you have chosen. Take notes about the articles. Use your notes to support your opinion about your issue.

3. Write your speech. Be sure to explain your opinion. Remember to think about what makes a good speech.

4. Read your speech over a few times. Then put it aside. Deliver your speech to the class. Remember to relax!

DISCUSSION AND WRITING TOPICS

Discuss these topics in a small group. Choose one of them and write a short essay about it. Use the vocabulary from the chapter.

1. As Reading One notes, technology has allowed public officials to speak to growing numbers of people. At the same time, it has focused more and more attention on public officials, so that presidents, mayors, and other leaders have almost no private life: everything they say becomes public. Do you think that technology has basically a positive effect on the way officials interact with the public, or it is basically negative?

2. Lee Iacocca, one of the most famous businessmen in the world, said: "A speech is a sales opportunity," and Steve Jobs, founder of Apple, often spoke to the public. Convincing the public to buy products through *sales pitches* (oral arguments made in order to sell things) is easier if a person is a good public speaker. Do you know any other businesspeople who are good public speakers? Do you think their success depended on their expertise in public speaking? Explain.

3. Many public speakers, especially in academic settings, use PowerPoint to illustrate what they are saying. However, other people do not. Do you think that PowerPoint helps speakers make a better oral presentation or not? What other types of technology might be useful with giving speeches? How could they be used?

VOCABULARY

Nouns	Verbs	Adjectives
abolition	convert*	articulate
address	dedicate	celebrated
attribute*	paralyze	committed*
awareness*	plead	convincing*
compassion	secure*	critical
complexion		sincere
conviction		stirring
delivery		
depth		
exhortation		
gesture		
impression		
judgment		
liberty		
orator		
posterity		
trustworthiness		

* = AWL (Academic Word List) item

SELF-ASSESSMENT

In this chapter you learned to:

- ○ Skim by reading topic sentences
- ○ Understand rhetorical modes
- ○ Examine footnotes
- ○ Guess the meaning of words from the context
- ○ Understand and use word forms and word usage
- ○ Use dictionary entries to learn different meanings of words
- ○ Research a person or topic and use a chart to group ideas

What can you do well? ☑

What do you need to practice more? ☑

CHAPTER 9

PEACE STUDIES:
The Change Makers

PEACE STUDIES: an interdisciplinary field concerned with promoting world peace, justice, and security

OBJECTIVES

To read academic texts, you need to master certain skills.

In this chapter, you will:

- Find definitions in a text
- Understand pronoun references
- Read case studies
- Guess the meaning of words from the context
- Understand and use word forms and synonyms
- Use dictionary entries to learn different meanings of words
- Take notes on numbers in a text and take notes to prepare for a test

A **Consider These Facts**

How much do you know about world poverty? Read the facts below and fill in the blanks with your guess. Then check your answers at the bottom of the page.

1. There is no sanitation in _____ percent of the world.

2. Women in developing countries have to walk _____ miles to get water each day.

3. Globally, women earn _____ percent less than men.

4. The richest 20 percent of the world's population earns _____ percent of the world's income.

5. Worldwide, _____ children die from poverty every day.

B **Your Opinion**

Answer the questions. Check (✓) the appropriate box. Then discuss your answers with a partner. If you answered yes, give more details.

	YES	No
Have you ever . . .		
1. felt strongly about a serious world problem?	☐	☐
2. been involved in a group project?	☐	☐
3. taken on a leadership role?	☐	☐
4. had an idea about how to improve the lives of others?	☐	☐

ANSWERS
1. 33, 2. 4, 3. 50, 4. 75, 5. 30,000

A **Warm-Up**

An *entrepreneur* is a person who operates a business, especially a new one. A *social entrepreneur* approaches a social problem with a business model. Read the list of qualities of a good social entrepreneur. Rank them in order of importance (1 being the most important) in solving serious social problems. Then share your ideas with a partner.

_____ knowing powerful people

_____ having close friends

_____ being idealistic

_____ being young and energetic

_____ having innovative ideas

_____ having a lot of money

_____ being creative

_____ your own idea: _____

B **Reading Strategy**

Finding Definitions

If you are unfamiliar with an important word or concept in a text, especially if it is in the title or appears more than once, **scan the text carefully to find whether it is defined.** You will often find an explanation of important words immediately before or after them.

Look at the title of the reading and then scan the text to find answers to the questions.

1. Who are social entrepreneurs, and what do they do?

2. What characteristics do social entrepreneurs have?

Now read the text. If you come across unfamiliar words, scan the text to find the definitions.

SOCIAL ENTREPRENEURSHIP

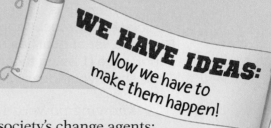

WE HAVE IDEAS: Now we have to make them happen!

1   At the age of 80, sculptor Henry Moore said: "The secret of life is to have a task, something you do your entire life, something you bring everything to, every minute of the day for your whole life. And the most important thing is: It must be something you cannot possibly do." With these words, he captured the idealism and determination of one of the fastest growing programs of study: social entrepreneurship. Although this term was not commonly used until the 1970s, today there are programs in the field in some of the highest-ranking universities in the world.

2   Social entrepreneurs identify **daunting** world challenges. For example, they may see the need to protect the environment, provide universal health care, or promote **literacy**. They look for creative new ideas to implement large-scale, long-term change in the world. Many social entrepreneurs have a background in business, but they also have persistence, vision, **courage**, and commitment. Their projects typically involve large numbers of people working in their own communities.

3   Social entrepreneurs are people who are trying to improve the lives of others, especially those living in underserved[1] communities. The Skoll Foundation, an organization committed to peace and **sustainability**, defines them as "society's change agents: creators of innovations that disrupt the status quo[2] and transform our world for the better."

4   Social entrepreneurs are said to share various characteristics:
Ambitious: They tackle major social issues. These might include increasing the college enrollment rate of low-income students or fighting poverty in developing countries.
Mission-Driven: Although their projects may be profitable, they measure their success in terms of the social progress they are able to make.
Strategic: They improve systems, create solutions, and invent new approaches. They are intensely focused and **relentless** in their **pursuit** of a social vision.
Resourceful: Because they have limited access to capital[3], social entrepreneurs are **exceptionally skilled** at gathering and **mobilizing** human, financial, and political **resources**.
Results-Oriented: Ultimately, social entrepreneurs produce measurable returns. These results transform existing realities, open up new pathways for the marginalized and disadvantaged, and unlock society's potential to effect social change.

5   Of course, the idea of innovation and social transformation is not new, but the models used by social entrepreneurs are fresh and exciting.

---

[1] **underserved:** inadequately provided with essential services

[2] **the status quo:** the way things are

[3] **capital:** wealth or financial assets

COMPREHENSION

(A) Main Ideas

Complete the sentences with a phrase from the box. Check your answers with a partner.

> **a.** is an organization committed to promoting peace
>
> **b.** is an important world challenge
>
> **c.** was a sculptor who had big life lessons
>
> **d.** is a growing field of study
>
> **e.** are two qualities many social entrepreneurs have
>
> **f.** may have a background in business

1. Henry Moore _____c_____.

2. Social entrepreneurship _____.

3. Social entrepreneurs _____.

4. The Skoll Foundation _____.

5. Protecting the environment _____.

6. Being ambitious and strategic _____.

(B) Close Reading

Read each statement. Cross out the one answer that does not complete the statement correctly.

1. According to Henry Moore, the secret of life is ____. (*paragraph 1*)

   a. becoming involved in something very interesting

   b. finding a difficult challenge to solve

   c. finding the easiest way to make a living

2. Social entrepreneurs try to do things that ____. (*paragraph 2*)

   a. can be used on a big scale

   b. have obvious solutions

   c. require creative thinking

(continued on next page)

3. Social entrepreneurs are committed to _____. (*paragraph 3*)

   a. improving the lives of others

   b. changing the world for the better

   c. staying out of underserved communities

4. The Skoll Foundation defines social entrepreneurs as people who _____. (*paragraph 3*)

   a. make large profits

   b. promote positive change

   c. improve the lives of others

5. Characteristics of social entrepreneurs include _____. (*paragraph 4*)

   a. the ability to define an issue and work hard toward it

   b. the knowledge that most problems can be easily overcome

   c. the ability to promote change that can be measured

Jeff Skoll, founder of the Skoll Foundation, accepts an award from the Environmental Media Association.

VOCABULARY

A Guessing from Context

Read the conversation and guess the meanings of the words in bold from the context. Then match the words with their meanings.

BILL: I'm trying to decide on a major. What do you think about social entrepreneurship? What I'm really interested in is climate change. You know, people talk about protecting the environment all the time, but then nothing changes. I really want to do something to change the status quo.

NIGEL: Wow. That's no small goal. Protecting the environment is a **daunting** challenge. How would you go about that?

BILL: Look, Nigel, we have to begin somewhere. We should be looking at more creative ways to cut down on waste, as well as trying to recycle everything we use. We can't give up—we have to be **relentless** at educating people about the risks of climate change.

NIGEL: But it's such a hopeless situation. Do you really think there is anything one person can do?

BILL: I know what you mean, but I'm not talking about only one person making a change. I'm interesting in **mobilizing** a lot of people to work together. I mean, think about the future. What kind of world do you want to leave to your children and grandchildren? We have to think about the **sustainability** of the projects we design to protect the environment.

NIGEL: Well, good for you. I think that's an **exceptionally** good major.

_c_ 1. daunting	a. very	
____ 2. relentless	b. putting into motion	
____ 3. mobilizing	c. very difficult or challenging	
____ 4. sustainability	d. extremely determined or committed	
____ 5. exceptionally	e. the process of keeping something alive for a long time	

B Word Forms

1 Fill in the chart with the correct word forms. Some categories can have more than one form. Use a dictionary if necessary. An *X* indicates there is no form in that category.

	NOUN	VERB	ADJECTIVE
1.	courage	X	*courageous*
2.	literacy	X	literate/
3.	pursuit		X
4.	resource	X	
5.		X	skilled/

2 Complete the paragraphs with the correct form of the words. Choose from the forms in the chart.

Maria Montessori was the first female doctor in Italy. She was not only a _____*skilled*_____ doctor, but a person who wanted to
1.
change educational methods so that individual children's needs were recognized. She was particularly interested in promoting a high level of

_____ among the children she worked with, since
2.
many of them could not read. She _____ her mission
3.
so relentlessly that her success is still evident a century later.

Jane Addams was a strong supporter of women's rights. She concentrated her efforts in a poor neighborhood in Chicago, which

was a _____ task for a woman to undertake in
4.
1889. Although at first she did not have much money, she was very

_____, and she managed to do a lot with very little.
5.
As a result of her efforts, laws were passed to protect women and children.

C **Using the Dictionary**

1 Read the dictionary entry for *resource*.

> **resource** *n.* **1** a place where you can get something you need, or a person who helps you get what you need **2** money **3** natural sources of essential elements, such as fossil fuels

2 Read the sentences. Determine which meaning (1, 2, or 3) is being used. Compare answers with a partner.

_____ a. The world's **resources** are disappearing.

_____ b. I can't go to the party. I don't have the **resources**.

_____ c. I'm doing some research on economic development, and the library is a great **resource**.

_____ d. I'm trying to find someone who has experience working with poor people. Can you ask your sister to help me? She would be a great **resource**.

CRITICAL THINKING

Discuss the questions with a partner. Be prepared to share your ideas with the class.

1. Have you ever heard of a college program in social entrepreneurship? Do you think this would be an interesting field of study? Why or why not?

2. What lessons do you think social entrepreneurs can learn from the business world? How do you think social entrepreneurship is similar and different from business entrepreneurship?

3. Why do you believe social change is interesting to young people? Do you believe that young people tend to be idealistic, creative, and energetic? If so, why?

A **Warm-Up**

Read the nursery rhyme about how small things can make a big difference. Then discuss the questions with a partner.

For want of a nail, the shoe was lost;
For want of a shoe, the horse was lost;
For want of a horse, the battle was lost;
And all for the want of a horseshoe nail.

1. What do you think the nursery rhyme is trying to teach? _____

2. How would you complete the sentences?

   a. If there had been a nail, _____

   b. If we take care of small things, _____

   c. Sometimes little details _____

B **Reading Strategy**

Understanding Pronoun References

As you read, it is important to make sure you understand who or what the **pronouns** (*he, it, their,* etc.) in the text refer to.

Example:
Almost half the world — over three billion people — live on less than $2.50 a day. **They** *do not have access to basic needs.*

They refers to *almost half the world* or *over three billion people*.

Read the sentences, paying attention to the pronouns in bold. Scan the reading to find the correct reference. Then match the pronouns with their references.

_____ 1. She was trying to raise **her** children on next to nothing. (*paragraph 2*)

_____ 2. He would go to people's houses, trying to understand **their** life. (*paragraph 2*)

_____ 3. More than 100 countries worldwide have been inspired by **its** success. (*paragraph 4*)

a. the Grameen bank

b. people in villages in Bangladesh

c. Sufiya Begum, a basket maker

Now read the website and pay attention to the pronoun references.

A Poverty-Free World

1   According to official statistics, almost half the world —over three billion people—live on less than $2.50 a day. They do not have access to the basic needs of food, water, **shelter**, clothing, health care, and education, and they have little hope of ever escaping from their situation. Millions more live on much less than that.

Muhammad Yunus (left) received the Nobel Peace Prize for his work with the poor.

2   Muhammad Yunus was troubled by the cycle of poverty[1] in his native land, Bangladesh, one of the poorest countries on earth. He started visiting villages across the country, where he would go to people's houses and talk to them, trying to understand their life. He was **struck** by the fact that a small amount of money could make so much difference in their lives. For example, he met a 21-year-old basket maker, Sufiya Begum, trying to raise her three children on next to nothing. He realized that if she could get a **loan** of just a few dollars, she could operate more efficiently and her business could be **transformed**, but no bank would lend her any money, saying she would never pay it back.

3   Yunus felt that, poor or not, people should be able to borrow money. He believed in human potential and thought that, given a chance, even the illiterate and the uneducated could build on the skills they had and pull themselves out of poverty. Yunus founded the Grameen Bank ("gram" means "village" in Bangla), to give small loans to the world's poorest, especially women. In addition to microfinancing[2], the bank also distributed educational information about health, farming, and innovative technological ideas so that people could take their **destiny** into their own hands. Respect, dignity, and opportunity were among the goals they **envisioned** for the world's poorest citizens. Yunus and Grameen were awarded the Nobel Peace Prize in 2006. **Incidentally**, 97 percent of **borrowers** do pay back their loans.

4   Grameen has had an impact on many people. More than 100 countries worldwide have been inspired by its success and have created similar programs. Yunus is hopeful for the future. He said: "We have created a slavery-free world, a smallpox-free world, an apartheid[3]-free world. Creating a poverty-free world would be greater than all these **accomplishments** while at the same time reinforcing them. This would be a world that we could all be proud to live in."

---

[1] *cycle of poverty:* a set of events by which poverty, once it starts, is most likely to continue

[2] *microfinancing:* making small amounts of money available temporarily

[3] *apartheid:* an official policy of racial segregation, formerly practiced most notably in South Africa

COMPREHENSION

A **Main Ideas**

Answer the questions based on the main ideas of Reading Two. Compare answers with a partner.

1. Reading Two begins with a shocking statistic. What is it?

   Almost half the world lives on less than $2.50 a day.

2. According to the reading, what are some basic human needs?

   _____

3. What did Yunus do to try to understand poor people's situation better?

   _____

4. What is the Grameen bank?

   _____

5. How has Yunus been rewarded?

   _____

6. What world problems have we successfully overcome?

   _____

B **Close Reading**

Read the quotes from Reading Two. Match the words that most closely correspond with the ideas. Share your answers with a partner.

a. worried, upset, devastated	**d.** determined, hopeful, idealistic
b. amazed, surprised, impressed	**e.** trusting, sincere, serious
c. proud, happy, inspired	

___a___ 1. "Muhammad Yunus was troubled by the cycle of poverty in his native land." (*paragraph 1*)

_____ 2. "He was struck by the fact that a small amount of money could make so much difference in [poor people's] lives." (*paragraph 2*)

_____ 3. "He believed in human potential and thought that even the illiterate and the uneducated could pull themselves out of poverty." (*paragraph 3*)

_____ 4. "Yunus and Grameen were awarded the Nobel Peace Prize." (*paragraph 3*)

_____ 5. "He said: We have created a slavery-free world, a smallpox-free world, an apartheid-free world. Creating a poverty-free world would be greater than all these accomplishments." (*paragraph 4*)

VOCABULARY

A Synonyms

Cross out the word or phrase that is NOT a synonym for the word in bold. Use a dictionary if necessary. Compare answers with a partner.

1.	**shelter**	house or home	~~factory or workplace~~
2.	**loan**	money made available temporarily	finished project
3.	**destiny**	past project	future fate
4.	**accomplishments**	important goals	significant achievements
5.	**envision**	imagine	discuss

B Word Forms

1 Fill in the chart with the correct word forms. Use a dictionary if necessary. An *X* indicates there is no form in that category.

	NOUN	VERB	ADJECTIVE	ADVERB
1.	borrower	borrow		X
2.		X		incidentally
3.	X		striking	
4.		transform		X

2 Read the paragraph. Complete the paragraph with the correct form of the words. Choose from the forms in the chart.

When he was traveling through his native country, Bangladesh,

a relatively insignificant _____ seems to have
1.
had an enormous impact on Yunus. When he realized that a young

mother's life could be _____ if she were able to
2.
_____ a small amount of money, he began to think about
3.
the potential of microfinancing. He was _____ by the
4.
far-reaching consequences of a minor loan.

NOTE-TAKING: Taking Notes on Numbers in a Text

> When you take notes on an informational reading, make sure you correctly identify what any **numbers** in the reading refer to.
> **EXAMPLE:**
> 3 billion (*paragraph 1*) = the number of people in the world who live on a very small amount of money.

Read the numbers in bold. Go back to Reading Two. Circle the numbers. In your own words, write down what the numbers refer to. Share your responses with a partner.

1. **half** (*paragraph 1*): <u>fraction of the world that lives on a very small amount of money</u>

2. **$2.50** (*paragraph 1*): _____

3. **21** (*paragraph 2*): _____

4. **2006** (*paragraph 3*): _____

5. **97** (*paragraph 3*): _____

6. **100** (*paragraph 4*): _____

CRITICAL THINKING

Discuss the questions in a small group. Be prepared to share your opinions with the class.

1. Why do you think Yunus was interested in visiting people's houses and speaking to them face to face? What was the value of this personal interaction?

2. How do you think microfinancing can help people succeed? Do you believe this is a good strategy? Explain.

3. Yunus refers to the elimination of slavery, smallpox, and apartheid. What other problems, in your view, do we need to end and why?

4. How does the nursery rhyme before the reading represent Yunus's strategy?

LINKING READINGS ONE AND TWO

With a partner, fill in the mind map with as many ideas as you can from Readings One and Two. Then share your ideas with the class.

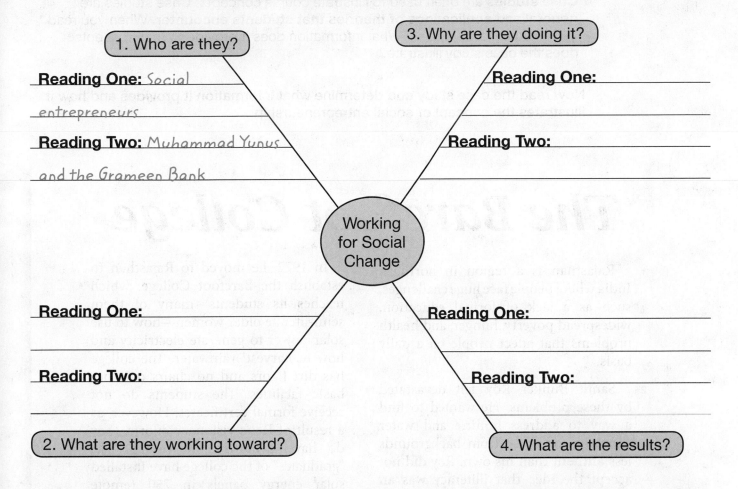

1. Who are they?

Reading One: *Social*
entrepreneurs

Reading Two: *Muhammad Yunus*
and the Grameen Bank

3. Why are they doing it?

Reading One:

Reading Two:

Working for Social Change

Reading One:

Reading Two:

2. What are they working toward?

Reading One:

Reading Two:

4. What are the results?

READING THREE: The Barefoot College

A **Warm-Up**

Look at the photo and describe what you see to a partner. Explain the feelings that you experience.

Reading Case Studies

Case studies are often used to illustrate course concepts. Case studies are **generalized applications of theories that students encounter**. When you read a case study, ask yourself: What information does it provide? What concepts does the case study illustrate?

Now read the case study and determine what information it provides and how it illustrates the concept of social entrepreneurship.

The Barefoot College

1   Rajasthan is a region in northern India where people face huge challenges, such as a lack of formal education, widespread poverty, hunger, and health problems that affect people on a daily basis.

2   Sanjit Bunker Roy felt devastated by these problems. He wanted to find a way to address **famine** and water **shortage** for those from backgrounds less **affluent** than his own. Roy did not accept the idea that illiteracy was an **insurmountable** barrier to progress. He did not think a **lack** of education should necessarily prevent people from developing their skills. Instead, he **emphasized** the idea that the very poor should have access to modern ideas that could help them address problems that were immediate and relevant to them. In addition, he saw potential in what local villagers *did* know. For example, in Rajasthan there are examples of rainwater-collecting mechanisms that are hundreds of years old. Roy showed that in an educational environment that **targets** concrete problems, people are capable of rapidly learning about new technology and combining it with their existing skills.

3   In 1972, he moved to Rajasthan to establish the Barefoot College, which teaches its students—many of them semi-literate older women—how to use solar power to generate electricity and how to harvest[1] rainwater. The college has dirt floors and no chairs or other basic facilities. The students do not receive formal certificates. However, as a result of Roy's visionary efforts, they do have **demonstrable** results. The "graduates" of the college have installed solar energy panels in 750 remote villages and made drinking water and **sanitation** available to over 2½ million children.

4   Roy's critics thought he would not be able to succeed. He was inspired by the words of Gandhi[2], who said: "First they ignore you, then they laugh at you, then they fight you, and then you win." The Barefoot College model has now spread to over 28 countries in the least developed parts of the world.

---

[1] *harvest:* collect

[2] Mahatma Gandhi (1869–1948) inspired Roy. He supported civil rights and freedom, and worked tirelessly to improve the situation of the poor.

COMPREHENSION

A Main Ideas

Check (✓) the ideas that are included in the reading.

- ☐ **1.** an explanation of why Roy became interested in Rajasthan
- ☑ **2.** some details about Roy's background
- ☐ **3.** a story about a student who attended the Barefoot College
- ☐ **4.** an example of local knowledge in Rajasthan
- ☐ **5.** the date when the Barefoot College was opened
- ☐ **6.** the reaction Roy's family had to his plan
- ☐ **7.** a description of the college's graduation ceremony
- ☐ **8.** a person who inspired Roy

B Close Reading

Read the statements. Cross out all the answers that are not correct. Share your answers with a partner.

1. According to the reading, problems in Rajasthan include _____.
   - **a.** hunger
   - **b.** a lack of formal education
   - **c.** a high level of crime

2. Roy did not believe that _____.
   - **a.** illiteracy was common in the area
   - **b.** progress was possible in Rajasthan
   - **c.** a lack of education should stop people from making progress

3. Students at the Barefoot College _____.
   - **a.** do not receive formal certificates
   - **b.** do not have demonstrable results
   - **c.** enjoy few basic facilities at the college

4. Roy _____.
   - **a.** was inspired by Gandhi
   - **b.** listened to those who thought he would not succeed
   - **c.** established a successful educational model

VOCABULARY

A **Guessing from Context**

Read each sentence and guess the meaning of the word in bold from the context. Then match the word with its meaning.

1. In many areas of the world, food and water are not available. Widespread **famine** affected large areas of Africa last year.

2. In regions where there is poor **sanitation**, there is always a big risk of disease.

3. Social entrepreneurs often **target** large-scale problems and look for large-scale solutions to address them.

4. Although many of the world's problems may seem **insurmountable**, people are making progress every day toward addressing them more creatively.

_____ 1. famine   a. too big to overcome

_____ 2. sanitation   b. a serious condition in which there is no food

_____ 3. target   c. having a clean environment with an adequate supply of clean water

_____ 4. insurmountable   d. to aim or direct your efforts

B **Using the Dictionary**

1 Read the dictionary entries for *shortage* and *lack*.

> **shortage** *n.* a situation in which you cannot obtain enough of something you need
>
> **lack** *n.* a situation in which you do not have something

2 Now read each sentence. Decide whether you should use *lack*, *shortage*, or could use either one. Circle *lack*, *shortage*, or both words.

1. There is a **lack/shortage** of teachers in many cities.

2. The class was out of control today. There was a complete **lack/shortage** of respect for the teacher.

3. In some villages, there is a **lack/shortage** of drinking water.

C Word Forms

1 Fill in the chart with the correct word forms. Some categories can have more than one form. Use a dictionary if necessary. An *X* indicates there is no form in that category.

	NOUN	VERB	ADJECTIVE
1.	affluence	X	affluent
2.			demonstrable
3.	X		surmountable/
4.		emphasize	
5.	sanitation	X	
6.	shortage	short	

2 Complete the sentences with the correct form of the words. Choose from the forms in the chart.

1. Power and _____ affluence _____ are two elements that are commonly associated with successful business executives.

2. Roy _____ that a simple idea could have a far-reaching impact.

3. Roy was able to _____ some of the challenges of rural areas and put a mechanism into place to address the regions' problems.

4. The region's residents live in conditions that are not very _____. For example, they probably have no running water.

5. Drinking water in the region is in _____ supply.

6. Roy _____ that although a person is poor, with some education, that person can succeed.

NOTE-TAKING: Taking Notes to Prepare for a Test

> One of the most important reasons for **taking notes is to prepare for a test**. A useful strategy is to make your own questions and then answer them based on your notes.

1 Go back to Reading Three and take notes. Use your notes to answer the questions. Share your notes with a partner.

1. Where is Rajasthan? *Rajasthan is in northern India. It is a very poor region.*

2. What is the Barefoot College? _____

3. Who is Sanjit Bunker Roy? _____

4. Who goes to the Barefoot College? _____

5. What have its graduates succeeded in doing? _____

2 Write three other questions that the reading answers. Share your questions with a partner. Using your notes, answer each other's questions.

1. _____

2. _____

3. _____

CRITICAL THINKING

Discuss the questions with a partner. Be prepared to share your thoughts with the class.

1. Roy says that a lack of education should not prevent people from being successful. Do you think this is realistic? Why or why not?

2. Compare the achievements of Sanjit Bunker Roy and Muhammad Yunus. What are the similarities and the differences?

3. Roy was inspired by Ghandi to help people. Has anyone ever inspired you? If so, how and to do what?

BRINGING IT ALL TOGETHER

Review the characteristics of social entrepreneurs that Reading One lists. Then work with a partner. Explain whether you believe Yunus and Roy have these characteristics. Give specific examples.

READING ONE: SOCIAL ENTREPRENEURS	READING TWO: MUHAMMAD YUNUS	READING THREE: SANJIT BUNKER ROY
• ambitious		Sanjit Bunker Roy was very ambitious because he wanted to tackle a huge problem — famine.
• mission-driven		
• strategic	Muhammad Yunus was very strategic. His strategy was to make small amounts of money available to very poor people.	
• resourceful		
• results-oriented		

WRITING ACTIVITY

Read the examples of organizations that are promoting positive change in the world. Choose the one that interests you the most and write a paragraph explaining why. Use some of the vocabulary from the chapter (for a complete list, go to page 229). Share your paragraph with the class.

1. Free the Children is dedicated to eliminating child labor and to freeing young people all over the world from poverty, thirst, and disease.

2. *Cidade Saludable* (Healthy City) aims to educate the public and engage public officials to reduce the amount of garbage.

3. International Bridges to Justice has transformed legal systems in many developing countries and made torture illegal.

4. Citizen Schools uses volunteers to transform after-school programs in disadvantaged neighborhoods.

DISCUSSION AND WRITING TOPICS

Discuss these topics in a small group. Choose one of them and write a paragraph or two about it. Use the vocabulary from the chapter.

1. Why do you think social entrepreneurship is becoming more popular these days? Explain.

2. Do you think it is possible to combine making money with making social change? Explain.

3. There are many songs that reflect the spirit of social entrepreneurship, like "We Are the World" and "Heal the World." Do you think that song is a good way to spread important ideas about social concerns, or do you believe that most people just listen to these kinds of songs without thinking about what they mean? Explain.

4. Yunus believed that everyone, rich or poor, should be able to borrow money. Do you agree? What other rights does everyone deserve to have? Explain.

VOCABULARY

Nouns	Verbs	Adjectives	Adverbs
accomplishment	emphasize	affluent	exceptionally
borrower	envision	daunting	incidentally*
courage	mobilize	demonstrable*	
destiny	target*	insurmountable	
famine	transform*	relentless	
literacy	strike	skilled	
lack			
loan			
pursuit*			
resource*			
sanitation			
shelter			
shortage			
sustainability*			

* = AWL (Academic Word List) item

SELF-ASSESSMENT

In this chapter you learned to:

○ Find definitions in a text

○ Understand pronoun references

○ Read case studies

○ Guess the meaning of words from the context

○ Understand and use word forms and synonyms

○ Use dictionary entries to learn different meanings of words

○ Take notes on numbers in a text and take notes to prepare for a test

What can you do well? ☑

What do you need to practice more? ☑

CHAPTER 10

URBAN STUDIES:
Living Together

URBAN STUDIES: a field that involves the study of cities and their surrounding areas. It includes the study of how people interact in urban environments.

OBJECTIVES

To read academic texts, you need to master certain skills.

In this chapter, you will:

- Read a fact sheet

- Read aloud to determine the main idea of a text

- Recognize the difference between narration and opinion

- Guess the meaning of words from the context

- Use dictionary entries to learn different meanings of words

- Understand and use word forms and positive and negative meanings of words

- Use abbreviations and symbols to take notes, and take notes on a timeline

A Consider This information

Complete the chart with cities you know. As a class, share what you know about the cities on your list.

ASIA	THE MIDDLE EAST	LATIN AMERICA AND CARIBBEAN	EUROPE	AFRICA	NORTH AMERICA
Tokyo Hong Kong	Istanbul Dubai	La Paz Santo Domingo	Paris Rome	Cairo Lusaka	Chicago Vancouver

B Your Opinion

1 Check (✓) the statements that you think are true about life in cities. Give an example to illustrate your opinion.

☐ People who live in cities have more independence than people who live in urban areas.

☐ There are better employment possibilities in cities.

☐ There is little personal contact among neighbors in urban areas*.

☐ People have more choices about the way they want to live in cities.

☐ Cities give people a strong sense of community.

☐ Cities are good places for children to grow up.

☐ Cities are more attractive to young people than small towns are.

☐ your own idea: _____

2 Share your ideas with a partner.

---

* *urban areas:* another term for cities

A **Warm-Up**

How much do you know about the place where you live or come from? Fill in the chart with as many ideas as you can. Then share your chart with a partner.

approximate size of the population	
interesting or famous people who have come from there	
important architecture	
historical importance	
reasons why people like to live there	
problems that residents experience	

B **Reading Strategy**

Reading a Fact Sheet

Fact sheets are designed to communicate a lot of different information quickly and clearly. To read a fact sheet, follow these instructions:
- Focus on the information it provides.
- Look at the different ways the information is presented. For example, are there different sections? Are there headings? Is there bulleted information? Is there a logical order to the information?
- Pay special attention to charts, pictures, and numbers.

Scan the fact sheet. With a partner, choose the correct answer to the questions.

1. What information does the fact sheet provide?
   a. information on the history of cities
   b. information on world population

2. How is the information presented?
   a. in sections and with headings
   b. in sections and with bullets

3. What do the charts, pictures, and numbers tell you?
   a. about the crime in cities
   b. about the world's population and where they live

Now read the fact sheet and see if your answers were correct.

City Fact Sheet

Did you know . . . . ?

1 The word *metropolis*, meaning *large city*, comes from the Greek μήτηρ, *mētēr,* meaning "mother" and πόλις, *pólis,* meaning "city" or "town."

2 The word *metro*, describing a transportation system, and *metropolitan*, (as in *Metropolitan Opera*) come from the same word.

3 A *megacity* is a city with over 10,000,000 people. Some of the world's cities have twice that number.

4 Less than 1% of the earth's surface is covered by cities, but cities use 75% of the world's energy. 70% of the world population is expected to live in **urban** areas by 2050 (up from 13% in 1900).

5 For the first time in history, the urban and rural populations of the world are approximately equal. Urban populations are constantly **rising**.

6 Many of the world's cities have incredible architecture, cultural institutions, and opportunities of all kinds. However, city dwellers[1] can face **massive** problems, such as:

- *Transportation*. Large cities often have inadequate transport networks.
- *Housing*. Worldwide, over 1 billion people live in slums[2], and that number is expected to double in the next few **decades**.
- *Urban sprawl*[3]. As cities grow larger and larger, they **spread** out over large areas. People who live on the **peripheries** have difficulties **commuting** to work.
- *Health and safety*. Mortality[4] rates are high in **densely populated** areas.

---

[1] **city dwellers:** people who live in cities

[2] **slum:** very poor, overcrowded area

[3] **urban sprawl:** disorganized, unattractive urban growth

[4] **mortality:** death

The World's Megacities
(with populations exceeding 10 million)

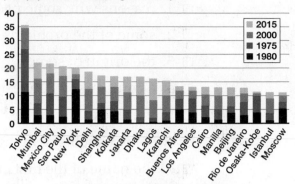

World's megacities, 1950–2015

The Urban and Rural Population of the World, 1950–2030

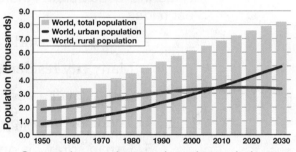

Comparison, urban and rural populations

Transportation is a problem in many cities.

COMPREHENSION

A Main Ideas

Check (✓) the information that is shown in the fact sheet. Discuss your answers with a partner.

- ☐ 1. reasons why some people prefer living in the country
- ☑ 2. some of the problems faced by people living in cities
- ☐ 3. the origin of some words associated with cities
- ☐ 4. a comparison between urban and rural areas
- ☐ 5. the size of the biggest cities in the world
- ☐ 6. some benefits of living in cities
- ☐ 7. the name of the first city
- ☐ 8. the world's biggest city

B Close Reading

Read the ideas below. Find the section in the fact sheet that best shows each idea.

- __3__ 1. Some of the world's cities are extremely large.
- _____ 2. Many city residents live in very poor areas.
- _____ 3. Cities cover a very small percentage of the world's area.
- _____ 4. There are many opportunities in cities.
- _____ 5. Urban sprawl is one of the problems created by large cities.
- _____ 6. The populations in cities and in urban areas is almost equal.

VOCABULARY

(A) Guessing from Context

Read each sentence and guess the meaning of the word in bold from the context. Then match the word with its definition.

1. There has been a **massive** increase in the number of people living in cities. A century ago, only about 2 out of every 10 people lived in cities, but now that number is about 5 out of 10.

2. In the next **decade** or so, the problems faced by urban areas are expected to grow. By 2025, there will be so many people that cities will be faced with the problems of pollution, and inadequate transportation and health care.

3. As urban sprawl **spreads**, so does obesity. As a result of limited public transportation in urban areas, people drive more and walk less.

4. Health is also a concern in **densely** populated city centers, which often do not have enough hospitals or health care facilities for the large number of people who live there.

_____ 1. **massive**	**a.** ten years	
_____ 2. **decade**	**b.** crowded closely together	
_____ 3. **spread**	**c.** extend over a large area	
_____ 4. **densely**	**d.** very large	

(B) Using the Dictionary

> Dictionaries often have a "thesaurus" section that puts words into groups with other words that have a similar meaning.

Read the dictionary entries for *periphery*, *outskirts*, and *suburbs*. Notice that they have a similar meaning.

periphery *n.* the outside area or edge of a city or town

outskirts *n.* the parts of a city or town that are farthest from the center

suburbs *n.* the area away from the center of the city

Now read each sentence. Decide if the sentence makes sense. Check (✓) the appropriate box. If not, change it so it makes sense. Discuss your answers with a partner.

	MAKES SENSE	DOESN'T MAKE SENSE
1. I grew up in the old quarters of the city, but now I live in the **suburbs**.	☐	☐
2. I live on the **outskirts** of the city, so I have a short commute to my job downtown.	☐	☐
3. Because of urban sprawl, fewer people are now living on the **periphery** of the city.	☐	☐

C Word Forms

1 Fill in the chart with the correct word forms. Some categories can have more than one form. Use a dictionary if necessary. An **X** indicates there is no form in that category.

	NOUN	VERB	ADJECTIVE
1.	commute/	commute	X
2.			populated
3.		rise	
4.		urbanize	urban

2 Complete the conversation with the correct form of the words. Choose from the forms in the chart.

NANCY: Hi, Sheila. Are you all right? You look really exhausted.

SHEILA: Yes, I'm OK. There was a delay coming into work today, so I'm

feeling a bit stressed.

NANCY: How long is your _____?
1.

SHEILA: Usually it's about an hour, but it took me almost two hours today.

NANCY: Well, that's one of the problems of _____ living!
2.

SHEILA: I know. Apparently there was a water main break downtown. And what's the _____ of the city? Almost 8 million? There must be a lot of angry people today.

                3.

NANCY: Yeah, and I think that as the number of people living in the city _____, the problems are going to get worse, too.

                4.

NOTE-TAKING: Using Abbreviations and Symbols to Take Notes

Using abbreviations and symbols can help you organize your notes more efficiently. You should develop your own system of abbreviations and symbols.

Examples:

Abbreviations	Symbols
prob (problem)	→ (causes)
urb (urban)	↗ (increase)

1 Read the sentences below and take notes. Use abbreviations and symbols. Then share your notes with a partner.

1. As urban areas get bigger and bigger, the problems faced by residents are increasing.

    _____

2. The percentage of people living in cities is growing.

    _____

2 Go back to Reading One and read it again. Choose three sentences. Take notes on the sentences, using abbreviations and symbols.

CRITICAL THINKING

Discuss the questions with a partner. Be prepared to share your opinions with the class.

1. As you have learned, cities are growing faster than ever. In your opinion, what are the main reasons why people choose to live in cities?

2. What do you think are the main differences between life in a large city and life in a town or rural area?

3. How do relationships between people change when they move to an urban environment?

Ⓐ Warm-Up

These cities are mentioned in Reading Two. Work with a partner and find the cities on the map. Write the correct number next to each city. Check your answers at the bottom of the page.

a. _____ Bangkok   e. _1_ New York

b. _____ Cairo   f. _____ Prague

c. _____ Hyderabad   g. _____ São Paulo

d. _____ Lagos   h. _____ Venice

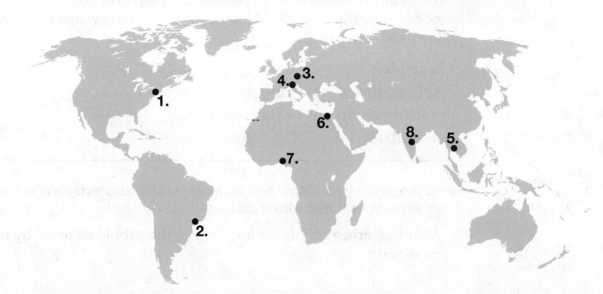

Ⓑ Reading Strategy

Reading Aloud

When you face a difficult text, try **reading parts of the text aloud**. This can help you to determine the main idea of the text. When you read, divide the sentences into "thought groups" of a few words each and pause between thought groups.

Read paragraph 1 of the magazine article aloud, dividing the sentences into "thought groups."

EXAMPLE: There was a time/when big cities/thrilled and amazed people.

Now read the entire article. If you have difficulty understanding any of it, read it aloud.

The Future of Cities

1   There once was a time when big cities **thrilled** and amazed people. "It is the metropolis of the universe, the garden of the world," Ibn Khaldun, the Arab historian, wrote of Cairo in 1382. In 1611, English traveler Thomas Coryat described Renaissance Venice as a "beautiful queene." French artist Marcel Duchamp, in 1915, called New York City "a complete work of art." Since their appearance about 3000 B.C., cities have always been the natural center of everything that mattered: the temple, the court, the market, the university. Of course, even though cities have been the fountains of civilization, many thinkers, from Rousseau (1712–1778) to Jefferson (1743–1826) to Thoreau (1817–1862), have also regarded them as the source of **corruption** and evil.

2   However urban life strikes you, cities worldwide have been growing ever more rapidly. Some of this growth has occurred in the developed world, but the most **dramatic** increase has been in the developing world. In the future, almost all the world's population growth will take place in the cities of developing countries. By the year 2030, for the first time in history, 60 percent of the world's people will be living in cities.

3   This is actually good news in some ways. "Cities are the fundamental building blocks of **prosperity**," says Marc Weiss, chairman of the Prague Institute for Global Urban Development, "both for the nation and for families. There's the crazy notion that the way to deal with a city's problems is to keep people out of them, but the problems of rural life are even more serious than those of the city." For better or worse, urban-watchers are clear on one point: The quality of life for most people in the future will be determined by the quality of cities.

4   To discover how people are coping with **drastic** urban growth, I went to São Paulo, Bangkok, Lagos, and Hyderabad. I was prepared to be **overwhelmed**, and I was. But it wasn't the shapeless turmoil[1], the choking[2] air, the crushing slums, and mindless skyscrapers that left the deepest impression. It was the people, so tenacious, gallant, ingenious[3], and hopeful. These massive cities are not, as they may first appear, overloaded ships sailing in no direction. In the **anonymous** city peripheries and the teeming[4] old quarters, I found that what appeared to be each city's greatest **burdens**—all those people—are in fact her richest **resources**.

---

[1] *turmoil:* lack of organization

[2] *choking:* making it difficult to breathe

[3] *tenacious, gallant, ingenious:* persevering, brave, good at finding ways to solve problems

[4] *teeming:* very crowded

COMPREHENSION

Ⓐ Main Ideas

Read the main ideas from Reading Two. Put them in the correct order from 1 to 6. Discuss your answers with a partner.

___1___ **a.** the original date when cities began to appear

_____ **b.** experts' opinion about cities

_____ **c.** a discussion about the future of cities

_____ **d.** the impression that cities have made on the author

_____ **e.** opinions about cities from the 14th to the 20th century

Ⓑ Close Reading

Read the quotes from Reading Two. Circle the statement that best explains each quote. Share your answers with a partner.

1. "Of course, even though cities have been the fountains of civilization, many thinkers . . . have also regarded them as the source of corruption and evil." (*paragraph 1*)

   a. Most people believe that cities are full of dishonest people.

   b. Cities seem to have both positive and negative characteristics.

   c. The benefits of cities are greater than their disadvantages.

2. "However urban life strikes you, cities worldwide have been growing ever more rapidly." (*paragraph 2*)

   a. Cities are becoming bigger and bigger, whether we like city living or not.

   b. Living in a city makes it difficult to appreciate their growth.

   c. Cities are not growing as quickly as they did in the past.

3. "For better or worse, urban watchers are clear on one point: The quality of life for most people in the future will be determined by the quality of cities." (*paragraph 3*)

   a. City life is beneficial for most people.

   b. Cities affect our quality of life.

   c. It is important to make sure that cities have a high standard of living.

4. "These massive cities are not, as they may first appear, overloaded ships sailing in no direction." (*paragraph 4*)

   a. Large cities show good planning, which is important because they are full of people.

   b. Cities are like ships, and it is difficult to make them change direction.

   c. Although cities seem to have no direction, this is not true.

VOCABULARY

A **Guessing from Context**

Read the news reports. Complete each report with words from the box.
Use the context of the reports to help you select the correct words. Compare
answers with a partner.

anonymous	burden	dramatic	drastic	resources	thrilled

REPORT 1

According to official statistics, there has been a _____ _drastic_ _____

1.

increase in the number of people riding the subway. One official said: "We

understand that people are upset about crowding on the trains, but we don't

have the _____ to add more trains right now." He

2.

added: "We are replacing miles of tracks, but this is currently placing an

additional _____ on the organization. However, within a

3.

few months, the public is going to see an improvement in the system."

REPORT 2

A new museum opened its doors downtown today. The museum will

house the work of new artists, and its _____ rooftop

4.

views are sure to please visitors. One _____ reviewer,

5.

who did not want to be named, said: "I am _____ about

6.

this great new cultural institution in our city. It shows that we are taking the

lead in the arts."

B Meanings

1 Read each sentence. Look at each word in bold. Decide whether it has a *Positive* or *Negative* meaning. Check (✓) the appropriate box. Discuss your answers with a partner.

	POSITIVE	NEGATIVE
1. I was **thrilled** when I found a new apartment near the park. It's going to be wonderful to live in such a great neighborhood.	✓	☐
2. Did you read the news? The mayor of the city has just been accused of **corruption**! I never trusted him.	☐	☐
3. I have to get my own place to live. I don't want to be a **burden** on my parents any more.	☐	☐
4. Look at this newspaper article. It says: The city has had a period of **prosperity**, but now the economic situation is getting worse.	☐	☐
5. I've always wanted to start my own business, and now I finally have the financial **resources**.	☐	☐
6. When I saw the traffic on the highway during rush hour, I knew I'd be late. I really felt **overwhelmed**.	☐	☐

NOTE-TAKING: Taking Notes on a Timeline

When you read a text that includes dates or factual information about past events or thinkers, it is helpful to **take notes on a timeline**. This will allow you to make better connections between the ideas that you read.

Go back to Reading Two and read it again. Take notes on the timeline with information about cities, as well as any events and thinkers that are mentioned in the reading.

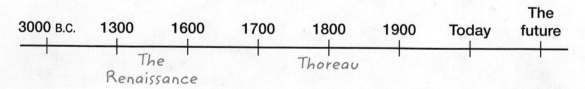

```
3000 B.C.   1300      1600      1700      1800      1900     Today   The
  |----------+---------+---------+---------+---------+--------+-------future
                  The                    Thoreau                      |
              Renaissance
```

CRITICAL THINKING

Read the ideas from Reading Two. Decide whether you agree or disagree with them. Check (✓) the appropriate box. Discuss your ideas with a partner. Be prepared to share your opinions with the class.

	AGREE	DISAGREE
1. Cities are the source of all evil.	☐	☐
2. Cities are the fountains of civilization.	☐	☐
3. Cities are fundamental blocks of prosperity.	☐	☐
4. Cities are places of shapeless turmoil.	☐	☐
5. Cities are like overloaded ships sailing in no direction.	☐	☐

LINKING READINGS ONE AND TWO

Read the facts about cities. Then fill in the chart with the main ideas from Readings One and Two. Share your chart with the class.

FACT	READING ONE	READING TWO
Cities are very large.	A megacity is a city with over 10,000,000 people.	
Cities have many benefits.		
Cities have created many problems.		
In the future, more and more people will live in cities.		

A Warm-Up

1 Use the items chart to talk about your relationships with your neighbors. Talk to another class member about item 1. Then switch to another class member and talk about item 2. Continue changing partners until you have finished discussing item 6.

1. Find five adjectives to describe your neighbors.	**2.** Talk about a neighbor you would like to know more about.
3. Talk about a neighbor who you find strange or annoying.	**4.** Talk about an activity you would never do with a neighbor.
5. Talk about three activities you would be happy to share with a neighbor.	**6.** Discuss what you can do to avoid being lonely in the city or suburbs.

2 Look at the cartoon. Discuss the questions with a partner.

1. Do you think the cartoon is funny? Why or why not?

2. What do you think the cartoon says about being neighbors?

3. Do you think most people want to know their neighbors better, or do they prefer more privacy? Explain.

Recognizing the Difference between Narration and Opinion

Many narratives (stories) also convey opinions. As you read, **try to distinguish between the narration** (what the author has done) **and the author's opinion or observations** (what the author believes).

EXAMPLES:

Narration	*I began to telephone my neighbors.*
Opinion	*We divide ourselves with invisible dotted lines.*

Read the sentences. Decide whether they are narration or opinion. Check (✓) the appropriate box. Discuss your answers with a partner.

	NARRATION	OPINION
1. We often don't know the people who live next door.	☐	☐
2. When Lou awoke that morning, he and I shared breakfast.	☐	☐
3. I was privileged to be his friend.	☐	☐
4. He told me about his grandparents' immigration.	☐	☐

Now read the story and pay attention to the narration and the author's opinion.

Won't You Be My Neighbor?

By Peter Lovenheim

1   The alarm on my cell phone rang, and I awoke to find myself in a twin bed in a spare room at my neighbor Lou's house.

2   Lou was 81. His six children were grown and **scattered** around the country, and he lived **alone**, two doors down from me. His wife, Edie, had died five years earlier. "When people learn you've lost your wife," he told me, "they all ask the same question. 'How long were you married?' And when you tell them 52 years, they say, 'Isn't that wonderful!' But I tell them no, it isn't. I was just getting to know her."

3   The previous evening, as I'd left home, the last words I heard before I shut the door had been, "Dad, you're crazy!" from my teenage daughter. Sure, the sight of your 50-year-old

(continued on next page)

father leaving with an overnight bag to sleep at a neighbor's house would **embarrass** any teenager, but "crazy"? I didn't think so.

4 There's talk today about how as a society we've become **fragmented** by ethnicity, income, city versus suburb, red state versus blue.[1] But we also divide ourselves with invisible dotted lines. I'm talking about the property lines that **isolate** us from the people we are physically closest to: our neighbors.

5 Why is it that in an age of cheap long-distance rates, discount airlines, and the Internet, when we can create community anywhere, we often don't know the people who live next door?

6 Maybe my neighbors didn't mind living this way, but I did. I wanted to get to know the people whose houses I passed each day—not just what they do for a living and how many children they have, but the depth of their experience and what kind of people they are.

7 What would it take, I wondered, to penetrate the **barriers** between us? I thought about childhood sleepovers and the insight I used to get from waking up inside a friend's home. Would my neighbors let me sleep over and write about their lives from inside their own houses?

8 I began to telephone my neighbors and send e-mail messages; in some cases, I just walked up to the door and rang the bell. The first one turned me down, but then I called Lou. "You can write about me, but it will be boring," he warned. "I have nothing going on in my life—nothing. My life is zero. I don't do anything."

9 That turned out not to be true. When Lou awoke that morning, he and I shared breakfast. Then he lay on a couch in his study and, skipping[2] his morning nap, told me about his grandparents' immigration, his Catholic **upbringing**, his admission to medical school despite anti-Italian quotas[3], and how he met and courted[4] his wife, built a career and raised a family.

10 Later, we went to the Y.M.C.A.[5] for his regular workout[6]. We ate lunch. He took a nap. We watched the business news. That evening, he made us dinner and talked of friends he'd lost, his **concerns** for his children's futures and his own mortality.

11 I was **privileged** to be his friend until he died, just this past spring.

12 Our political leaders speak of crossing party lines to achieve greater **unity**. Maybe we should all cross the invisible lines between our homes and achieve greater unity in the places we live. Probably we don't need to sleep over; all it might take is to make a phone call, send a note, or ring a bell. Why not try it today?

---

[1] "Red" and "blue" describe political beliefs. Red refers to the Republican party, and blue refers to the Democratic party.

[2] *skipping:* not doing

[3] In the early 20th century, it was common for official limits, called "quotas," to restrict admission to various institutions on the basis of national origin.

[4] *courted:* became romantically involved with

[5] *Y.M.C.A.:* gym run by the Young Men's Christian Association

[6] *workout:* exercise routine

COMPREHENSION

A Main Ideas

Read each statement. Decide which describe the author's life *(A)* and which describe his neighbor Lou's life *(L)*.

_A_ 1. As a child, he sometimes slept at his friends' houses.

____ 2. He wanted to get to know his neighbors.

____ 3. He had six children.

____ 4. His wife died.

____ 5. His daughter thought he was crazy.

____ 6. He was married for 52 years.

____ 7. He thinks we need greater unity among our neighbors.

____ 8. He went to medical school.

B Close Reading

Read the quotes from Reading Three. Circle the statement that best explains each quote. Share your answers with a partner.

1. "There's talk today about how as a society we've become fragmented by ethnicity, income, city versus suburb, red state versus blue." (*paragraph 4*)

   a. City life makes people more divided.

   b. Our different backgrounds and beliefs often separate us from each other.

   c. If we had better communication, we would be more united.

2. "Maybe my neighbors didn't mind living this way, but I did." (*paragraph 6*)

   a. The author doesn't like his neighbors' houses.

   b. The author's neighbors are unfriendly toward him.

   c. The author didn't like the way he lived.

3. "I have nothing going on in my life—nothing. My life is zero. I don't do anything." (*paragraph 8*)

   a. Lou didn't think his life was very interesting.

   b. Lou didn't want to be more involved with his neighbors.

   c. Lou was trying to make friends with the author.

4. "Our political leaders speak of crossing party lines to achieve greater unity." (*paragraph 12*)

   a. Politicians believe people understand each other.

   b. Politicians think we should overcome our differences.

   c. Politicians want people to support their own political parties.

VOCABULARY

Ⓐ Guessing from Context

Read the paragraph and guess the meanings of the words in bold from the context. Then match the words with their meanings.

A new study of suburban life focuses on how to promote more **unity** among neighbors. Many people choose to live in the suburbs because they are concerned about their children's **upbringing** and want a give them a quiet, safe place to live. However, many neighborhoods are very **fragmented** and do not provide opportunities for people to interact with each other. Houses, schools, parks, and shopping areas are **scattered** over a wide area, so residents tend to spend a lot of time in their cars. Large gardens look beautiful, but they can **isolate** people from each other, and fences are like **barriers** between houses. The big challenge for urban planners is how to find a way to build neighborhoods that provide both privacy and community. There are **concerns** that this balance is becoming harder and harder to find.

_a_	**1. unity**	**a.** being together
___	**2. upbringing**	**b.** separated into many parts
___	**3. fragmented**	**c.** things that keep people separate
___	**4. scattered**	**d.** the way parents raise their children
___	**5. isolate**	**e.** distributed over a large area
___	**6. barriers**	**f.** to separate from other people
___	**7. concerns**	**g.** worries

Ⓑ Using the Dictionary

1 Read the dictionary entries for *alone*, *by yourself*, *on your own*, and *lonely*. Notice that the first three are synonyms.

> **alone** *adv.* without any other people: *He lived alone.*
>
> **by yourself** *adv.* completely alone: *He lived by himself.*
>
> **on your own** *adv.* alone: *He lived on his own.*
>
> **lonely** *adj.* unhappy because you are alone: *He felt lonely.*

2 Now complete each sentence with the correct word or expression. Choose from the word or expression in parentheses.

1. Lou was married for 52 years, but when the author met him, he lived

   _____ (alone/lonely).
   (alone/lonely)

2. The author believed, that Lou often felt _____.
   (by himself/lonely)

3. Since his wife died, Lou got used to doing things _____.
   (lonely/on his own)

   For example, he would go to the gym or cook.

4. Lou always ate meals _____ because he had no one to
   (lonely/alone)

   share them with.

C Meanings

Look at each word. Find the word in the reading. Decide whether it has a *Positive* or *Negative* meaning. Check (✓) the appropriate box. Discuss your answers with a partner.

	POSITIVE	NEGATIVE
1. scattered	☐	☑
2. embarrass	☐	☐
3. unity	☐	☐
4. fragmented	☐	☐
5. privileged	☐	☐
6. isolate	☐	☐
7. concerns	☐	☐
8. alone	☐	☐

CRITICAL THINKING

Discuss the questions in a small group. Be prepared to share your opinions with the class.

1. What do you think of the author's experiment? Do you believe, like his daughter, that his idea was a little crazy, or not? Could it work for other people? Explain.

2. Why do you believe Lou said he had nothing going on in his life? Do you think that's true? What do you think his children thought of his friendship with the author?

3. Do you agree that people create invisible lines separating themselves from other people? If so, why do you think they do this?

4. The author thinks it is strange that although we have many ways to connect with other people, such as phones, the Internet, and cheap forms of travel, we are also very isolated from others. Do you think that these devices make our connections with others stronger, or weaker? Explain.

AFTER YOU READ

BRINGING IT ALL TOGETHER

1 Read the quotes. With a partner, explain what they mean in your own words. Then discuss your reactions.

1. "Cities are the greatest creations of humanity."

   —*Daniel Libeskind, architect, 1946–*

2. "City life is millions of people being lonesome together."

   —*Henry David Thoreau, author and environmentalist, 1817–1862*

3. "Cities force growth, and make men talkative and entertaining, but they make them artificial."

   —*Ralph Waldo Emerson, author and naturalist, 1803–1882*

2 Find an idea from Reading One, Two, or Three that illustrates each of the quotes. Complete the chart. Discuss the ideas in your chart with a partner.

	QUOTE	READING	IDEA
Ex.	Libeskind	Reading Two	emphasizes the positive aspects of cities
1.	Libeskind		
2.	Thoreau		
3.	Emerson		

WRITING ACTIVITY

Choose one topic and write a short essay. Use some of the vocabulary you studied in the chapter (for a complete list, go to page 252).

1. Write a story (true or fictitious) about an exciting, frustrating, lonely, frightening, or liberating experience of life in the city.

2. Write a story about a neighbor of yours that you like or dislike.

DISCUSSION AND WRITING TOPICS

Discuss these topics in a small group. Choose one of them and write a paragraph or two about it. Use the vocabulary from the chapter.

1. There are nicknames for many famous cities. For example, New York is often called "the Big Apple," Chicago is called "the Windy City," and Denver is called "the Mile High City." Do you know of any other city nicknames? Why do you think cities often have nicknames?

2. The older generation is often very conscious of the differences between today's urbanized society and the simpler world they grew up in. What do the older people in your family or community have to say about life in cities today? Do you think they find it harder than young people to live in an urban environment? If so, why?

3. Many characteristics of city life can be both good and bad, depending on your viewpoint. For example, some people may dislike living among many other people, but others may find it exciting. Some people find city living lonely, but others like the anonymity it sometimes provides. What is your opinion about life in the city? Is it mostly positive, or negative? Explain.

Chicago, the Windy City

VOCABULARY

Nouns	Verbs	Adjectives	Adverb
barrier	commute	alone	densely
burden	embarrass	anonymous	
concern	isolate*	dramatic*	
corruption	scatter	drastic	
decade*	spread	fragmented	
periphery		massive	
prosperity		overwhelmed	
resource*		privileged	
unity		populated	
upbringing		rising	
		thrilled	
		urban	

* = AWL (Academic Word List) item

SELF-ASSESSMENT

In this chapter you learned to:

○ Read a fact sheet

○ Read aloud to determine the main idea of a text

○ Recognize the difference between narration and opinion

○ Guess the meaning of words from the context

○ Use dictionary entries to learn different meanings of words

○ Understand and use word forms and positive and negative meanings of words

○ Use abbreviations and symbols to take notes, and take notes on a timeline

What can you do well? ✓

What do you need to practice more? ✓

VOCABULARY INDEX

The number following each entry is the page where the word, phrase, or idiom first appears. Words followed by an asterisk (*) are on the Academic Word List (AWL). The AWL is a list of the highest-frequency words found in academic texts.

CREDITS

TEXT CREDITS

Page 210 Written by Kim Sanabria: characteristics quoted from http://thejustlife.org/home/agents-of-change/missional-entrepreneurs/; **Page 239** Erla Zwingle, "Cities: Challenges for Humanity." Erla Zwingle/National Geographic. Adapted with permission; **Pages 245, 246** Peter Lovenheim,"Won't You Be My Neighbor?," *The New York Times*, June 6, 2008. Copyright © 2008 by The New York Times Company. All rights reserved. Reproduced by permission; **Dictionary Entries** From *Longman Advanced American Dictionary*, Courtesy of Pearson Education.

PHOTO CREDITS

Page 1 Corbis Super RF/Alamy; **p. 4** vetal1983/Fotolia; **p. 10** The Art Gallery Collection/Alamy; **p. 11** Marc Scott-Parkin/Shutterstock; **p. 16** Win Initiative/Getty Images; **p. 29** (top) Liz Van Steenburgh/Shutterstock, (bottom) sommai/Fotolia; **p. 35** Corbis Cusp/Alamy; **p. 36** Dorling Kindersley/Getty Images; **p. 50** (top) Horizons WWP/Alamy, (middle) Tyler Olson/Fotolia, (bottom) Maridav/Fotolia; **p. 53** (top) BSIP SA/Alamy, (bottom) Jeff Greenberg/Alamy; **p. 54** AFP/Getty Images/Newscom; **p. 68** Sergey Yarochkin/Fotolia; **p. 72** BeTa-Artworks/Fotolia; **p. 77** Digital Vision/Getty Images; **p. 93** matka_Wariatka/Fotolia; **p. 94** Renaud Thomas/Shutterstock; **p. 108** Suprijono Suharjoto/Fotolia; **p. 121** ZUMA/Newscom; **p. 124** Gary Lee/Photoshot/Newscom; **p. 130** Paul Bradbury/Alamy; **p. 132** Andrew Innerarity/MCT/Newscom; **p. 139** (left) Cusp/SuperStock, (right) Yuri Arcurs/Fotolia; **p. 146** (left) BESTWEB/Shutterstock, (right) Classic Image/Alamy; **p. 156** GeoPappas/Fotolia; **p. 159** Jennifer Gottschalk/Shutterstock; **p. 170** pzAxe/Fotolia; **p. 176** (top) Reeed/Shutterstock, (middle) amlet/Shutterstock, (bottom) Behyar/Shutterstock; **p. 178** Vorobyeva/Shutterstock; **p. 180** (top) Universal Images Group/SuperStock, (middle top) SuperStock/SuperStock, (middle) Everett Collection Inc/Alamy, (middle bottom) Teutopress/Ullstein Bild/Glow Images, (bottom) Jan Sochor/Alamy; **p. 183** Everett Collection/SuperStock; **p. 186** (top) The Protected Art Archive/Alamy, (bottom) GL Archive/Alamy; **p. 190** Ryan McVay/Getty Images; **p. 193** Antonio Gravante/Fotolia; **p. 197** Inc-Photo/Getty Images; **p. 207** Imagesource/Glow Images; **p. 212** Frederick M. Brown/Getty Images; **p. 216** nikolay chervonenko/Fotolia; **p. 217** ABIR ABDULLAH/EPA/Newscom; **p. 221** ROBERTO SCHMIDT/AFP/Getty Images/Newscom; **p. 230** rabbit75_fot/Fotolia; **p. 233** JTB MEDIA CREATION, Inc./Alamy; **p. 245** Ed Metz/Shutterstock; **p. 251** Andrew Bayda/Fotolia.

ILLUSTRATION CREDITS

Page 20 Andrew Bock; **p. 47** Accurate Art; **p. 66** John Kurtz; **p. 77** Albert Tan; **p. 86** Accurate Art; **p. 98** Albert Tan; **p. 158** Accurate Art; **p. 183** Albert Tan.